Perceptual Changes
in Psychopathology

Perceptual Changes in Psychopathology

EDITED BY

WILLIAM H. ITTELSON

AND

SAMUEL B. KUTASH

CONTRIBUTING EDITORS

LEONARD ABRAMSON

BERNARD SEIDENBERG

RUTGERS UNIVERSITY PRESS

NEW BRUNSWICK, NEW JERSEY

Copyright © 1961 by Rutgers, The State University

Library of Congress Catalogue Number: 61-10263

Manufactured in the United States of America
by Quinn & Boden Company, Inc., Rahway, New Jersey

Preface*

In February, 1953, a research proposal entitled *Perceptual Changes in Psychopathology* was approved by the Veterans Administration, and under the terms of this proposal a continuing research program was established in the Fall of that year at the East Orange Veterans Administration Hospital. This book represents a progress report on this project.

The general scope of the research and the assumptions underlying it were set forth in the original proposal in the following words:

"It is proposed to investigate experimentally the perceptual distortions which are encountered in certain types of psychopathology and the perceptual changes which occur in the course of psychotherapy, with the aim of adding immediately to the empirical knowledge of this area and ultimately leading to a comprehensive theory of perceptual change, particularly as related to psychopathology."

The underlying assumption which has been made in the research carried out under the proposal is that much of psychopathology can be conceptualized as distortions either of perceptual content or of perceptual processes, and that the course of psychotherapy can be conceptualized as a course of perceptual change.

The general way in which the project was set up and developed under this enabling proposal is described below.

* Much of this preface originally appeared in the *Journal of Counseling Psychology,* 2, 63-66, 1955.

THE SETTING OF THE PROJECT

The East Orange Veterans Administration Hospital is a General Medical and Surgical Hospital of approximately 960 beds including a Neurology and Psychiatry Service containing 250 beds. The clinical psychiatric population consists entirely of active treatment patients of all types. Every form of modern therapy is used including individual and group psychotherapy. The Psychology Service consists of a Chief of Psychology Service, eight staff members, and an average number of twelve transient Veterans Administration Trainees in Clinical, Counseling, and Social Psychology, whose stay varies from six to twelve months. The formal functions of these staff members consist of providing needed hospital services, suitable training experiences, and research. Until the Fall of 1958 there were no formal research positions on the staff, although as part of their training a number of trainees are expected to complete the research for their dissertations during their stay at the hospital. In addition, the services of a Perception Research Consultant are available, as well as those of a number of other research and clinical consultants in various specialities of psychology and psychiatry.

This staff operates in a modern hospital, formally dedicated in 1952, which offers up-to-the-minute physical facilities, and, more important, provides an atmosphere of eager interest in research in all areas of medical science. This interest is expressed at the highest levels of VA administration, through the provision of tangible funds and less tangible but equally important interest and support, and at the highest levels of hospital administration, where both the Manager and the Director of Professional Services have provided enthusiasm, co-operation, and support.

The net result has been a fully equipped perception research laboratory, a staff whose research interests are recognized and encouraged, and an atmosphere of interest and co-operation on the part of the entire hospital organization. During the period covered by this book there was no formal research organization as such, although the subsidiary duties of one of the regular clinical psychology staff members consisted of general administrative cognizance of the research activities. In November, 1958, the position of Co-ordinator of Research was established. In February, 1959, a half-time research assistant in the Perception Laboratory was appointed.

In addition, some of the work reported here was supported in part by U. S. Public Health Service Grant M—2503, to Brooklyn College in co-operation with the East Orange VA Hospital.

THE STRUCTURE OF THE PROJECT

It was in this favorable environment that it was decided to establish a long-term, large-scale research project. After considerable discussion among all interested administrative personnel, an approach evolved which, in retrospect, can be labeled a philosophy of "freedom within structure." This was a logical outgrowth of two views which were fairly generally shared by all concerned. First, it was felt that research which is dictated to a subordinate by a superior (unless the subordinate is specifically hired for that purpose) may redound to the fame of the superior but is deleterious to the self-esteem and professional development of the subordinate. This, coupled with a belief that fruitful research in untried areas most frequently results from an alert investigator diligently following his own interests wherever they may lead him, led to a general view that a high degree of structure is undesirable in a research project of this sort. On the other hand, it was equally strongly felt that to allow each individual staff member complete freedom to pursue his every transient interest would result in an over-all research product which would be chaotic, fragmentary, and incoherent, and which would not represent the best possible utilization of the available facilities. It was therefore decided to provide a certain degree of structure in terms of theoretical orientation, subject matter, and experimental apparatus. Within this definite but loose structure, each individual is permitted complete freedom to develop his own particular interests. The theoretical orientation which was adopted is that which has come to be labeled "Transactional psychology"; the subject matter was perceptual processes as related to psychopathology, and the apparatus the Ames demonstrations in perception.

Transactional psychology is a broad systematic approach to psychological theory which has grown out of studies principally concerned with visual perception. Its basic tenet holds that neither a perception nor an object-as-perceived exists independent of the total life situation in which both perception and object are a part. It is meaningless to speak of either as existing apart from the situation in which it is encountered. The word *transaction* is used to label such a situation. For the word "transaction" carries the double implication (a) that all parts of the situation enter into it as active participants, and (b) that they owe their very existence as encountered in the situation to this fact of active participation and do not appear as already existing entities merely interacting with each other without affecting their own identity. Within this context, perceiving has been defined as that part of the process of living by which each one of us, from his own particular point of view, creates for himself the world within which he has his life's experiences and through which he strives to gain his satisfactions. (Ittelson, 1960.)

This theoretical view was chosen as being at once congenial to clinical and counseling psychologists, yet stemming from outside the confines of their immediate field of specialization. It offers a framework within which the clinical and counseling psychologist each has an opportunity both to expand his own horizons in a somewhat new direction and to bring his own special knowledge and experience to bear on evaluating and refining a theory which comes from outside his own province, yet purports to have something of value to say to him.

The general subject matter of perceptual processes in psychopathology represents an obvious area of overlap between the emphasis in transactional psychology on perceptual processes and the clinician's interest in psychopathology. This, coupled with the fact that perception generally represents an area of growing and basic interest to clinicians and personality theorists, made the choice of this subject a compelling one. To repeat, the underlying assumption which is made in most of the research carried out under this project is that much, if not all, of psychopathology can be conceptualized as distortions of perceptual content or of perceptual processes, and that the course of psychotherapy can be conceptualized as a course of perceptual change.

It should be noted that in this book we are presenting only the work done at the East Orange Veterans Administration Hospital that deals directly with the problems of perceptual change. Much additional research, which is not reported here, has been carried out under the Psychology Service on other psychological problems. This book, in other words, is in no sense a complete report of all psychological research done at the Hospital, but is rather an attempt to summarize our approach to one particular problem.

Two ways of studying perceptual change have been carried out concurrently. These are represented in the two sections into which the book has been divided. First, we have attempted to work out a theory of perceptual change as it relates to over-all personality functioning and to develop a suitable experimental methodology by which such a theory can be tested in the laboratory and related to clinical practice. Summary statements of our conclusions in this area of theory and methodology comprise Section I.

Second, a number of different specific aspects of perceptual change have been investigated. Numerous variables, processes, and determinants have been selected; the individual reports represent an interest both in devising suitable methodology and in arriving at substantive findings. These studies are reported in Section II under the general heading of "Correlates of Perceptual Change." Six different "correlates" have been specified.

It should be noted that there are three main sources for the work reported here: (a) long term studies involving all staff members, (b) co-operative studies involving a number of staff members, and (c) Ph.D. dissertations by trainees. The work reported in Section I represents an example of the first categories and is appropriately credited in individual footnotes. Co-operative group projects have been found valuable in making possible the investigation of problems which are beyond the scope of a single person, either because of the intrinsic nature of the problem or because of its magnitude. Ph.D. thesis research, on the other hand, seems ideally suited to the intensive and detailed study of a more limited problem. Here, every effort is made to encourage the student to develop his own research interests, both in terms of theory and experimentation. Complete co-operation with the training university with which the student is affiliated is maintained at all times, and the university, of course, retains full authority over its students' theses.

It should be clear that the work reported here is the joint product of a number of people working co-operatively and congenially together. The following staff members and trainees have contributed to this volume:

> Leonard S. Abramson—Chapter 14
> Dorothy Block—Chapter 8
> Alfred L. Brophy—Chapter 12
> Robert A. Buhler—Chapter 7
> Erasmus L. Hoch—Chapter 5
> William H. Ittelson—Chapters 1 and 5
> George Kaufer—Chapters 4 and 5
> Samuel B. Kutash—Chapter 2

Gerald J. McCarty—Chapter 6
Paul Perez—Chapter 3
Allen Raskin—Chapter 10
Ammon C. Roth, Jr.—Chapter 9
Bernard Seidenberg—Chapter 5
Rebecca Snyder—Chapter 11
Daniel E. Sugarman—Chapter 14
Eugene H. Walder—Chapter 12
Arthur Willner—Chapter 5

Special thanks are due to Martin Scheerer for contributing Chapter 11 together with Rebecca Snyder.

In addition the entire volume has been revised by the editors who assume full responsibility for the point of view represented and such errors as may appear.

Contents

Perceptual Changes
in Psychopathology

Section I

An Approach to Perceptual Change: Theory and Methodology

· 1 ·

Perceptual Theory and Personality Dynamics*

Interest in the interrelationship between perception and psycho-pathology is a most ancient one, and the work reported in this book in this sense fits into a long tradition in human thought. Certainly the capacity to see things that no one else sees and to hear things that no one else hears has always been a mark of psychological distinction. Usually, but by no means always, it has been considered pathological. Sometimes, of course, and more frequently in some cultures than in others, quite the opposite occurs and saintly qualities are attributed to the individual so endowed. But whether judged favorably or otherwise, such perceptual anomalies have probably always been thought important. It is not suprising, therefore, that early work in psychopathology put great emphasis on perceptual disorders, describing them in great detail in texts and relying heavily upon them in setting up diagnostic categories.

Today, however, interest in the interrelationships between perception and psychopathology is proceeding along a radically new direction. While the importance of perceptual abnormalities as a clinical problem is by no means underestimated, emphasis is more and more shifting toward perception as a basic psychological process through which we can gain greater understanding of the over-all functioning of the person. And this shifting emphasis has been brought about largely through growing contact between two initially diverse subjects for inquiry within the science of psychology, the

* This paper was originally presented in slightly different form by W. H. Ittelson at the University of Kansas "Symposium on Perception and Psychopathology," April, 1956.

experimental study of perception on the one hand, and the clinical study of personality on the other.

Perceptual studies, as we know, initiated the modern era of scientific psychology, and a look at the course of development of the study of perception since that time gives us a bird's-eye view of the course of development of the entire field of psychology. The early perceptual work fell within what has come to be known as the tradition of stimulus determination. This is the view that the external stimulus determines the perception. Emphasis was placed on a detailed analysis of the characteristics of the external stimulus and the search was for universal "laws" relating the physical environment on the one hand and the subjective experience on the other. Within the limits of this approach it was gradually found necessary to enlarge the subject matter to include the study of the sensory apparatus and of neural processes and central functioning as well. This line of approach has been and continues to be actively pursued and productive of important findings.

Within the past decade or so, however, the experimental study of perception has received a tremendous impetus from a point of view almost directly opposed to this. The early work started with the object and went to the person. It asked the question, "What does the environment do to the perceiver?" Present day thinking reverses this, starts with the perceiver and works toward the object. This apparently simple change has produced a revolution in thinking, so that today we ask, "What does the perceiver do to the environment? What is actually done by the individual when he perceives?" The shift, then, is from considering perception as a passive reaction to external events, toward considering perceiving as a process actively carried out by the perceiver.

In short, the over-all trend of contemporary perceptual studies has been away from the earlier stimulus orientation, based on the assumption that external stimuli determine perceptions, and toward the treatment of perceiving as an essentially creative process actively carried on by the organism. This trend is based on the assumption that the individual acts in any situation in terms of the way he perceives that situation. Perception, then, becomes a crucial process intimately involved in the effective functioning of the individual. It need hardly be pointed out that such an approach has necessarily led the experimental study of perception into a consideration of problems which had previously been considered sacred to that branch of psychology labeled "personality."

Actually, the meeting has been at the half-way point. More and more, personality theorists and practicing clinicians have become interested in the perceptual process, and an analogous trend can be traced from this starting point. Certainly the most fruitful clinical approaches currently in use in psychodiagnosis and psychotherapy rely on a theoretical basis which assumes a relationship between perception and personality. Psychoanalysis, of course, has always assumed that the individual structures his world through his experiences. The direct importance of perceptual processes in shaping the content of these experiences is specifically stressed by most contemporary psychoanalytic writers. The relationship of perception to phenomenological personality theory is more direct and obvious. The projective theorists have, of course, always maintained this position, and in a sense are today coming into their own. Rorschach himself referred to his test as an "experiment in perception." It is safe to say that personality studies have been approaching perception as rapidly as perceptual studies have been approaching personality. The two have met with an impact that has vitally affected contemporary psychology.

Before proceeding, it may be well to point out that this recognition of the close relationship between the study of perception and the study of personality has had at least one perhaps unfortunate by-product, in that the awareness of similarities has tended to obscure fundamental differences. One need only look at the many books and articles bearing some variant of the title *Perception and Personality* to see that there is a tendency to consider these two as if they were co-measurable. They are not; no more than apples and oranges. Perception is a process actively carried on by the individual linking him with the world about him. Personality is not a process but rather a description of a particular pattern of processes, of which perception is perhaps the most important. It may be that in time the distinction between these two terms will be erased, but as long as the dichotomy remains, it is well to bear in mind just where the differences lie. It is certainly clear, however, that the study of perception and the study of personality are intimately related. And since pathology in experiencing and pathology in behavior can both fruitfully be conceptualized in terms of disorders of the perceptual process, it is small wonder that research in perception represents one of the major fields of endeavor in the study of psychopathology today.

II

It is clear that such a broad approach to perception demands that we have a definition of our subject matter which will encompass the area of inquiry with which we are concerned, and a conceptualization of perceptual theory which will provide us with fruitful hypotheses and further our understanding of particular problems. In short, it must on the one hand be concrete and specific and narrow enough to permit of rigid experimentation, and on the other hand be abstract and general and broad enough to admit of all the complexities of human activity.

For a working definition of perception we shall use the one briefly referred to in the introduction, which was previously suggested in another context. It does not seem to be in need of serious modification. This defines perceiving as that part of the process of living by which each one of us from his own particular point of view creates for himself the world within which he has his life's experiences and through which he strives to gain his satisfactions.*

There is not time, nor is this the appropriate place, to indicate in detail the theory of perception which is implied by such a definition. Rather we shall briefly note four aspects of perceiving which are directly relevant to our discussions here. First, there is the way in which perception enters into the total life situation of the individual, which is most adequately handled under the concept of transaction. Second, there is the way in which perception links the experience of inner and outer events, which is subsumed under the heading of externalization. Thirdly, we will consider the question of perceptual change, and finally, the problem of perceptual validation, which leads us into the role of action.

Perceiving is not only an inseparable part of all waking activity, but even more important, perceiving never occurs independent of some other activity. This is simply another way of saying that perceiving is an abstraction from concrete experience and must be treated as such. We cannot somewhat isolate a perception in its "pure" state as a chemist might isolate a pure chemical or a biologist a pure strain, and then proceed to study it in isolation. Perceiving never takes place "by itself." It can only be studied as part of the situation in which it operates.

---

* Much of the following discussion is based on and some of it directly quoted from W. H. Ittelson, *Visual Space Perception*, New York: Springer, 1960.

Of course, the abstraction of some very simple act of perceiving from the rest of an on-going situation for purposes of experimentation is frequently necessary, but this is always done at the risk of seriously distorting the subject matter. The starting point for perceptual studies must always be perceiving as it is encountered in concrete, real-life situations. This, of course, places severe restrictions upon the experimental study of perception, involving important methodological and procedural as well as theoretical implications. No matter how much he may wish to do otherwise, the student of perception is frequently forced to obtain data under conditions quite remote from those in which perception normally operates. But when he does so, he must always be sensitive to the limitations of attempting to treat such data as if they had relevance to real-life situations. Possibly the safest way out of this dilemma is to treat an experiment in the perceptual laboratory not as a reflection of how one perceives in another kind of situation but rather as a concrete situation in itself in which the observer is perceiving.

Neither a perception nor an object-as-perceived exists independent of the total life situation of which both perception and object are a part. It is meaningless to speak of either as existing apart from the situation in which it is encountered. The word *transaction* is used to label such a situation, for this word carries the double implication (1) that all parts of the situation enter into it as active participants, and (2) that they owe their very existence as encountered in the situation to this fact of active participation and do not appear as already existing entities, merely interacting with each other without affecting their own identity.

The term "transaction" was first used in this general context by Dewey and Bentley (1949), for whom it took on far-reaching philosophical significance. What they mean by this term can best be gathered by their own words: "Observation of this general 'transaction' type sees man-in-action not as something radically set over against an environing world nor yet as merely action 'in' a world but as action of and by the world in which the man belongs as an integral constituent." Under this procedure all of man's behavior "including his most advanced knowings" are treated as "activities not of himself alone nor even as primarily his but as processes of the full situation of organism-environment." "From birth to death every human being is a *party* so that neither he nor anything done or suffered can possibly be understood when it is separated from the fact of participation in an extensive body of transactions—to which a given human being may contribute and which he modifies but only in virtue of being a partaker in them."

Dewey and Bentley distinguish this transactional procedure from two other procedures which they feel have largely dominated the history of science up till now. First is what they call the antique view of "self action where things are viewed as acting under their own powers." Second is the interaction view of classical mechanics "where thing is balanced against thing in causal interconnection." In transactional observation "systems of description and naming are employed to deal with aspects and phases of action without final attribution to 'elements' or other presumptively detachable or independent 'entities,' 'essences,' or 'realities,' and without isolation of presumptively detachable 'relations' from such detachable 'elements.'"

Speaking more specifically of visual perception, Bentley has said, "We do not, however, take the organism and environment as if we could know about them separately in advance of our special inquiry but we take their interaction itself as subject matter for study. We name this *transaction* to differentiate it with interaction. We inspect the thing seen not as the operation of an organism upon an environment nor the environment on an organism but as itself an event." (Bentley, 1954)

Just as no single aspect of the transaction can be said to exist in its own right apart from the transaction, so not even the transaction itself can be treated as existing in its own right. Using the term transaction is not to be construed as simply a new way of breaking the subject matter into larger but still discrete elements or events. This view, which we shall try to avoid in this discussion, is analogous to the narrow, archaic view of Newtonian physics in which the belief was held that the observer somehow stood outside of the system which he was observing and which was independent of the fact of observation. Rather, we shall assume that every transaction has within it as an integral part of its being its own unique reflection of all past transactions and its own unique presentment of future transactions.

"An event has contemporaries. This means that an event mirrors within itself the modes of its contemporaries as a display of immediate achievement. An event has a past. This means that an event mirrors within itself the modes of its predecessors as memories which are fused into its own content. An event has a future. This means that an event mirrors within itself such aspects as the future throws back into the present; or, in other words, as the present has determined concerning the future . . . These conclusions are essential for any form of realism for there is in the world of our cognizance memory of the past, immediacy of realization and indication of things to come." (Whitehead, 1949) Similarly, aspects of the transaction which cannot be reached from any other point can be known only by the particular participant and are unique to him.

Each one of us is, therefore, constantly playing a dual role. First, we are experiencing our own unique participation with all its intellectual and valueful overtones, many of which cannot even be verbalized without being lost. Secondly, we are constantly trying to abstract from this total experience those aspects which are or can be experienced at the time by other participants. It is here that we are constantly in danger of falling into what Whitehead has called the "Fallacy of Mis-Concreteness" if we assign greater concreteness, that is, a higher degree of external "reality," to the abstracted aspects than to the total experience from which they are abstracted.

III

Probably the most obvious aspect of the experience of perception is that it is externally oriented—that is, the things we see, and hear, and taste, and touch, are experienced as existing outside of ourselves and as possessing for themselves the characteristics which we perceive in them. But it is also clear that perception is part of the experience of the individual. One essential feature of perception, then, is the external orientation of certain aspects of experience. In perceiving, parts of our own experience are attributed to events external to ourselves in whose independent existence we firmly believe. "The act of perceiving in itself so implies the act of considering it real that the latter can be called an attribute of the act of perceiving." (Schilder, 1953) When we perceive, we externalize certain aspects of our experience and thereby create for ourselves our own world of things and people, of sights and sounds, of tastes and touches. Without taking any metaphysical position regarding the existence of a real world independent of experience, we can nevertheless assert that the world-as-experienced has no meaning and cannot be defined independent of the experience. *The world as we experience it* is the product of perception, not the cause of it.

Certain aspects of experience are definitely and surely attributed to the external world. "Perception," as Bridgman has pointed out, "we have always had with us and we take it completely for granted. We *see things* out there in space moving about, and that is all there is to it. We accept these perceptions at their face value and, on them as a foundation, we build the pattern of our 'reality.' To this reality, we ascribe an absolute existence transcending its origin." (Bridgman, 1954)

Clearly, not all experience is externalized, however; other aspects are just as definitely considered to be personal, subjective, and having no external reference. Still other aspects lie in a never-never-land in between. It is important, therefore, to ask such questions as: What aspects of experience are viewed as representing something independent of the experience? And what aspects are not? Why, indeed, does anyone ever come to believe in the independent existence of an external world? And what are the factors that determine which aspect of experience is selected as representing this external reality? The answers to these questions lie beyond the scope of the present work, but the problems raised by them always lurk behind any study in the field of perception.

It should be noted that it is not immediately and simply evident what kinds of experience can profitably be externalized. Some people on some occasions may externalize experiences which might more effectively be considered as subjective or vice versa. One important part of psychotherapy, then, may well be learning to externalize some aspects of experience which have heretofore not been externalized, and, probably more important, learning not to externalize many experiences which in the past have been externalized—that is, to recognize as one's own experience certain things which have in the past been attributed to external events.

IV

Any present perceptual experience consists of a total complex of significances. All previous experiences have been similarly composed. Through the course of experiencing, certain significances are found by the perceiver to have high probabilities of being related to each other. Other relationships have a low probability of occurring. The probabilities, high or low, are in turn weighted in terms of the relevance of the unique situation in which they have occurred to the larger purposes and values of the experiencing person. All this is accomplished through a largely unconscious process and results in a set of *assumptions* or weighted averages of previous experiences which are brought to the present occasion and play a principal role in determining how the occasion is experienced. For each of us the sum total of these assumptions can be said to constitute our *assumptive world*. The assumptive world of any particular individual at any particular time determines his perceptions. It is therefore in a very real sense the only world which he knows.

Each of us goes about building up his assumptive or form world largely in an unconscious and nonintellectual way in the process of adjustment and development as he goes about the business of life, that is, as he tries to act effectively to achieve his purposes. We often use many of our assumptions without being at all aware of them, such as those involved in habits, stereotypes, and a whole host of perceptual activities. We become aware of other assumptions from time to time as they become relevant to the situation at hand, such as loyalties, expectancies, ideals. Still others, such as intellectual abstractions, can be brought to voluntary recall. Our actions cannot be effective unless and until each one of us builds up an assumptive world that has some degree of constancy and verifiability.

Perhaps the most significant point to be made concerning assumptions as they concretely enter into the transaction is that they are not always, if ever, in complete harmony. On the contrary, any concrete experience involves the achievement of some sort of resolution of a host of more or less incompatible and sometimes directly contradictory assumptions. This resolution is accomplished by means of an unconscious *weighting process*, in which the italics are taken to indicate that this is a figurative description of an as yet imperfectly understood function. The particular weight given to each assumption in this unconscious calculation is a product of at least three factors. First, each assumption is undoubtedly weighted on a probability basis. That is, assumptions which have frequently and consistently proved valid in the past will tend to be weighted most heavily. This point has been made, in other terminology, by Brunswik (1956), in whose "probabilistic functionalism" weightings are determined on the basis of "ecological validity." Brunswik is in error, however, when he assumes that weights are based solely on a probability basis. A second criterion for the weight given an assumption lies in the over-all significance to the individual of each particular experience into which it entered and the importance of the assumption within that experience. This consideration makes possible extreme cases of traumatic weighting, but also undoubtedly figures less dramatically in every experience. Finally, an assumption will be weighted in the immediate situation depending upon its relevancy to the specific purposes of the moment. Each assumption, then, enters into the weighting process with a weight determined on a probability basis adjusted in terms of its previous importance to the individual and its relationship to the immediate transaction.

V

It follows from these considerations that perceptions can change through two quite different processes. One process takes place within the already existing framework of assumptions and consists of altering the weight without changing the assumptions themselves. The effects of this *perceptual reweighting* process become evident only when conflicts are present. In a conflict situation, however, the particular resolution achieved, and hence the resultant experience, will be changed in accord with the newly assigned weights. The second process of perceptual change is quite different and calls for the acquiring of totally new assumptions. This *perceptual relearning* process is more fundamental and can change the entire perceptual experience of the individual.

Perceiving, as we have seen, provides us with predictions of the significance of the external situation only by experiencing the consequences of our own actions. The experienced consequences of every action provide a check on the perceptual prediction on which the action was based. In this sense the perceptual process constantly operating in all of us is quite analogous to the process of scientific inquiry. Every action can be thought of as an experimental test of an hypothesis which is appropriately modified or confirmed as the result of our test through action. One psychological result of any action, then, is a change in the probabilities unconsciously assigned to the particular assumptions on which that action was based. The probability is changed in proportion to the weight given to that particular experience, resulting in new assumptions, new predictions, new externalized significances.

There are, however, two ways in which assumptions, and consequently perceptions, change through experiencing the effects of our actions. It is important that these be differentiated. First, every action we undertake is a check on an assumption. Hence, every action affects the subjective probability assigned to that assumption. But second, and of much greater importance, are those actions which bring about changes in the assumptions themselves or the formation of any assumptions. These are actions whose experienced consequences are either directly contradictory to an assumption or not related to any existing assumption. In such cases the consequences of our actions directly contradict the predictions on which they are based. These are "unsuccessful" actions resulting in surprise, disappointment, frustration, or the awareness of a new problem to be resolved.

VI

If such an approach to a theory of perception is to have any value for us, we must be able to translate it into terms which either help us understand concrete problems or help us to formulate new problems for empirical study.

The therapeutic situation is the concrete transaction with which we are at the moment concerned. And the word *concrete* is used advisedly: that is the reality with which both therapist and patient must deal. Whitehead's fallacy of misplaced concreteness is appropriately considered here when either participant introduces abstractions from outside of the situation and attempts to treat them as if they represented reality. It cannot be emphasized too strongly that from the point of view here presented, the only real concrete situation is the total transaction as it unfolds as an ongoing process.

The characteristics of this transaction are a product of the participants and more important, the characteristics of the participants are determined by the nature of the transaction. The therapist does not enter as therapist nor the patient as patient, but both as active participants, and neither one of them can be defined or studied or known in any way without considering this very fact of their participation.

Each such transaction represents a unique occurrence which cannot be duplicated. The therapist has never been just that therapist, nor the patient just that patient, in any other situation. To the extent that the therapist ceases to be a unique participant and seeks to become the generalized therapist, or to the extent that the patient seeks to become the generalized patient, the nature of the transaction is altered and the therapeutic value diminished. This fact of the uniqueness of every transaction has led to a multitude of divergent theories and notions about the nature of the therapeutic process. However, out of this diversity certain general principles have emerged. The first of these we have just referred to. That is, the importance of the concrete therapeutic situation. Next, we shall consider some of the implications of the way the participants perceive each other within this transaction.

The patient perceives the therapist in terms of all his past experiences primarily with authority figures and love objects. He brings to the situation all his acquired assumptions about such people and he will in turn base his actions within the therapeutic situation on predictions which he characteristically makes on the basis of these assumptions. The patient successively runs through his whole range of important people as he tries out his entire repertoire of assumptions in an effort to find some way of perceiving the therapist which will give him relatively stable directives for acting. He gradually discovers that such predictions can be made only to the extent that he experiences the therapist as a unique individual uniquely participating in the concrete transaction.

The therapist in turn perceives the patient in a variety of ways dependent on his own previous experiences with other patients and other important figures of one sort or another. He must necessarily do this since his own experiences are all he can or does bring to the transaction. However, he also has a greater flexibility in changing his perceptions as they prove inadequate. Danger to therapy stems not from misperceiving the patient—that is inevitable—but from the need to persist in misperceptions.

Because the therapist is more closely linked to the concrete transaction he is less likely to do this. But it should be noted that since the patient is presumably constantly changing, misperceptions by the therapist are not only inevitable, they are desirable. A correct perception of the patient is not a static thing to be acquired once and for all, but rather a constantly changing product of the situation which will always remain to a certain extent elusive as long as the transaction retains its dynamic qualities.

This serves to emphasize the fairly obvious fact that change is the *sine qua non* of therapy. And from the point of view of this discussion, change in therapy can be conceptualized as a progressive sequence of perceptual changes. The patient initially changes his perception of the therapist and gradually expands his new ways of perceiving to include other aspects of his world. And since perceptions provide the bases for action, these changing perceptions bring about changing ways of behaving and eventually a whole new mode of acting and experiencing emerges.

What was said earlier about perceptual change, then, can be carried over bodily into this context. First, we must assume that the person who comes for therapy has certain misperceptions of the world about him. And here by misperceptions we mean specifically perceptions which give him predictions for actions which do not in turn provide him with the satisfactions he seeks. That is, his perceptions lead to actions which do not, for him, have the consequences he expects.

In the process of therapy he will change these perceptions through the two processes of perceptual change, initially always in direct, concrete transactional relationship with the therapist. What we have referred to as perceptual reweighting undoubtedly takes place first. Here there is no basic change in the individual's assumptions but rather a reordering, a reshuffling, and a shifting of relative importances of modes of perceiving which he has already brought with him to the occasion. While dramatically different perceptions and hence different ways of acting may emerge from this process, nothing basically new has been added. This is probably the kind that occurs in relatively short-term or supportive therapy in which no basic changes in personality are achieved. The second kind of perceptual change, which we have referred to as perceptual relearning, involves the formation of entirely new and different assumptions. As such, it does, in a very real sense, involve the creation of something new, something which the patient did not bring with him. It corresponds to the changes which occur in deep therapy with attendant basic personality changes.

All of this implies that the focus of therapy is, as we have previously stated, not inappropriate behavior but rather inappropriate modes of perceiving. Psychotherapy aims at changing perceptions, not changing overt behavior. Of course changing perceptions are related to changing actions in the way we have indicated. Changing perceptions lead to new predictions on which actions are based, and to the extent that these predictions are valid, that these actions provide the experienced consequences the individual seeks, to that extent will they become established as part of that person's characteristic, habitual ways of experiencing the world and acting in it.

So this process of perceptual change involves a never-ending sequence of new perceptions, new directives for acting, new actions, and a reassessment of the perception in terms of the experienced consequences of the action. All of this takes place usually quite gradually and almost entirely without any specific awareness. Characteristically, a patient may become aware of his changed behavior only after it has become a well-established part of his life.

VII

The general problem of therapeutic change, then, has been approached from the standpoint of a theory of perceptual change. Such a theory stems from laboratory findings and must constantly be in contact with experimental procedures. We shall turn now to some laboratory procedures which are currently proving useful in this connection.

One problem which is certainly of basic importance in the understanding of perceptual change is the question of perceptual conflict. The way in which an individual handles perceptual conflicts can lead to an understanding of both perceptual processes in general and the personality processes unique in that particular individual. For purposes of definition we shall call "perceptual conflict" any situation in which two incompatible modes of perceiving are both indicated. While this is a fairly loose definition, and difficult to specify operationally, it makes the main points that (1) there must be at least two different modes of perceiving, (2) each one of these must, by itself, lead to a stable and consistent perception, and (3) the two perceptions must not be able to be maintained simultaneously.

A simple laboratory example can be taken as an illustration. Presumably one cannot see something both near and far at the same time. If we have one set of cues which indicate that an object is near, and another set of cues which indicate an object is far, and we combine these two sets of cues, we have met the criteria for perceptual conflict. The two perceptions "near" and "far" cannot be maintained at the same time. The advantages of this approach to the experimental study of conflicts are several. First, the process is unconscious in the sense that an individual so presented with a perceptual conflict situation is not in general aware that there is any anomaly in the situation he is perceiving. He is seeing something; he does not see a conflict. The resolution of the conflict, then, occurs without specific awareness on the part of the perceiver. Second, perceptual conflicts can be controlled experimentally; they can be quantified. And third, they can be varied along a continuum from very simple to very complex. An example of a relatively simple perceptual conflict is given by the case of aniseikonic glasses. These glasses present a perceptual conflict between monocular cues on the one hand and binocular cues on the other. There is a straightforward perceptual conflict, and subjects react to it in fairly consistent ways. Typically when a person puts on a pair of these glasses, he sees a gradual and progressive change in the world in front of him in whatever surfaces or objects he is looking at. This change consists of a shift from the monocular appearance to the binocular one. This, then, is a relatively simple perceptual conflict involving perceptual processes about which we know a great deal, and which we can study quantitatively.

An example of a more complex perceptual conflict is the rotating trapezoid. This is more complex in that the number of different sets of cues indicating different incompatible perceptions is very great, and also the underlying perceptual processes involved are not as well understood. Both the aniseikonic lenses and the rotating trapezoid have been effectively used in the laboratory study of perceptual conflicts.

In general, the findings obtained in perceptual conflict studies parallel those arrived at in other conflict studies, e.g., conflicts in motor performance and conflict as found in clinical practice. The most common form of resolution of the conflict between two opposing sets of visual indications is in terms of compromise, i.e., the resultant perception falls somewhere in between that which would occur in the absence of one set of cues and that which would occur in the absence of the other set. For example, referring back to the earlier example, given one set of indications that taken alone would show an object near and another set which alone would result in a perception of the object as far, these actually combine in a resultant perception of the object somewhere in the middle, i.e., the object is seen at an intermediate point which corresponds to none of the actual cues. This is the most common resolution of a perceptual conflict situation and is the one most commonly referred to in the literature. However, it is by no means the only resolution possible. There can be complete suppression of one or another set of indications, with the observer apparently reacting as if the second conflicting set of indications were simply not there. Other forms of resolution are temporal alternation in which first one perception and then the other is seen, and there may be a time delay, in which case nothing happens immediately following the introduction of conflict, and then some time later the perception changes. These are the four most frequently encountered ways of resolving a perceptual conflict. They roughly correspond to the kinds of resolutions of conflict that one encounters in personality theory and in clinical practice. They also resemble the kinds of resolutions that have been obtained in studies of motor conflict. This suggests that the process of resolving conflicts may be a general one and also indicates that perceptual conflicts give us a technique for studying this problem quantitatively.

In closing, one other kind of perceptual change will be described, which we have referred to as perceptual relearning. It involves the establishing of some new mode of perceiving which the individual did not have prior to the experimental procedure. One example will serve for illustration. The distorted room presents a complex situation in which the room is physically of one shape and is perceived as another shape. The problem is how the observer can be taught, one way or another, to perceive the room in its true shape. A learning procedure can be set up to accomplish this, although the details of the processes involved are not clear. An important complicating problem stems from the awareness on the part of the observer that he is facing a peculiar situation, which is not the case in perceptual conflict. But here any learning procedure must show him the incompatibility between the way things appear and the way they are experienced in some other way. The difficulty of perceptual relearning experiments of this sort arises from the fact that the subject can utilize intellectual processes. An advantage of course is that the study of the relationship between intellectual and perceptual processes can be carried out in this general context of perceptual relearning.

It is hoped, in conclusion, that this brief outline of a theory and some related laboratory procedures has indicated, at least, that it is worth-while to have a perceptual theory, that hypotheses fruitful for clinical practice do stem from such a theory, and that the specific theory outlined here does lead to useful hints in understanding the therapeutic process, and to useful hypotheses for studying these hints carefully and quantitatively in the simplified situation within the laboratory.

The remainder of this book will be devoted to a more detailed description of specific experiments carried out within this general framework.

· 2 ·

Perceptual Flexibility and Mental Health*

In a recent address on "Psychology and the Mental Health Movement," Fillmore Sanford stated that "it is safe to say that nobody knows exactly what is mental health." He went on to assert that "it is even safer to say that no two people agree on what mental health is." Most of our notions about mental health have been derived from the field of medicine with its branches of psychiatry and neurology and from the work in psychopathology. According to the medical tradition mental health is usually defined in terms of the absence of pathology or symptoms. This type of conception of mental health, however, is perhaps as unsatisfactory as the psychiatric descriptive nosology for mental illness upon which it depends. It is a negative definition stating what mental health is not, failing to define it in positive terms in a way which would make it possible to measure and appraise it more scientifically.

Experience in clinical psychology and psychiatry has shown that there can be people who show symptoms who are nevertheless mentally healthy and people who do not show symptoms who are mentally unhealthy. Tyhurst (1955), for example, from his studies of disaster situations, has introduced the concept of transitional periods during which the healthiest people normally developed mental and emotional symptoms which actually served a positive function for them. We are coming to realize that the absence of symptoms, while important, is not the essence of mental health.

On the other hand, a host of definitions of mental health may be

* This chapter is based on a paper originally presented by Samuel B. Kutash at the University of Pittsburgh, 1958.

19

subsumed under the cultural approach based on a consideration of how the individual fits into the culture. The sociological emphasis defines mental health in terms of the absence of social symptoms such as antisocial behavior, social inadequacy, and the like. Mental health has also been described in terms of the absence of sexual disturbance or maladjustment. Even the newer schools of psychoanalysis, while they define neurosis as a difficulty in living happily and effectively, do not tell us what mental health is. Equally unsatisfactory is the statistical definition of normality. There is need today for a purely psychological definition of mental health which would be based on the positive attributes of the normal personality rather than the absence of symptomatology as the major criterion. Some attempts have been made at this, such as Maslow's eleven "manifestations of psychological health." (Maslow, 1951) The difficulty here is in agreeing on the definition of each of the eleven categories.

The advent of psychological science into the mental health field has brought new, fresher approaches which are only now beginning to bear fruit. Psychology has long been interested in the basic process of perceiving. Perception is more and more being considered as a basic psychological process through which we can gain greater understanding of the over-all functioning of the person. Ittelson, as we have seen, has defined perceiving as "that part of the process of living by which each one of us from his own particular point of view creates for himself the world within which he has his life's experiences and through which he strives to gain his satisfactions." Blake and Ramsey (1951) present the view that the study of perceptual activity provides a basic approach to an understanding of personality and inter-personal relations and that "perceptual activity supplies the materials from which the individual constructs his own personally meaningful environment." Similarly, Witkin (1954) and his collaborators studied the way in which personal characteristics of the individual influence his perception.

Through the convergence of perception and personality studies and of the experimental and clinical approaches there has emerged a possible essential criterion of mental health. Neither the content of perception nor the perceptual process itself are static characteristics of an individual, but rather change continually as the individual changes. This capacity to change one's perception, or perceptual flexibility, is the overriding process which may give us the clue to a workable, operational definition of mental health.

In the course of everyday life experiences, effective living demands a balance between two contradictory tendencies, conservation and change. The person who never or rarely changes is helpless in the face of new and changing conditions. At the other extreme the person who changes with every shift of the wind is at the mercy of the transient whims of his surroundings. Somewhere between lies a region of effective functioning.

If perceptual flexibility—or the capacity to change one's perceptions of persons, objects, situations, and events could be measured directly, quantitatively and qualitatively, and the optimal range of perceptual flexibility could be determined experimentally, we would have a criterion of mental health which would prove useful in clinical and experimental work and would avoid the shortcomings of the pathological, cultural, and statistical definitions. This would make it possible to have an objective base line for prognostications about the effectiveness of treatment or psychotherapy and for a method of grading severity of psychopathology and of diagnosing the existence and extent of mental disturbances.

In the course of psychotherapy the patient as well as the therapist is faced with an important dilemma. If the patient resists change too rigidly, he is unable to benefit from psychotherapy. If he changes too readily he fails to develop a stable personality structure on which he can rely in the future. He must, somehow, with the aid of the therapist, keep up a continuous process of change while at the same time maintaining a sufficiently stable, though changing, structure to serve as a foundation to which each change is added; a springboard, as it were, from which each succeeding jump is taken. This whole process is, of course, complicated by the fact that it takes place largely on an unconscious level.

Many of the changes which take place in psychotherapy and in everyday living as well can be conceptualized as perceptual changes. A patient's capacity for changing his perceptions, i.e., his perceptual flexibility, may well reflect his capacity for benefiting through psychotherapy as well as his potentialities for effective living following therapy.

With the above background in mind we shall proceed to describe the researches in the area of Perceptual Changes in Psychopathology and of Perceptual Flexibility and Mental Health at the East Orange Veterans Administration Hospital.

At the outset, three general types of perceptual change were differentiated for the purpose of the projected studies. The first was called *perceptual learning,* which involves a change in the perception of a single, constant aspect of the environment, the learning of a new significance in the place of the one already there. The second, *perceptual conflicts,* involves a change in the perception of a total situation due to a shift in the relative ways different conflicting aspects enter into the perception, a reweighting of the significances that are already there. Thirdly, the special problems of *psychopathological distortions* were introduced. The changes based on perceptual learning and perceptual conflicts can occur in varying degrees in different pathologies. Unique pathological factors also may enter. It was proposed to study all three of these areas experimentally using specially designed apparatus in conjunction with already established psychological techniques. Subjects would be drawn from patients displaying all varieties of psychopathological symptoms, including psychosomatic disorders, as well as normals. The areas of investigation outlined were sufficiently broad so that any one of the available psychology staff and research personnel could develop projects in line with his own individual interest, at the same time maintaining an over-all coherence in the program.

We shall turn now to a review of some selected completed studies from the perception research program. These will be used to illustrate the nature of the work and the findings in the areas of perception and psychopathology, the effects of stress on the perceptual process, the perception of interpersonal relationships, perception of the self and self-products, intraindividual consistence, and changes in perception as a result of verbalization. After this is accomplished, the major long-term project on perceptual flexibility and the prediction of perceptual change will be discussed. All of the studies are reported in detail in Part II of this book.

A number of studies in the Perception Laboratory have aimed at investigating the possibilities of various perceptual tasks and measures as diagnostic differentiators between various clinical psychopathological groups and normal individuals. An example of this is the study by Dr. Paul Perez, who undertook to investigate the size-constancy perception of a group of schizophrenic subjects and a group of nonschizophrenic or so-called normal subjects under two different conditions of experimental instructions, objective and analytic. In addition, three different standard stimuli were used. All were white cards 9 centimeters square. On one was drawn a nonsense figure, on one an alphabetic block, and on the third, a skull. Each subject also took the Witkin Embedded Figures Test, which gives a measure of ability in separating a configuration from a complex field.

The performance of schizophrenic subjects in this task differs in two respects from that of nonschizophrenic subjects. They demonstrate a higher degree of size-constancy than do nonschizophrenics, regardless of the type of instructions used or the content of the standard stimulus. The ability of schizophrenics to comply with analytic instructions is related to their ability to separate a configuration from a complex field. The results suggest the greater perceptual rigidity of the schizophrenic as compared to the normal.

In another type of study, Dr. George Kaufer investigated the relationship between personality orientation and size-distance perception, using certain measures of personality orientation and characteristic modes of perceiving as manifested in reactions to emotionally valent material. Among the related problems Kaufer dealt with were such specific aspects as whether there was a correlation between emotional valence and the perception of an object by an individual within the context of a particular personality orientation.

The personality orientations were defined, in Horney's terms, as tendencies to move toward, against, or away from people. For each subject, three judges determined the general personality orientation, the orientation toward men and the orientation toward women. Kaufer concluded, generally, that personality orientation is related to characteristic modes of perception. His study did not reveal any differential effect of emotional valence or verbalization.

The first study on person-perception completed in our Laboratory, by W. H. Ittelson, Erasmus L. Hoch, and George Kaufer, dealt with group therapy. Each patient in a therapy group made settings of a photograph of each of the following persons: (a) that other member of the group whom the subject most liked, in the opinion of the cotherapists of the group; (b) that other member of the group whom the subject least liked, in the opinion of the cotherapists; (c) the two therapists; and (d) himself. Significantly different settings were obtained between the self and the least liked, and the most liked and least liked, indicating that the relationship between individuals does affect the way they see each other.

In a psychiatric ward study by Arthur Wilner, this approach was further elaborated. Sociometric measures were obtained from patients on a psychiatric ward, and each patient subsequently made settings of photographs of himself and other patients who were liked, disliked, and neutral, selected on the basis of sociometric data. Results again show significant effects for the self-picture and that both highly liked and highly disliked persons are equivalent in this task and are both different from relatively neutral persons.

One general conclusion can clearly be drawn from the above studies. The apparent metric properties of photographs of persons, as measured in this experimental situation, are influenced by the affective relationship between the subject and the person photographed. Exactly what are the important aspects of the affective relationship, however, remains unclear. Furthermore, subjects seem to differ in the direction of the effect, and increasing the magnitude of the emotional loading increased the effect in the direction peculiar to that subject. Subjects who tend to set all emotionally loaded objects further than relatively neutral objects will tend to set heavily loaded objects still further than less loaded objects. In other subjects, the entire effect is reversed. One can speculate as to whether this may not represent basic differences in personality structure and ways of dealing with the world. Again, it is certainly significant that all the effects observed are greatest when we are dealing with photographs of the self. Surely this suggests the possibility of an experimental approach to problems of self-image to which we shall return.

In another approach to the effect of interpersonal relations on perception, Gerald J. McCarty investigated the variables of visual perceptual behavior and small group verbal interaction as they are related to the independent variables of attitude, structure of the situation, and structure of the group. Each member of a pair of subjects was given aniseikonic glasses that had the opposite apparent distortion to his partner although they were not so informed. The perceptual distortion experienced each time was measured for each subject independently of the partner, without either being aware of the other's response.

Following their initial perceptual measurements, each pair of subjects was given a period of free interaction with permissive instructions to discuss what they saw, how they saw it, and to try to reach agreement on these points as well as their reactions and associations. After the interim settings the experimenter became authoritarian and in a very directive manner controlled the discussion, more or less forcing the subjects to try to reach agreement. He read off a list of cues that were monocular and cues that were binocular asking the subjects to talk it over and come to some agreement. Following this the final perceptual measure was taken.

McCarty found, among other things, that there is a greater amount of perceptual change in the permissive, less-structured situation than in the more-structured situation. Just the opportunity for interaction results in perceptual change. Of those who change the tendency is for more to show a decrease in the amount of perceived distortion in both types of situation. However, more individuals perform in this manner in the less-structured situation than in the more-structured one. The implications of the above for therapy are obvious and confirm the clinical intuition that interaction and permissiveness promote perceptual change.

Of interest from another point of view are studies dealing with the effects of stress on the perceptual process, since they have implications concerning the causes of mental illness. For example, Robert A. Buhler confirmed previous observations in clinical and experimental situations that psychological stress and anxiety produce marked changes in perceptual functioning as measured by flicker fusion. Specifically, he established that Flicker Fusion Threshold is a valid, sensitive, and reliable index of anxiety level. Increase in psychological stress and anxiety tended to lower FFT markedly and was accompanied by significant increases in the intraindividual variability of FFT.

Dr. Dorothy Block, in a study of the effect of stress on resolving the conflict between monocular and binocular cues using the aniseikonic lenses and Leaf Room, found that under stress the anxious group showed less perceptual flexibility, thus taking longer to resolve the conflict. Ammon C. Roth, Jr. studied the effects of experimentally induced stress on three measures of visual perception—the Thereness-Thatness Table, the Double-Flash Generator, and the aniseikonic lenses and Leaf Room. Roth concluded from his data that stressful conditions resulted in reduced perceptual efficiency as measured by the fusion-discrimination threshold, confirming Buhler's results. Experimentally induced stress produced significantly greater interference with perceptual discriminations among females than among males. In resolving the perceptual conflict involved in the Leaf Room, all three stressed groups took longer than in the nonstress condition, thus confirming Block's findings, although these results did not achieve statistical significance.

Another series of experiments was performed studying perception of self and self-products. Alfred L. Brophy and Eugene H. Walder studied the modification of the self under a condition of praise of performance on an ego-involved task. They hypothesized that praise increases acceptance of the self. The subjects were 18 female nurses employed at the East Orange VA Hospital. The self-acceptance scale of the Bills Index was used as a measure of manifest self-acceptance. Settings on the Thereness-Thatness Demonstration were used as measures of latent perceptions of the self and other objects. The Aptitude Test for Nursing of the George Washington University Series was the ego-involved task for which the experimental subjects were praised. They found a curvilinear relationship between manifest self-acceptance and several measures of implicit perception of the self. Both highly and lowly self-accepting subjects implicitly perceived themselves in a manner different from subjects in a middle range of self-acceptance. Praise of performance of an ego-involved task tended to effect an increase in manifest self-acceptance, but produced no measurable change in implicit perception of the self.

Dr. Daniel Sugarman made a study of the effects of atmosphere of failure and success upon the subsequent rating of one's self-product and the readiness to recognize it.

Both normal and schizophrenic subjects who made their products in an atmosphere of failure took longer to recognize their products and also rated their products more negatively, the following week, than subjects in either the success or control groups. Judgment of one's own product under neutral conditions is usually positive. It would seem that people do not recognize either some aspect of themselves or something they have made when that object or aspect has become associated with unpleasant experience.

A study closely related to psychotherapy was carried out in our Laboratory by Dr. Leonard S. Abramson. Verbalization is, of course, a salient feature of most forms of psychotherapy. Verbalization is assumed under the special conditions of therapy to be instrumental in altering perception. This problem was investigated by Abramson using 40 nonneuropsychiatric hospitalized male veterans as subjects who were assigned randomly to an experimental and control group. Each of the groups was put through three steps, a pretest on the "thereness-thatness" apparatus, an interstitial step during which the experimental group verbalized their responses to TAT cards while the control group did not, and a posttest to evaluate the effects of verbalizing and not verbalizing.

The results were that the experimental condition of adding verbalization to the subject's responding to the standard stimuli of the TAT cards produced greater idiosyncratically-determined perceptual change and related handling of the stimulus materials.

A final group of studies investigated intraindividual consistency in perceptual functioning. Dr. Allen Raskin found that associating electric shock with a particular stimulus object resulted in changed size perception of that object as measured by four quite different tasks—tactual size, reproduced size, size-distance setting, and recognition. Furthermore, the magnitude of the effect was related to the unpleasantness of the shock.

In another important study which can only be briefly mentioned here, Dr. Rebecca Snyder investigated consistencies between personality constriction and a variety of perceptual measures and skeleto-muscular activity. She found these measures to be interrelated, and also that the alleviation of internal stress resulted in greater flexibility of performance on both perceptual and skeleto-muscular tasks.

The common element that pervades all of these studies is the matter of perceptual flexibility or the capacity to change one's perceptions. In addition to studying specific correlates of perceptual change, we are studying experimentally the entire relationship between the capacity to change perceptions and personality health as well as neuropsychiatric prognosis. It is hypothesized that the ways in which an individual changes his perceptions are related to his capacity to change in personality organization, to his capacity to benefit from therapy or treatment, to personality health, and perhaps also to diagnostic groupings. Specifically, we postulate that there is an optimum range of perceptual flexibility for each subprocess of perceptual change such as perceptual reweighting and perceptual relearning; that flexibility in perceptual reweighting is related to superficial or short-term changes in personality during treatment and may be an index to short-term prognosis; and that flexibility in perceptual relearning is related to the more fundamental personality changes aimed for in deep or insightful types of psychotherapy and may be related to long-term prognosis. A prime objective of the research is to relate measures of perceptual flexibility for a hospitalized psychiatric population to their short-term prognosis within the hospital and their long-term prognosis following discharge. Other objectives are to obtain normative data on nonhospitalized populations and so-called well-adjusted people; to develop predictive indices for indicating psychotherapy; to relate perceptual measures to conventional diagnostic categories; to develop indices of intensity of mental illness; and to continue exploratory research and experiments expanding and developing hypotheses as they grow out of the findings.

While much of this work remains for the future, substantial steps have been taken. We have developed a "Perceptual Flexibility Battery" and a Manual for it which standardizes procedure for securing various quantitative measures of flexibility on several of the Ames demonstrations. Thus, on the Leaf Room with aniseikonic lenses we secure the *Distortion Time* or the time taken to reach a final resolution of the perceptual conflict, and the *Distortion Magnitude* or the magnitude of the induced distortion. On the Thereness-Thatness Table we have the *Range of Settings* for familiar and neutral objects, a measure of the consistency of these settings which we have called the *Ratio*, and a measure of *Shift* following an intervening suggestion experience which evaluates that effect in altering these settings. On the Rotating Trapezoid we have an over-all or *Total* score which is a composite of ratings based on a check list of the verbal report under various viewing conditions. Usually the subject enters the Perception Laboratory and is tested first on the Snellen chart. This examination serves as an anxiety reducer, since it is a familiar task in a strange black-painted room filled with strange and unfamiliar objects, and as a check on the adequacy of vision. In all questionable cases the staff ophthalmologist is consulted.

The subject is seated near the door, in order to view the trapezoid from the length of the room, and an eye patch is placed to cover the left eye. The room lights are turned off, the trapezoid itself is illuminated, and the rotation begun. When the large end of the trapezoid is perpendicular to the subject, the examiner steps out of the line of vision, and asks the subject to describe what he sees. This is repeated first with a red cube attached to the top of the small end, and then with a green bar clipped to the center of the middle frame of the window-like trapezoid. The measure is a scaled evaluation on a check list of the spontaneous comments, emotional reactions to the perceptual conflicts, and responses of the subject to questions as he monocularly perceives this situation which is entirely new and contradictory to his previous experiences. Cubes ordinarily do not take off and fly by themselves as this one does, nor do bars slice through or bend around windows!

We then turn the subject's attention to the Thereness-Thatness Table and explain what he is to do. The apparatus is a long table, with a middle partition the length of it. Along the left side of the table are fived spaced lucite posts illuminated from beneath. On the right side is a cart on a pulley which the subject moves with a knob. Objects are placed on the cart and are also illuminated. The subject, seated at one end of the table, can see only the posts with his left eye. He can see both the posts and the objects with his right eye. A small-sized playing card is presented first and the subject is requested to set it to the second and then to the fourth post. A large-sized playing card is then shown him represented as the one being used on the cart, following which the subject again makes settings of the normal-sized playing card. The difference of the two settings is calculated, a measure of the influence of the intervening presentation, and thus a measure of perceptual learning.

The Leaf Room, an 8 by 8 by 8-foot cube, is so named because of the specially treated leaves intertwined in the wire mesh covering all sides of the room except the doorway at which the subject sits and looks into the room while wearing the axis-90 aniseikonic glasses. He wears these glasses first with the distorting lens over the right eye, then over the left eye, and then both placements are repeated. With his right hand, he turns a selsyn knob to keep a white rod across the room apparently lined up parallel to the top edge of the back wall. He is instructed that the glasses may make the room appear to change shape while he looks at it, but that whatever it does he is to keep the rod always lined up with the top edge, moving it as fast or as slowly as the edge moves. The examiner starts his stop watch and records the subject's settings at ten-second intervals up to three minutes or until a stable condition is reached. The binocular cues making for distortion of the appearance of the room are compelling. The floor and one side, depending upon which eye looks through the aniseikonic lens, slope eerily and drop away. The measures obtained are the time taken to reach a final resolution of the perceptual conflict and the magnitude of the distortion.

This *Perceptual Flexibility Battery* is administered to psychiatric admissions together with the regular psychodiagnostic tools and interviews. The patients admitted to the Psychiatry and Neurology Service range from people suffering with severe neuroses to those having mild and severe functional and/or organic psychoses. There is also a considerable sample of neurologically and organically impaired individuals. An average of five new patients a week are admitted and given psychological testing, psychiatric and medical evaluations, as well as psychiatric social work interviews. All these data are available on each patient. Usually the patient receives, among other tests: the Rorschach examination, Wechsler-Bellevue Adult Intelligence Scale, Bender-Gestalt, Figure Drawings, and other techniques as indicated by the nature of the individual case.

To these are added, wherever possible, the Perceptual Flexibility Battery and hospital and posthospital adjustment rating scales to evaluate behavioral changes during and after the patient's hospitalization.

Patients are seen on three occasions: prior to discharge from the hospital; one year following discharge; and three years following discharge. A record of all treatment during hospitalization is made, together with detailed progress notes concerning each psychotherapy session and other modalities of treatment. A current evaluation of ward behavior will be made at the time of discharge from the hospital. Pooled judgments of the ward psychiatrist and the clinical psychologist are to be integrated to arrive at a joint evaluation of the patient's status at the time of discharge. The psychological tests given in the initial work-up will be repeated.

Thus, we shall have ample operational criteria of functioning covering the patient's adjustment in interpersonal, social, and economic activities, such as nonrecurrence of hospitalizations, job stability, marital adjustment, self-evaluation on a questionnaire, and similar measures. Normative data will be obtained from a non-hospitalized population, using the same measures insofar as they are applicable. These subjects will be examined with a parallel set of apparatus. Normal subjects will be readministered the Perceptual Flexibility Battery for purposes of evaluating the reliability and consistency of the measurements obtained from the battery.

Much of this over-all project remains in the future but considerable progress has been achieved and preliminary findings can be reported. The following data all refer to two groups of patients who were administered the Perceptual Flexibility Battery. The patients were randomly selected from psychiatric referrals. The first group consisted of 57 subjects, while the second group numbered 21. It should be emphasized that the second study was conducted completely independently of the first, approximately one year later for the purpose of replication.

Table 1 indicates the mean scores for the two groups in the various measures. None of these measures is significantly different statistically for the two groups, and indeed the numerical values are almost identical in most cases.

The question can be asked whether the various measures of perceptual flexibility are interrelated. From Table 2, which shows the correlations between the various measures, it can be seen that the great bulk of these correlations are not significantly different

TABLE 1

Mean Scores on Perceptual Flexibility Measures

1st Study (Total N = 57)

T	(Time in Leaf Room)	=	17.6	N = 36
M	(Magnitude in Leaf Room)	=	7.9	N = 36
Tr	(Trapezoid)	=	22	N = 54
Rg	(Range in Thereness-Thatness)	=	141.2	N = 54
Ra	(Ratio in T.-T.)	=	.550	N = 54
S	(Shift in T.-T.)	=	10.1	

2nd Study (Total N = 21)

T	=	10.5	N = 16
M	=	9.6	N = 16
Tr	=	23.2	N = 20
Rg	=	133.0	N = 18
Ra	=	.582	N = 18
S	=	11.3	N = 18

TABLE 2

Intercorrelations between Flexibility Measures

1st Study

	T	M	Tr	Rg	Ra	S
T	—	.01	−.46	.07	—	—
M	—	—	.11	—	—	.01
Tr	—	—	—	.05	.01	—
Rg	—	—	—	—	−.23	—
Ra	—	—	—	—	—	−.43
S	—	—	—	—	—	—

In addition: Fisher's rigidity scale correlates −.35 with Trapezoid.

2nd Study

	T	M	Tr	Rg	Ra	S
T	—	—	.20	—	—	—
M	—	—	−.51	—	—	—
Tr	—	—	—	—	.18	—
Rg	—	—	—	—	−.19	−.19
Ra	—	—	—	—	—	−.57
S	—	—	—	—	—	—

from zero. Except for certain transient cases, the measures of perceptual flexibility seem to be unrelated and we can safely say that they are tapping different parts of the process.

We now turn to the diagnostic make-up of the groups. In the first group of 57, diagnostic material was available for 43 cases. These fell roughly into four broad diagnostic categories: Anxiety Reaction, Schizophrenic Reaction, Psychosomatic Reaction, and Conversion Reaction, in the following numbers:

Anxiety reaction	15
Schizophrenic reaction	6
Psychosomatic reaction	12
Conversion reaction	6
Miscellaneous	4

Since the schizophrenic group did not seem to be distinguished on the flexibility measures from the anxiety group, it was decided to combine these categories. The four miscellaneous diagnoses were assigned either to this combined category or to the psychosomatic group on the basis of whether or not they manifested any major somatic involvement. The resulting diagnostic make-up was as follows:

Anxiety and/or psychotic (No somatic symptoms)	23
Psychosomatic reaction	14
Conversion reaction	6

Using the same criteria, the make-up of the second group was as follows (six cases not diagnosed):

Anxiety and/or psychotic	8
Psychosomatic	6
Conversion	1

The two groups are compared in Table 3.

Predictive criteria separating the three diagnostic groups were derived *post hoc* from an analysis of the data for the first group. These criteria are given in Table 4. They were then applied directly to the second group.

Table 5 shows the results in predicting a three-way grouping of the patients as compared to the actual diagnostic findings. It will be noted that for the first study 24 correct predictions were made as opposed to 12 incorrect. On replication, 10 correct and only 4 incorrect predictions were made.

Even more impressive results are obtained if we divide the patients into two groups simply on the basis of whether or not their symp-

TABLE 3

Diagnostic Make-up of Experimental Groups

		1st Study	2nd Study
No Somatic Involvement	Anxiety reaction and/or possible psychosis	23	8
Major Somatic Involvement	Primarily Psychosomatic Symptoms	14	6
		20	-7
	Primarily Conversion Symptoms	6	1
	Total Diagnosed	43	15
	No Diagnosis	14	6
	Total N	57	21

TABLE 4

Flexibility Measures Used to Predict Diagnostic Groups

	Numerical	Qualitative
Anxiety and/or Psychotic	Trapezoid—mean or above Ratio—less than mean .05	Trap.—high Ratio—low
Psychosomatic	Trapezoid—mean or below Ratio—mean .05	Trap.—low Ratio—middle
Conversion	Ratio—above mean Shift—negative	Ratio—high Shift—negative

TABLE 5

Predictions Based on Flexibility Measures Compared with Actual Diagnostic Grouping

First Group—Actual Diagnosis

		Anxiety and/or Psychosis	Psycho- somatic	Con- version	
Predicted Diagnosis	Anxiety and/or Psychosis (No Soma- tization)	12	4	0	16
	Psychosomatic	5	7	0	12
	Conversion	1	2	5	8
		18	13	5	

Second Group—Actual Diagnosis

		Anxiety and/or Psychosis	Psycho- somatic	Con- version	
Predicted Diagnosis	Anxiety and/or Psychosis	5	—	—	5
	Psychosomatic	2	4	—	6
	Conversion	—	2	1	3
		7	6	1	

tomatology includes any somatic involvement. As shown in Table 6, 24 correct predictions were made in the first study as against only 10 incorrect. On replication in the second study 10 correct and only 2 incorrect predictions were made.

It is quite clear that the predictive criteria based on measures of perceptual flexibility are very significantly related to the presence or absence of somatic symptoms. The study is still in its early phases and the measures are still crude. It is to be expected that greater refinement of the measures and the predictive indices will result in still greater accuracy and sharper diagnostic distinctions.

Since there is much work to be done on the perceptual flexibility study, we can conclude this discussion of the over-all project with the general statement that the possibilities seem promising. All of the

TABLE 6

Predictions of Somatization vs. Nonsomatization Compared
with Actual Symptomatology

1st Study

		Actual		
		Somatic	Nonsomatic	
Predicted	Somatic Involvement	12	6	18
	No Somatic Involvement	4	12	16
		16	18	

2nd Study

		Actual		
		Somatic	Nonsomatic	
Predicted	Somatic	5	2	7
	Nonsomatic	—	5	5
		5	7	

data point toward positive results in terms of being able, eventually,
to differentiate clinical groups, as well as the emotionally ill, from
the normal by perceptual flexibility measures. It is also likely that
we shall, in the future, be able to prognosticate better a patient's
response to psychotherapy and other modalities of treatment by using
the criterion of whether he scores within the optimal range of perceptual flexibility. If it proves that these two preliminary findings
hold up after cross-validation and a complete analysis of the data
together with the follow-ups, we shall have developed a new and
fruitful approach to many of the problems in the fields of mental
illness and health. New instruments will be available for evaluating
patients initially, evaluating their progress and the changes that take
place in the course of their illness, and for clarifying our views concerning the nature of mental illness and of mental health. All of this
can provide a scientific underpinning for many of the hunches that
we have all had concerning the importance of flexibility in human
living.

Section II

Correlates of Perceptual Change:
A. Psychopathology

· 3 ·

Size-Constancy in Normals and Schizophrenics*

The present study is concerned with the relationships between particular classes of environmental, intermediate, and personal determinants as they affect size-constancy. The specific environmental determinant investigated was the content of the standard stimulus object. The specific intermediate determinant investigated was the type of experimental instructions used. The personal variable chosen for this study was manifest schizophrenia.

The results of previous investigations indicate that each of these variables affect size-constancy perception. However, the interactions between these pertinent variables have not been systematically investigated. Manifest schizophrenia was chosen as the personal determinant to be investigated because it was felt that this represented an extreme personal reaction. In addition, the empirical data indicated that schizophrenia is a relevant variable in terms of size-constancy reactions.

In order to develop experimentally testable hypotheses concerning the size-constancy perception of schizophrenic subjects, we had to have some ideas or theories about the nature of schizophrenic perception. These theories had not only to be consistent with previously obtained results in size-constancy experiments, but had to be consistent with other known perceptual and behavioral characteristics of schizophrenia. A theory which adequately "explains" one

* This chapter was prepared by Paul Perez and represents a condensation of a doctoral dissertation entitled "Experimental Instructions and Stimulus Content as Variables in the Size-Constancy Perception of Schizophrenics and Normals," submitted to the Graduate School of Arts and Science of New York University.

perceptual phenomenon but is contradicted by another, is, at best, of very limited value and is more likely to prove untenable.

One such theory could be termed a "defensive" theory of schizophrenic perception. In such a theory a schizophrenic is thought of as an individual who withdraws from an environment with which he cannot cope; the peculiarities or deviations from normality of his perceptual behavior are attributed to an attempt at defending himself against intruding stimulation from the external world of reality. Such considerations led Bruner (1951) to make the prediction that withdrawal from object relations would lead to lower size-constancy in schizophrenics, as compared to normals. Experimental evidence indicates that this is not the case; in fact, the reverse seems to hold. Rausch (1952), for example, was forced to change his hypothesis from that suggested by Bruner's prediction. He attributed the higher degree of constancy which he obtained from schizophrenics to restitutional efforts. Rauch concluded that the schizophrenic defends himself through the projection of stability onto the environment, that his world is overly-structured and overly-organized in contrast to the variability of the reality situations which he meets. Thus, what might be termed a general defense theory of schizophrenic perception has the dubious advantage of being able to account for deviations from normal size-constancy perception regardless of the direction of deviancy. Higher constancy is attributed to defense of the self by means of projected stability and lowered constancy would be attributed to defense by withdrawal from reality.

The rationale for the hypotheses of the present study was derived from consideration of the nature of schizophrenic deviations in perceptual behavior, rather than from consideration of the purposes or reasons which may logically necessitate such deviations. In other words, we are concerned with the question, "How does schizophrenic perception differ from normal perception?" rather than, "Why does the schizophrenic perceive his world in the way he does?" The second type of consideration is probably more basic, but it was felt that it would prove more fruitful to investigate and describe a phenomenon before considering the purposes it may serve.

The results of previous studies have indicated that schizophrenic subjects in a size-constancy experiment show higher constancy indices than do normal subjects. This would suggest that in their judgments of size-at-a-distance, the schizophrenic subjects may be more responsive to cues for distance than are normals. If we consider cues which are features of the field rather than that of the object itself as "peripheral" cues, it can be inferred that schizophrenics are more responsive to peripheral cues than are normals. In general, all perceptual processes involve some selectivity of cues; for example, we can respond to size differences between objects even though they are the same color, or respond to similarity in color regardless of differences in size. In other words, we respond to those cues which are most appropriate to the task and tend to ignore those which are less appropriate. There is some evidence to suggest that this ability is impaired in schizophrenics; that the perceptual behavior of schizophrenics is characterized by something analogous to the "over-inclusion" which Cameron (1947) considers to be a characteristic of schizophrenic thinking.

A type of response on the Rorschach test which has been considered to be pathognomonic of schizophrenia is the "contaminated" response. Klopfer (1946) has defined this as a response in which the subject gives to one stimulus configuration two entirely incompatible interpretations. For example, for the green details on card IX, an F response, "bear," may be used, or a C response, "grass" . . . the schizophrenic subject puts these two responses together to create a new concept—as for example, "grass bear." Thus the normal who responds to the stimulus of color is able to ignore the then inappropriate cue for form and give the response "grass." The schizophrenic does not exert this selectivity, but responds to both cues. Using the term "peripheral" in a broader sense to include cues that are inappropriate to the task or intentions of the observer, we can say that the schizophrenic is responding to peripheral cues which the normal is able to ignore.

A phenomenon of schizophrenic behavior that may indirectly support our contention is the "clang association," a response to a stimulus word which is determined by the sound of the stimulus word rather than by any sense relationship. Rapaport (1946) found clang associations practically absent in his normal, neurotic, and depressed groups, but his schizophrenics and pre-schizophrenics gave a significant number of clang associations such as "beef-weef" and "man-tan." In this situation, schizophrenics respond to a less appropriate cue (the sound of the stimulus word) that the normal is able to ignore when he responds to a more appropriate aspect of the stimulus word (its meaning).

The "loose" concept span which Shafer (1948) has found to be characteristic of many schizophrenics on a Sorting Test, appears to be relevant to our concept of schizophrenic perception. When he includes more objects in a group than are embraced by the usual conception process, or groups together two or three objects which conventional concept formation almost never relates to each other, the schizophrenic can be said to be responding to inappropriate relationships, which might be considered as peripheral, in the sense of being secondary in importance to the more conventional relationships that the normal uses in concept formation.

The Size-Constancy Experiment

If the schizophrenic is more responsive to peripheral cues than is the normal, we could predict certain differences between schizophrenics and normal subjects in a size-constancy situation. We predicted that schizophrenics would be more able to comply with "objective" or "bet" instructions which require the subject to respond to distance cues, than would normals. "Bet" instructions require the subject to estimate the actual physical dimensions of the standard stimulus. To do this, he must respond adequately to the cues for distance as well as to the optic angle subtended by the distant stimulus. On the other hand, we expected schizophrenic subjects to be less able to comply with "analytic" or "look" instructions. "Look" instructions require the subject to respond only to the optic angle and to ignore consciously the cues for distance. To use Singer's (1952) term, the subject is required to impose a "functional reduction screen" on the field, that is to say, to respond as if the field cues were not available to him. "Bet" instructions are designed to elicit a response based on distal stimuli, while "look" instructions require a response to proximal stimuli. Previous investigations into the differential effect of "analytic" and "objective" instructions have not included mental patients as subjects. Singer, for example, drew his subjects from a postgraduate student population. It was felt that the language of his instructions might be difficult for the subjects in our experiment to understand. For these reasons our instructions were essentially simplified versions of the "look" and "bet" instructions originally used by Singer.

Singer found that meaningful stimulus content led to enhancement of apparent size in an experiment similar to the present one, but using normal subjects. This enhancement due to content was most apparent when "look" instructions were used, that is, when the set was to ignore field cues. Objectively speaking, stimulus content is an irrelevant cue when the task or intention is size estimation.

Therefore, the general theory that schizophrenics are more responsive to peripheral and irrelevant cues than are normals would lead to the prediction of a greater degree of size enhancement due to stimulus content in the schizophrenic group as compared with the normal group. Just as meaningfulness is an irrelevant cue in the context of size estimation, so is "emotional impact" or "affective value." Singer found no significant difference in size-enhancement between his "happy face" and his "sad face" stimuli. His results may have been a function of (a) his two meaningful stimuli not differing sufficiently in affective value to elicit differences in enhancement, or (b) normal subjects not being responsive to affective content but being responsive to meaningfulness. The present experiment attempted to avoid the first possibility by using two meaningful stimuli with presumably greater difference in emotional impact than those used by Singer. Whether such stimuli lead to differential enhancement in nonschizophrenic subjects or not, the general theory that schizophrenics are more responsive to irrelevant cues than are normals, led to the prediction of differential enhancement effects due to the factor of emotional value being present in the one stimulus and relatively absent in the other.

The first general hypothesis was derived from the findings of other investigators who have separately investigated environmental, personal, and intermediate determinants of size-constancy. On the basis of their findings, it was predicted:

1a. that schizophrenic subjects give larger values in estimating the size of a distant standard stimulus than nonschizophrenic subjects.

1b. that objective "bet" instructions elicit larger values in the estimation of the size of a distant standard stimulus than do analytic "look" instructions.

1c. that meaningful stimuli are perceived as larger than nonmeaningful stimuli, that a meaningful and affective stimulus is perceived as larger than a meaningful but nonaffective stimulus.

The second general hypothesis was concerned with the predicted interactions of the three determinants based on the general theory that was suggested previously. It was predicted:

2a. that there is a significant interaction, *diagnosis by instructions,* with differences in size judgments between schizophrenic and nonschizophrenic subjects being greater following "look" instructions than following "bet" instructions.

2b. that there is a significant interaction, *instruction by content*, with the size-enhancing effect of stimulus content being greater following "look" instructions than it is following "bet" instructions.

2c. that there is a significant interaction, *diagnosis by content*, with schizophrenic subjects showing more enhancement of size due to meaningfulness and affective value of stimulus content than do nonschizophrenic subjects.

2d. that there is a significant triple interaction, *diagnosis by content by instruction*, with the difference in size-enhancement effect of stimulus content between "bet" and "look" trials (the difference predicted in Hypothesis 2b) being less for the schizophrenic group than for the nonschizophrenic group.

The Embedded Figures Test

As a further test of the theory relating differences in perceptual constancy to differences in responsiveness to irrelevant stimuli, the Embedded Figures Test, an elaboration of the Gottschalt figures developed by Witkin (1950), was utilized. High scores on this test indicate difficulty in breaking up a complex field in order to locate a hidden figure. The use of this instrument permitted the testing of some of the assumptions on which the predictions as to the outcome of the size-constancy experiment were based. The first assumption was that schizophrenics are more responsive to peripheral and irrelevant cues than are normals. If this were so, they would have more difficulty in breaking up a complex field in order to locate a hidden figure. We therefore predicted that schizophrenics would make significantly higher scores on the Embedded Figures Test than would nonschizophrenic subjects.

The second assumption was that this hypothesized characteristic of schizophrenic perception is related to performance in the size-constancy experiment. Specifically, we assumed that the relatively higher constancy predicted for the schizophrenic subjects is related to their relatively greater responsiveness to those aspects of the field which make up cues for distance. If this were the case, a positive correlation between scores on the Embedded Figures Test and some representative size-constancy scores would be expected. In other words, the more field-dependent the individual, the greater his responsiveness to distance cues and the higher his constancy scores. Thus, a positive correlation between the mean scores of the three "bet" trials and the scores on the Embedded Figures Test was predicted.

Another assumption was that an individual's ability to comply with "look" instructions is related to his ability to ignore certain aspects of a field and respond to others. If this were the case, a negative correlation between scores on the Embedded Figures Test and scores representative of the individual's ability to comply with "look" instructions would be expected. Thus, a negative correlation between individual scores on the Embedded Figures Test and the difference between the mean of the three "bet" trials and the three "look" trials was predicted.

It was also assumed that individuals who have relatively more difficulty in ignoring relative aspects of a situation are affected more by differences in the content of the standard stimulus and that this is reflected in their size estimates. If this were the case, a positive correlation between scores on the Embedded Figures Test and scores representative of the effect of different stimulus content on the individual's size judgments would be expected. Thus, a positive correlation was predicted between individual scores on the Embedded Figures Test and the difference between trials using a meaningless stimulus figure and trials using a meaningful and affective figure.

Summarizing these hypotheses, it was predicted:

3a. that the mean of the Embedded Figures Test score of the schizophrenic group is significantly greater than that of the non-schizophrenic group.

3b. that there is a significant positive correlation between individual Embedded Figures Test scores and the mean score of the three "bet" trials for each subject.

3c. that there is a significant negative correlation between individual scores on the Embedded Figures Test and the difference between the mean of the three "look" scores for each subject.

3d. that there is a significant positive correlation between individual scores on the Embedded Figures Test and the difference between the mean of the two trials using a meaningless figure and the mean of the two trials using a meaningful and affective figure.

METHOD

Subjects

The subjects in this experiment were hospitalized male patients at the East Orange Veterans Administration Hospital. Only veterans of World War II or the Korean campaign were considered in the selection of subjects. Each subject was tested for visual acuity by means of a Snellen Chart and only those with 20/20 binocular vision, corrected or uncorrected, were included. A total of 50 subjects were tested, 25 in the schizophrenic group and 25 in the nonschizophrenic group.

Subjects in the schizophrenic group were selected from among those patients in the Neuropsychiatric Service of the hospital who carried a diagnosis of schizophrenic reaction and who met the requirements of military service and visual acuity referred to previously. Each patient in this group was considered by a panel of judges consisting of the patient's ward psychiatrist, the clinical psychologist who had tested the patient, and a clinical psychologist who had seen the patient for individual or group psychotherapy. Where the psychologist concerned was a trainee, his diagnostic judgment had to be supported by his supervising staff psychologist.

The judges were asked to determine on the basis of the available hospital records, case histories, psychological test data, and clinical observation, whether or not each patient could be classified as schizophrenic in terms of a description of schizophrenic disorders taken from the USVA Technical Bulletin, "Nomenclature of Psychiatric Disorders" (TB 1-78). The "Latent Schizophrenic" type of reaction was excluded from the description of schizophrenic reactions used in this study. This was because of the difficulty in differentiating this condition from other nonschizophrenic classifications.

If all three judges independently concluded on the basis of all available information that a diagnosis of schizophrenic reaction (regardless of type), as defined above, was justified, the patient was included in the schizophrenic group. However, only patients who were reasonably well-oriented and co-operative at the time of the experiment were tested. Patients who were receiving electro-convulsive therapy at the time of the experiment were excluded.

The nonschizophrenic group consisted of patients from the Surgical Service of the hospital who had been hospitalized for some physical condition not involving the central nervous system. Any patient whose previous history, records of current hospitalization, or ward behavior as reported by the ward physician or charge nurse suggested the presence of mental disorder, "neurotic overlay," or psychosomatic illness, was excluded. Only patients on a convalescent status were included in this group.

The two groups were matched for age and for verbal intelligence, as determined by the Wechsler-Bellevue Scale (Form I).

Procedure

The Size-Constancy Experiment. The experiment was conducted in the Perception Laboratory of the East Orange Veterans Administration Hospital under controlled conditions of illumination, background, and procedure. Upon entering the room each subject was seated in a chair and his visual acuity was tested by means of a Snellen Chart. He was then told:

I'm going to ask you to make some size judgments, but I'm going to ask you to make them in two different ways. Half of the time I'll ask you to tell me which size you think a card *really* is and half of the time I'll ask you to tell me which size the card looks to you. As you know, things at a distance look smaller than they would close up. Let me show you what I mean.

The subject was asked to close one eye and two plain white square cards were placed in his field of vision. One, 4 inches square, was placed at a distance of 2 feet from his eye; the other, 8 inches square, was placed at a distance of 6 feet from his eye. The cards were placed so that they could both be seen in one fixation and did not overlap. The subject was then asked, "Which card *looks* larger?" They invariably indicated the nearer card. Then they were asked, "Which card *really* is larger?" and they invariably indicated the more distant card.

The training trials were then carried out by the subject. A blank white card 9 centimeters square was hung on a black wall directly in front of the subject at his eye level. The distance from card to subject was 20 feet. At an angle of 45 degrees to the right and at a distance of 2½ feet were the comparison stimuli. These consisted of a booklet of white squares on black grounds. The white squares increased in diameter by .25 centimeter increments from 3 centimeters to 10.50 centimeters. The booklet hung on a ring-stand so that the pages could be flipped over, exposing one white square at a time. The subject was first read the "look" instructions:

Compare each of these squares with the one in front. Tell me when one of these squares *looks* the same size as the one in front. Remember, I'm interested this time just in the way they look to you, their appearance, not when you figure them to be equal. Try not to think about the difference in distance.

The experimenter then presented the comparison stimuli in ascending order by turning over the pages of the booklet at a constant rate until the subject indicated when to stop. The size of the square chosen as "looking" the same as the 9 centimeters square was recorded. The experimenter then read the "bet" instructions:

> Compare each of these squares with the one in front. Tell me when you think that one of these *really* is the same size as the one in front. Remember, this time I want you to say when they actually are the same size, not just when they look the same. Think of it as though you had a bet on it. You should take into account the difference in distances.

The experimenter then repeated the presentation of the comparison stimuli. After the two training trials the subject was asked if he understood the difference between the two types of instructions, which were reread to those subjects who requested it. The experimenter undertook to answer any questions the subject asked, but did so only by repeating relevant parts of the standardized instructions. At this point two of the schizophrenic patients appeared too confused to understand the instructions and were excused; another schizophrenic subject declined to continue the experiment.

The procedure for the experimental trials was similar to that of the training trials. In the experimental trials, however, three different standard stimuli were each presented twice, one following "bet" instructions and one following "look" instructions, making a total of six experimental trials for each subject. The three stimulus cards consisted of a drawing of a nonsense figure, a drawing of a lettered block, and a drawing of a skull. Each card was 9 centimeters square. In drawing the figures an attempt was made to keep their structural characteristics as alike as possible. Thus the over-all dimensions, the thickness of the lines used, the areas enclosed, and the amounts of black surface on each figure, were equated as much as possible to those of the other figures.

These figures were chosen in order to obtain a relatively meaningless stimulus, a meaningful stimulus with relatively little emotional value, and a meaningful stimulus with relatively more emotional value. In further discussion the stimuli will be designated N, B, and S for the nonsense figure, block, and skull, respectively. The six trials will be designated LN, BN, LB, BB, LS, and BS; the first letter indicating the type of instructions ("look" or "bet") and the second letter indicating the stimulus card presented.

The six trials were presented to each subject in random order, the sequence for each subject having been previously determined by use of a table of random numbers. For each trial, the procedure used was the same as that during the training trials. The stimulus card for the first trial was placed against a back wall 20 feet from the subject at eye level. The booklet of comparison stimuli was placed 45 degrees to the subject's right at a distance of 2½ feet. The experimenter read the appropriate instructions for the first trial and then presented the comparison stimuli in ascending order at a constant rate until the subject indicated when to stop. The diameter of the comparison square chosen for this trial was recorded. This procedure was repeated for each of the five remaining trials, using the appropriate standard stimulus and instructions.

At the end of the final trial, the last stimulus card was removed and the subject was asked to describe the cards he had been shown. The examiners then asked, "I asked you to estimate the size in two different ways; what were they?" The subject's answers and any other comments on his part were recorded.

The Embedded Figures Test

This test was developed by Witkin (1950), who elaborated on figures originally developed by Gottschalk (1924). Essentially, the test consists of 24 complex figures and 8 simple figures. Each complex figure contains one of the simple figures. The simple figure is embedded in the complex figure in such a way as to be perceptually obscured. All but one of the complex figures are colored in such a way as to reinforce a given pattern and further obscure the simple figure. The simple figures are all uncolored. In addition to the test figures, there are a complex figure and a simple figure which are used for demonstration and practice at the beginning of the test. A detailed account of this test and reproductions of the figures may be found in Witkin (1950).

The procedure used in this part of the study was that prescribed by Witkin. At the beginning of the test the examiner read the following instructions:

> I am going to show you a series of colored designs. Each time I show you one of these designs, I want you to describe the over-all pattern that you see in it. After you examine each design, I will show you a similar figure which is contained in the larger design. You will then be given the larger design again and your job will be to locate the smaller figure in it. Let us go through one to show you how it is done.

The subject was then shown the practice complex figure and allowed to look at it for 15 seconds. It was then taken away and he was shown the practice simple figure for 10 seconds. Then the simple figure was replaced by the complex figure and the subject was told to locate the simple figure in the complex figure. When he had found it, he was asked to trace it so that the examiner could be sure it was the right one.

After the practice trial the examiner read the following instructions:

> That is how we will proceed on all trials. I would like to add that in every case the smaller figure will be present in the larger design. It will always be in the upright position. There may be several of the smaller figures in the same large design, but you are to look only for the one in the upright position. Work as quickly as you possibly can, since I will be timing you, but be sure that the figure you find is exactly the same as the original figure, both in size, and in proportion. As soon as you have found the figure, tell me at once. If you ever forget what the smaller figure looks like, you may ask to see it again. Are there any questions?

The subject was then given the first complex figure for 15 seconds, then the first simple figure for 10 seconds, and then the complex figure for as long as it took him to locate the embedded figure. The order in which the figures were presented was that indicated by Witkin (1950), which is so arranged that the simple figure to be located is never the same in any two successive trials. The score for each trial was the time taken to locate the simple figure correctly. However, if a subject had not located the figure within five minutes, his score for that trial was recorded as five minutes (F) and he went on to the next trial. The subjects were allowed to re-examine the simple figures whenever they wished, but the complex figure was always removed so that they never saw both figures at the same time. The stop watch was stopped while the subject was re-examining the simple figure, so that this time was not included in his final score. Subjects were allowed to examine the simple figure whenever they wished, the time of examination being noted. They were not, however, permitted to see it for longer than 10 seconds at a time. Each subject's score for the test was the sum of his scores for the 24 trials.

RESULTS

Table 1 shows the means of the size judgments of a 9 centimeters standard stimulus for each of the six experimental trials of the size-constancy experiment. Separate means and standard deviations are given for each of the two subject groups.

The data in Table 1 indicate that, for each of the six trials, the

TABLE 1

Mean Size Judgments of 9 Centimeters Standard Stimuli Following "Look" and "Bet"
Instructions for the Schizophrenic and Nonschizophrenic Groups (Data in Centimeters)

Groups	Look			Bet		
	Nonsense	Block	Skull	Nonsense	Block	Skull
S mean:	6.86	6.81	6.38	9.16	9.20	9.00
S.D.	.9800	.8696	1.0750	.5866	.5099	.5916
NS mean:	5.74	5.71	5.52	8.57	8.54	8.46
S.D.	.8558	.8357	.9998	.4273	.5643	.5508

mean size estimate of the schizophrenic group is larger than the
mean size estimate of the nonschizophrenic group. It will also be
seen that the mean size estimates elicited by "bet" instructions are
larger than mean size estimates (for the corresponding group and
stimulus figures) elicited by "look" instructions.

If we consider the trials made by each group following a particular type of instructions, the mean estimate of the skull stimulus
is smaller than mean estimates of the other two figures. This is the
case for all four instruction-group combinations. It will also be seen
that the mean estimates of the nonsense figure exceed those of the
block figure, except for the schizophrenic group following "bet"
instructions.

The analysis of variance for the size-constancy experiment is shown
in Table 2.

The results of the analysis of variance indicated that the difference between the diagnostic means is a reliable one (P < .01).
That is to say the size estimates of the schizophrenic group are
significantly larger than those of the nonschizophrenic groups. The
significant *instructions* variable (P < .01) indicates that the estimates elicited by "bet" instructions are significantly larger than those
elicited by "look" instructions.

The significant *content* variable (P < .01) indicates that the differences in size estimation due to stimulus content are reliable.
Since the difference between mean estimates of the nonsense figure
and the block figure are not significant, the significant *content*
variable is due primarily to the skull figure being estimated as
smaller than the two other figures.

The only significant interaction is the *instruction by content* interaction, which is significant at the .05 level. This significant interaction

TABLE 2

Analysis of Variance of the Size Judgments of Schizophrenic and Nonschizophrenic Subjects Following "Look" and "Bet" Instructions, Using Standard Stimuli of Differing Content

	ss	df	ms	F	P
Between					
Subjects	146.4127	49	2.9880		
Diagnosis	49.4102	1	49.4102	25.0064	.01
Error$_b$	94.8450	48	1.9759		
Within					
Subjects	615.1446	250	2.4606		
Instructions	527.3502	1	527.3502	396.0572	.01
Content	3.6579	2	1.8289	22.9185	.01
I × C	.6430	2	.3215	3.9400	.05
I × D	3.4669	1	3.4669	2.6038	—
C × D	.4775	2	.2388	2.9925	—
I × C × D	.1366	2	.0638	.8370	—
Error$_w$	79.4125	240	.3309		
Error$_{1\,w}$	63.9108	48	1.3315		
Error$_{2\,w}$	7.6655	96	.0798		
Error$_{3\,w}$	.8362	96	.0816		

Tests of significance were made as follows:

Instructions variable against error term Error$_{1\,w}$
Content variable against error term Error$_{2\,w}$
Diagnosis variable against error term Error$_b$
I × C interaction against error term Error$_{3\,w}$
I × D interaction against error term Error$_{1\,w}$
C × D interaction against error term Error$_{2\,w}$
I × C × D interaction against error term Error$_{3\,w}$

is due primarily to variations in size estimates of the different stimuli elicited by "look" instructions. The size judgments of the three stimuli elicited by "bet" instructions are relatively consistent.

The mean scores of each group on the Embedded Figures Test are shown in Table 3. The value of t for the difference of the means is 2.03, which is significant at the .05 level for 48 degrees of freedom.

TABLE 3

Mean Embedded Figures Test Scores (in Minutes) for the Schizophrenic and Nonschizophrenic Group

	S	NS
Mean	30.25	19.46
S.D.	23.61	14.68

TABLE 4

Product Moment Correlations between Embedded Figures Test Scores and Mean "Bet" Scores; the Difference between "Bet" and "Look" Scores; and the Difference between N and S Scores

Group	$\bar{B}$	$\bar{B} - \bar{L}$	$\bar{N} - \bar{S}$
S	.1516	−.4708 *	.1025
NS	.0977	−.0951	.1880
Both	.2425	−.3657 †	.1817

* Significant at the .05 level of probability.

† Significant at the .01 level of probability.

Table 4 shows the product moment correlations between scores on the Embedded Figures Test and representative measures of performance on the size-constancy experiment. The size-constancy measures were the mean of the three "bet" scores ($\bar{B}$); the difference between the mean "bet" and "look" scores ($\bar{B} - \bar{L}$); and the difference between the mean N stimulus score and the mean S stimulus score ($\bar{N} - \bar{S}$).

The mean of the three "bet" scores ($\bar{B}$) was chosen as a representative measure of the individual's ability to estimate the actual size of a distant stimulus object. The difference between the mean "bet" and "look" scores ($\bar{B} - \bar{L}$) was chosen as a representative measure of the effect of varying instructions on the individual's size judgments. The difference between the Mean $\bar{N}$ stimulus score and the mean $\bar{S}$ stimulus score was chosen as a representative measure of the effect of varying stimulus content on the individual's size judgments.

SUMMARY AND CONCLUSIONS

Summary

The present study undertook to investigate the size-constancy perception of a group of schizophrenic subjects and a group of non-schizophrenic subjects under the two different conditions of experimental instructions and using three different standard stimuli.

In the size-constancy experiment, each subject was required to make six size judgments of a square card 20 feet away by means of a series of comparison variables 2½ feet away. Three trials were made following objective instructions and three following analytic instructions. Three different standard stimuli were used. All were white square cards 9 centimeters wide. On one was drawn a nonsense figure, on one an alphabetic block, and on the third a skull. The six trials were presented in random order. Each subject also took the Witkin Embedded Figures Test, a test giving a measure of ability to separate a configuration from a complex field. The data from the size-constancy experiment were subjected to an analysis of variance and representative measures of size judgments were correlated with scores on the Embedded Figures Test.

Findings

1. Size-constancy values were significantly higher for schizophrenic than for nonschizophrenic subjects.

2. Size-constancy values were significantly higher following objective instructions than they were following analytic instructions.

3. The skull figure elicited significantly smaller size comparisons than did the nonsense figure and the block. No significant difference was found between the block and the nonsense figure.

4. The only significant interaction was *instructions by content*. The differences in size due to content were greater following analytic instructions than they were following objective instructions.

5. The *content by diagnosis, instructions by diagnosis,* and *instructions by content* by diagnosis interactions were not significant.

6. Only one significant correlation was found between measures of size-constancy performance and Embedded Figures Test scores. This was a significant negative correlation between Embedded Figures Test scores and a measure of the ability to comply with analytic instructions (mean of the "bet" trials minus the mean of the "look" trials). This correlation was significant for the schizophrenic group.

Conclusions

The performance of schizophrenic subjects in a size-constancy experiment differs in two respects from that of nonschizophrenic subjects. They demonstrate a higher degree of size-constancy than do nonschizophrenics, regardless of the type of instructions used or the content of the standard stimulus. The ability of schizophrenic subjects to comply with analytic instructions is related to their ability to separate a configuration from a complex field. This relationship does not hold for nonschizophrenic subjects. No other significant correlations between performance on the Embedded Figures Test and the size-constancy experiment were found. However, the mean Embedded Figures Test score for the schizophrenic group was significantly higher than that of the nonschizophrenic group. While the nature of the standard stimulus affects the apparent size of a distant object, the factor of "meaningfulness" did not lead to enchancement of apparent size. While the skull figure was seen as significantly smaller than the other two figures, the results of the study did not allow us to ascribe this to the affective symbolic value of the skull figure card. The effect of stimulus content on apparent size was significantly greater following analytic instructions than it was following objective instructions.

· 4 ·

Personality Orientation
and Size-Distance Perception *

This study was concerned with the relationships between certain measures of personality orientation and characteristic modes of perceiving as manifested in reactions to emotionally valent material on the "thereness-thatness" demonstration (Ittelson, 1952; Kilpatrick, 1952).

In order to pursue this investigation it was considered important to clarify a number of specific problems:

In the context of a particular personality orientation, is there a correlation between emotional valence and the perception of an object by an individual?

If such a correlation exists, is it reflected in the manipulation of the object or symbol on the "thereness-thatness" demonstration?

If the manipulations reflect such correlation, what is the effect on the direction of the placements?

Is the manipulation of neutrally-valent material significantly different from the manipulation of positively or negatively valent material?

Is an object or symbol negatively valent if it is unfamiliar and unstructured?

Is perception of an ambiguous object or symbol affected by verbal identification (labelling), and if so, how?

* This chapter was prepared by George Kaufer and represents a condensation of a doctoral dissertation entitled "An Investigation of Certain Aspects of the Relationship between Personality Orientation and Perceptual Defenses" submitted to the School of Education of New York University.

The conception of personality orientation used in this study is that of Horney (1945), involving a trichotomous classification of orientations called "moving-toward," "moving-against," and "moving-away." The orientations are defined as follows:

"Moving-toward": a personality orientation in which an individual needs, compulsively, "to be liked, wanted, desired, loved; to feel accepted, welcomed, approved of, appreciated; to be needed, to be of importance to others, especially to one particular person; to be helped, protected, taken care of, guided."

"Moving-against": a personality orientation in which "aggressive trends predominate." The primary need becomes one of control over others.

"Moving-away": a personality orientation reflecting "the need for detachment." This results in "intolerable strain in association with people. . . . What is crucial is this inner need to put emotional distance between themselves and others." The following hypotheses were tested:

1. The size of an object as perceived, and the distance at which it is placed by the subject on the "thereness-thatness" demonstration is related to the emotional valence which that object has for the subject as well as the subject's personality orientation.

a) The positional placement reflects the personality orientation.

"Moving-toward" subjects—which in this study also included individuals judged "moving-against"—tend to make perceptual under-placements (toward the subject) while "moving-away" subjects tend to make perceptual overplacements (away from the subject).

2. The placement of emotionally valent material differs significantly when compared with the manipulation of neutrally valent material.

3. The more unfamiliar and unstructured an object is, the greater is its negative valence.

4. Once an individual has labelled an object or symbol, his subsequent perception of it, as reflected in the positional placements on the "thereness-thatness" demonstration, will show a change.

METHOD

Subjects

The subjects for this study were selected from the veteran population of a Veterans Administration general medical and surgical hospital. A patient population was decided upon because individuals who are ill tend to overgeneralize their reactions to other people and the Horney classification can be found with greater frequency in such a population.

In view of the visual requirements of the experimental situation, only subjects with 20/20 (Snellen vision, corrected) were chosen.

The TAT protocol was an important criterion for determining a subject's personality orientation. Since more productive TAT protocols can be expected from subjects with normal or better intelligence, only patients who scored normal or better on the Wechsler-Bellevue test were selected.

No patients were selected who suffered from organic, cerebral damage or degeneration resulting from senility or trauma. But the fact that these patients were referred for psychological evaluation is, of course, an indication that there was suspicion of possible emotional difficulties. The diagnosis, however, was not a factor in the selection of patients for the study.

Of the 42 subjects employed in this experiment, 30 were from the neuropsychiatric service and 12 from the medical service.

Procedure

All psychologists, both trainees and regular staff members, were requested to include in their regular test battery the following materials:

1. Cards #3, 4, 6, 7, 9, 12, 13, of the Thematic Apperception Test
2. Sacks Sentence Completion Test
3. Rorschach
4. Draw-A-Person Test

When these tests were completed, the resulting protocols were studied to determine whether the patients met the requirements outlined earlier. Patients whose I.Q.'s were below normal limits and who, on the basis of physical examinations by physicians and psychiatrists, gave any indication of organic brain disorder, were eliminated.

The names of patients who met the preliminary requirements for the study were submitted to the ward physician, who then referred the patients for research.

Each patient who appeared for the experiment first met with the researcher, who explained to him, in a general way, the nature and purpose of the study. Following this, the patient's visual acuity was checked with the Snellen eye chart. Those patients who tested less than 20/20 vision, either with or without glasses, were rejected from the study. If the patient's vision proved satisfactory, he was then introduced specifically to the experimental situation.

Categories Used in Organizing Data

As discussed earlier, the Horney formulations were employed to place each of the subjects into one of three categories in terms of what the judges considered their characteristic manner of relating to people. The method of arriving at the judgments with regard to each subject will be detailed below.

In her discussions of these three characteristic personality patterns,—movements toward, against, and away from people—Horney tends to view them as symptoms of inner turmoil. She maintains that an individual's basic conflict has its source in childhood feelings of helplessness in relation to others. The individual learns to defend himself against these feelings, she believes, by adopting one of the three basic patterns of behavior. The pattern selected then permeates all of his later activities.

For the purpose of this study, Horney's descriptions of the three personality orientations were adopted as the criteria for categorizing the subjects.

In the Horney formulations, two of the three categories—the one moving *toward* people and the one moving *against* people—imply an orientation in which the individuals tend to approach others; one for the purpose of nurturing and satisfying dependency needs, the other out of hostility. It was this factor which furnished the rationale for combining these two groups in the study.

The need to combine the two groups arose because only 4 of the 42 subjects tested were judged to move primarily *against* people. Since it was considered impractical to continue testing patients until an adequate number of "moving-against" subjects had been found, it was decided, for statistical purposes, to put the two categories together.

While it is difficult to determine precisely why so few subjects in the "moving-against" category were found, some conjectures can be made. The installation at which this study was conducted was a general medical and surgical Veterans Administration Hospital. Almost all of the patients at this hospital are voluntary admissions. Under the circumstances, one might expect that with the exception of those who came to the hospital for emergency medical reasons, those seeking admission might be doing so either to escape—to isolate themselves—or to be taken care of as completely as is only possible in a hospital. Persons in the "moving-against" category might more readily be found in a nonvoluntary institution such as a jail or a neuropsychiatric hospital, where they might land as a result of open conflict with, or aggression against, people, if they have not found a way of sublimating their hostility in some socially-accepted or highly competitive enterprise.

Judgments of Personality Orientations

The test battery protocols for each of the subjects accepted for the study were submitted separately to three judges. All of the judges were male clinical psychologists with a Ph.D. and a minimum of five years of clinical experience. Each judge received a mimeographed form, "Instructions for Judging Personality Orientation," together with the rating form for each subject.

The judges were instructed to make judgments as to a patient's basic personality needs in accordance with the Horney definitions of "moving toward people," "moving against people," and "moving away from people," all three of which were quoted. They were asked to proceed on the basis that all people fit into one or the other of these classifications, and to record their judgments on the basis of the projective test materials which they had examined.

The judges were asked first to classify the subjects generally, and then to indicate the estimated strength of the orientation with respect to men and women, with an appropriate check against one of the four points from one to four on the rating scale. It was emphasized that this was not a balanced scale and that the four points indicated the positive strength of the tendency. What was called for in this connection was a subjective clinical judgment on the part of each of the judges.

In addition to the written instructions, the researcher met with each judge individually in order to clarify certain aspects of the instructions. In this interview it was stressed that the sole criteria for arriving at the judgments were to be the Horney formulations as quoted in the instructions, and the clinical impressions of the judge with regard to the subjects' test protocols.

It was further suggested that the judges attempt to concentrate on possible behavior, rather than on underlying personality dynamics. This was done because preliminary discussions indicated that any other approach would necessarily be further complicated by the individual theoretical biases of the judges themselves. The judges were further instructed to make their judgments as to a subject's general personality orientation *before* attempting to make the more refined judgments concerning orientation with respect to men and women.

The original plan for this study was to use only those subjects about whom there was one hundred per cent agreement among the three judges. However, this was found to be quite impractical. It was therefore decided to accept agreement by two out of the three judges as a satisfactory level. This decision created some difficulties when it came to judgments about the subjects' personality orientations toward men and women. In these instances, the subjects were judged not only as to their predominant movements with respect to men and women, but also as to the intensity of that movement.

Thus it became possible for two of the judges to agree that a given subject moved *away* from either men or women with an intensity of four, while the third judge could maintain that the subject moved *toward* with the same intensity. While instances as extreme as the example cited occurred only on a very few occasions, some rationale for these are, nevertheless, required.

The judges' own performance in terms of the consistency of their judgments is available. An analysis of these judgments lends weight to the conclusion that the judges' personal conflicts and biases played a role in the type of discrepancies of judgment obtained.

While an extensive analysis of the judges and the judgments cannot be presented here, it is appropriate to state that with regard to general personality orientation, the judges arrived at 100% agreement in 55% of the total number of cases, and at 67% agreement for the remainder, which resulted in a mean percentage of agreement of 85%.

Apparatus

1. The "thereness-thatness" demonstration. This consists of "essentially two basic parts, a binocular comparison field and a test field. The test field provides some basic means for viewing a test object where apparent distance is to be determined. The binocular field provides distance indications relative to which this apparent distance is to be judged." (Ittelson, 1952)

The test object was mounted on a carriage which the subject manipulated along the length of the table with a control wheel, in an attempt to align it with a designated distance indicator.

2. Test. The following forms were employed (Twitchell-Allen, 1948):

    a) #12, which is frequently seen as a female figure (F)

    b) #21, which is frequently seen as a male figure (M)

    c) #7, which is frequently seen as symbolic representation of male genitalia (MG)

    d) #1, which is frequently seen as symbolic representation of female genitalia (FG)

    e) a cube (C)

3. A playing card, three-quarters of regulation size (PC).

The letters in parentheses represent the symbols for the figures described and will be used later to designate the figures. Each subject was seen in the laboratory for a short orientation interview before the actual experiment was begun. This session served to accomplish a number of things. The subject was introduced, generally, to the nature of the research. It was explained to him that this experiment was part of a large-scale study centered in universities and a few hospitals. He was further introduced to the concept that the research was concerned with some nonphysiological aspects of perception. Following this brief general orientation, he was given the opportunity to withdraw from the experiment if, for any reason, he did not wish to participate. Care was taken to make this offer in a context wherein the patient was made to feel that withdrawing from the experiment was in no way prejudicial to him. Of all the patients who appeared for the preliminary interview, only two withdrew.

If the subject agreed to participate, he was given a Snellen eye test, and if his vision proved to be 20/20 corrected, he was then introduced to the apparatus, with all the lights in the laboratory on. Its operations were explained to him, and he was given an opportunity to manipulate it. He was then seated at the apparatus and all the lights were turned off. The laboratory itself was thoroughly lightproof. A five-minute period was allowed for the subject to become adapted to the dark. He was then instructed to feel for the headrest and to place his head on it. When this had been done, he was instructed to close his eyes.

The examiner then set the controls so that a predetermined level of illumination—the same employed for all the subjects—was attained for the distance standards. A shield in front of the subject's left eye was set so that he could see the distance standards with both eyes and the object to be manipulated only with the right eye. This was checked at intervals throughout the testing period.

When the apparatus was properly adjusted, the subject was again asked to close his eyes, and the playing card was mounted on the carriage. This was placed at some arbitrary distance from the subject. He was instructed to open his eyes, and, by manipulating the carriage, to move the object to where it looked best to him. He was then instructed to close his eyes again.

All of the objects were then, in turn, placed by the subject at the position of his choice. The first object was again mounted in the apparatus and was again placed at some arbitrary distance. The subject opened his eyes and was instructed to align the object with the third point on the distance indicators. Then, he was again instructed to close his eyes, continuing to do so between settings until all the position settings were made.

The following settings were made:

1. from an arbitrary setting to where it looked "best" to the subject
2. from an arbitrary setting beyond the center of the table, to the second marker
3. from an arbitrary setting on the near side of the center of the table, to the second marker
4, 5. from arbitrary settings on both halves of the table (Ittelson, 1952; Kirkpatrick, 1952) to the fourth marker
5, 6. from arbitrary settings on both halves of the table, to the third marker

The objects were presented in the following order:

1. the playing card
2, 3, 4, 5. the male and female symbols, presented in random order to minimize the possible order effects
6. the cube

The procedure described above was repeated with each subject and the distance settings were recorded for each. One day following his first performance another session was scheduled with the subject. Each object was then presented to him in turn and he was asked to identify it. The question put to him was, "What would you call this?" An interview inquiry was conducted with respect to each response. As many associations as possible were elicited and recorded.

When this procedure had been completed for each subject, the subject was again presented with the apparatus in the manner outlined above. The distance settings were again recorded.

It will be noted that the experimental objects were essentially of two types:

1. amorphous objects, which are considered emotionally valent, such as the male and female figures
2. well-defined, familiar objects, which are considered to be neutrally valent

Previous research has indicated that the latter type of objects are generally correctly perceived and placed appropriately on the "thereness-thatness" demonstration. In view of this fact, these objects were used as a means of differentiating the subject's tendency to misjudge emotionally valent materials.

The inquiry about each object and the arrangement by the subjects of all six objects on the like-dislike continuum were presented to the clinical judges for an evaluation as to the valence (like-dislike) which each object had for each subject.

The inquiry and the associations to the forms served to establish the subjects' feelings with regard to the objects they named. On the basis of their naming the objects and associating to them, projective material was elicited regarding their attitudes and their feelings about all of the objects. This information was necessary to attempt to relate personality orientation, emotional valence, and perception.

Clinical judges possessing the same qualifications as those who judged the personality orientations were employed for this portion of the experiment. On the basis of the inquiry protocols and the arrangement of the figures by the subject, the judges were required to decide whether the subject felt positively (liked) or negatively (disliked) toward a particular object. As was the case with the earlier judgments, a two-out-of-three level of agreement was accepted.

The judges were gathered together and each of them was presented with a form listing the number of each of the patients, the symbol for each figure and the arrangement of the figures on the continuum like-dislike, by the subject. The subject's associations to each figure was read to the judges, and they were asked to record, in the appropriate space, a plus (+) if they felt the associations were positive, a minus (−) if they felt the associations were negative, and a zero (0), if they felt there was no clear valence for that subject.

In all, the judges were required to make 252 judgments. Of these, there were 15 for which there was total disagreement. On the basis of 67% for two-out-of-three agreement, and 100% for complete agreement, the over-all mean percentage of agreement was 80%.

RESULTS

Six separate settings were obtained for each subject before verbalization and another six after verbalization. Each series of six settings consisted of two settings to each of three poles—the second, third, and fourth—on the apparatus. The mean of the six settings before verbalization and the mean of the six settings after verbalization represented, for each subject, the raw data for statistical analysis.

For the purpose of analysis, the data were organized according to the judgment of personality orientation. The first analysis concerned the mean settings for those subjects who had been judged to have a *general* personality orientation of moving toward people, and a *general* personality orientation of moving away from people. Then the mean settings of those subjects who were judged to be moving toward or away from men were analyzed. Finally the mean settings of those subjects who were judged to be moving toward or away from women were examined.

General Personality Orientation

Table 1 summarizes the statistical findings for those groups judged to have a general personality orientation of moving toward (or

TABLE 1

Comparison of Groups (before Verbalization) with Personality Orientations Moving Toward (or Against) and Away from People

Object	Rank Totals		Lower Rank Totals	Probability
	Toward	Away		
PC	525	378	378	App. .05
Cube	489.5	413.5	413.5	Between .20 and .30
M	501.5	401.5	401.5	App. .20
F	501	402	402	App. .20
MG	494.5	408.5	408.5	Between .20 and .30
FG	497	406	406	Between .20 and .30

against) people or moving away from people before verbalization. The Wilcoxon T Test was employed in the analysis.

Table 2 compares the performance of the two groups after verbalization.

TABLE 2

Comparison of Groups (after Verbalization) with Personality Orientations Moving Toward (or Against) and Away from People

Object	Rank Totals		Lower Rank Totals	Probability
	Toward	Away		
PC	515	388	388	Less than .10
Cube	496	407	407	Between .20 and .30
M	496	407	407	Between .20 and .30
F	484.5	418.5	418.5	Between .30 and .40
MG	514	389	389	Less than .10
FG	490	413	413	Between .20 and .30

While the probability for each lower rank total occurring on a chance basis is fairly high, it is noteworthy that both before and after verbalization the lower rank totals appear consistently in the moving-away groups. The probability of this occurring on a chance basis is at the 1% level of confidence when these themselves are subjected to a Wilcoxon T Test.

On the basis of the results tabulated, the hypothesis that the size of an object as perceived, and the distance at which it is placed by the subject on the "thereness-thatness" demonstration is related to the subject's personality orientation, is supported.

The results also support the hypothesis that the positional placements reflect the personality orientation.

The hypothesis that subjects with moving-toward orientations tend to make perceptual underplacements and subjects with moving-away orientations tend to make perceptual overplacements is not supported, since the moving-away group consistently set all objects closer than did the moving-toward group.

The hypothesis concerned with the emotional valence of the objects could not be analyzed statistically. Table 3 summarizes the valences of both groups.

Inspection of Table 3 reveals that with the one exception of the valences indicated for the moving-away group toward the female objects (F), there is no distribution of valences for any object which

TABLE 3

Summary of Valences—For Groups with General Personality Orientations Moving
Toward (or Against) and Moving Away from People

Object	Moving-toward				Moving-away			
	+	0	−	NA	+	0	−	NA
Pc	1	13	5	2	3	18	0	0
Cube	6	12	3	0	3	13	4	1
M	3	2	13	3	6	1	13	1
F	16	1	4	0	7	5	6	3
MG	0	0	20	1	0	3	18	0
FG	0	3	16	2	2	3	13	3

(+) = positive valence; (0) = neutral valence; (−) = negative valence; NA = no
agreement.

would lend itself to statistical analysis. Therefore, no conclusion can
be drawn as to the effect of emotional valence on perception.

It may be noted, however, that with the exception of the valences
indicated for the moving-away group toward the female figure,
there was a modal valence for each figure in both groups. It may be
further noted that with the exception of the female figure, the modal
valences for each figure were the same in both groups.

The information tabulated in Table 3 does not clearly support the
hypothesis that the more unfamiliar and unstructured an object is,
the greater its negative valence.

Although the evidence in support of this hypothesis is not definitive, a trend seems discernible. Those objects with the most clearly
delineated shapes or identifying markings—the cube and the playing card—have very few instances of negative valence. This is also
true of the most highly structured of the remaining objects, the
female figure. The significance of this, however, is obscured by the
general cultural tendency not to express hostile or negative feelings about women, and the tendency to view them as nurturing,
dependency figures. The male figure, and even more clearly the
genital symbols, appear to evoke a preponderance of negative associations and feelings. These three figures are structurally the least
familar of all the objects.

Verbalization. Table 4 summarizes the statistical findings of
changes resulting from verbalization for groups judged to have personality orientation moving toward (or against) people, and for
groups judged to have personality orientations moving away from

TABLE 4

Changes Resulting After Verbalization

Object	Lower Rank Totals			N	Probability
	Toward+Away	Toward	Away		
PC	355			42	App. .15
		104.5		21	Bet. .60 and .70
			66.5	21	App. .10
Cube	218			42	Less than .01
		28		21	Less than .01
			81.5	21	Bet. .40 and .50
M	360			42	Bet. .30 and .40
		98		21	Bet. .60 and .70
			84	21	Bet. .40 and .50
F	419			42	Bet. .60 and .70
		80 (+)		21	Bet. .40 and .50
			80	21	Bet. .40 and .50
MG	263			39	App. .05
		66.5		20	App. .15
			68	19	Bet. .60 and .70
FG	426 (+)			41	Bet. .70 and .80
		99		21	Bet. .60 and .70
			110	20	Pure chance

people. The Wilcoxon T Test for paired replicates was employed in the analysis.

The results summarized in Table 4 indicate no consistent findings which would support the hypothesis that once an individual has labelled an object or symbol his subsequent perception of it as reflected in positional placement of the "thereness-thatness" demonstration shows a change. The new relatively high levels of significance found cannot be seriously considered, since these might be expected on a chance basis in such an array.

Qualitatively, it might be observed, there are two instances where there was a reversal of the lower rank totals.

The subjects in the moving-toward group placed the female figure further away after verbalization than they did originally. The entire population tended to place the female genital symbol further away after verbalization than they did originally. Although the change is not significant in either instance, the fact that this occurred only with the two female figures is worth noting.

Personality Orientation Toward and Away from Men

As was explained above, the judges were required to make three types of judgment as to a subject's personality orientation—first his general orientation toward people; second, his orientation toward men; and finally his orientation toward women. Thus, each individual appears in three different arrays of the same data.

A given subject might be judged to be moving, generally, toward people, but moving away from men and toward women. On this basis, 29 of the 42 subjects were judged to be moving toward men and 13 of the 42 were judged to be moving away from men.

Table 5 summarizes the statistical findings for the groups judged to be moving toward (or against) or away from men, before verbalization. The T test was employed in the analysis.

TABLE 5

Comparison of Groups with Personality Orientations Moving
Toward (or Against) and Away from Men

| Object | Means | | t | Probability |
	Toward	Away		
PC	149.55	119.74	2.52	Between .01 and .02
Cube	161.36	134.82	1.85	Between .05 and .10
M	180.55	151.54	2.08	Between .05 and .10
F	183.00	149.44	2.39	Between .02 and .05
MG	158.60	132.49	1.77	Between .05 and .10
FG	154.66	126.08	1.77	Between .05 and .10

The probabilities for the six objects would lend some support to the hypothesis that, for these groups, the size of an object as perceived, and the distance at which it is placed by the subject on the "thereness-thatness" demonstration, are related to the subject's personality orientation.

Applying Wilcoxon's T Test to the differences between the two groups of means, it is found that consistent direction of the differences could occur by chance less than one time out of one hundred. Thus it is concluded that the hypothesis is supported, and that, furthermore, the positional placements do reflect the personality orientation, although not in the predicted direction. As was the case with the general personality orientation, the group judged to be moving away from people consistently placed the objects closer than the group judged moving toward people.

Valence. The findings in Table 3 apply equally to this group, inasmuch as it summarizes the valences for the total population and the modal valences are the same for both groups, with the exception of the female figure. No further statistical analysis was attempted; therefore, no statements can be made regarding the effects of emotional valence on perception.

Verbalization. The findings in Table 4 apply equally to this group, inasmuch as it summarizes the change following verbalization for the entire population. The hypothesis that once an individual has labelled an object or symbol, his subsequent perception of it as reflected in the positional placements on the "thereness-thatness" demonstration will show a change, is not supported.

Personality Orientation Toward and Away from Women

Table 6 summarizes the statistical findings before verbalization for groups judged to be moving toward and groups judged moving away from women. The T test was employed in the analysis.

TABLE 6

Comparison of Groups with Personality Orientations Moving
Toward (or Against) and Away from Women

Object	Means		t	Probability
	Toward	Away		
PC	138.75	142.22	−.2931	
Cube	154.17	151.89	.1518	
M	171.64	171.49	.011	(no statistical
F	171.07	174.47	−.2439	significance)
MG	149.29	152.00	−.1899	
FG	148.00	143.16	.3103	

Whatever results obtain could be attributable to purely chance variations of samples drawn from a common population. Two possibilities suggest themselves for this occurrence:

1. that the two groups were, in fact, drawn from the same population. By this is meant that the discrimination of the judges themselves did not define two separate groups.

2. that the measuring techniques, even if the subjects were drawn from different populations, have so much variability that the results could be attributable to this factor.

On the basis of the fairly definitive findings for the general personality orientation groups and the moving-toward and moving-away-from-men groups, there is no evidence of the second possibility.

Valence. The findings in Table 3 apply equally to this group inasmuch as it summarizes the valences for the total population and the modal valences are the same for both groups with the exception of the female figure. No further statistical analysis was attempted; therefore, no statements can be made regarding the effects of emotional valence on perception.

Verbalization. The findings in Table 4 apply equally to this group, inasmuch as it summarizes the change following verbalization for the entire population. The hypothesis that once an individual has labelled an object or symbol, his subsequent perception of it, as reflected in the positional placements on the "thereness-thatness" demonstration will show change, is not supported.

SUMMARY AND CONCLUSIONS

Summary

The purpose of this study was to determine the relationships between certain measures of personality orientation and characteristic modes of perceiving as manifested in reactions to emotionally valent material on the "thereness-thatness" demonstration.

The subjects employed in this study were 42 male veterans from the neuropsychiatric and medical services of the East Orange Veterans Administration Hospital in New Jersey. The subjects were limited to individuals with 20/20 (Snellen) vision, corrected, who had at least a normal Wechsler-Bellevue I.Q., and who gave no evidence on examination by physicians or psychiatrists of organic brain pathology.

A test battery, consisting of six TAT cards, the Sacks Sentence Completion Test, the Rorschach, and the Draw-A-Person Test were administered to each of the subjects. The protocols of these tests were submitted to three judges who determined on the basis of these protocols the personality orientations of each of the subjects.

The personality orientations were defined, in Horney's terms, as tendencies to move toward, against, or away from people. For each subject the judges determined the general personality orientation, the orientation toward men and the orientation toward women. Agreement by two out of three judges was accepted as adequate for categorizing the subjects.

Each subject was required to make two series of six settings to predetermined points on the "thereness-thatness" demonstration for each of six objects: a three-quarter sized playing card, a cube, a male figure, a female figure, a male genital symbol, and a female genital symbol. The two series of settings were made one day apart. Between the two, the subjects were interviewed with respect to each of the objects, at which time they were asked to identify the objects in the apparatus and associate to them.

The protocols of the interview inquiry were submitted to three judges, who were asked to determine the emotional valence of each object for the subject. Agreement by two out of the three judges was accepted as determining the valence of each object.

The mean settings for each object for each of the subjects were analyzed in terms of personality orientations. The Fisher test and the Wilcoxon nonparametric T test were employed.

Findings

1. For the population of this study, the general personality orientation, as judged, is significantly related to performance on the "thereness-thatness" demonstration.

2. For the population of this study, personality orientation in relation to men, as judged, is significantly related to performance on the "thereness-thatness" demonstrations.

3. For the population of this study, personality orientation in relation to women is not significantly related to performance on the "thereness-thatness" demonstration.

4. Subjects judged to have a general personality orientation of moving toward people tended to place their objects further away on the apparatus than subjects judged to have a general personality orientation of moving away from people. Similarly, subjects judged to have a personality orientation of moving toward men tended to place their objects further away on the apparatus than subjects judged to have a personality orientation away from men.

5. For the population of this study, no significant changes following verbalization were found.

6. The relationship between emotional valence and perception could not be studied because of a lack of data.

Conclusions

Based on the veteran population studied, the following conclusions are drawn:

1. Personality orientation is related to characteristic modes of perception.

2. With the exception of those groups judged moving toward and away from women, the subjects judged to be moving toward people perceived the stimuli as larger and closer, while the subjects judged to be moving away from people perceived them as smaller and further away.

3. In the present investigation no effects of verbalization on perception could be found.

4. For the population studied, each of the objects appeared to have had a valence common to most of the subjects.

5. In the present study, the relationship between the valence of an object and personality orientation could not be evaluated.

6. For the population studied, there seemed to be a tendency for subjects to feel negatively about the more unstructured and more unfamiliar objects.

Correlates of Perceptual Change:
B. Interpersonal Relationships

· 5 ·

Some Effects of Group Relationships
on Interpersonal Perceptions *

The general problem with which we are concerned in this chapter is whether or not the nature of the interpersonal relationship between two persons affects their perception of the physical characteristics of each other. The statement of the problem in this way indicates that there are two aspects to this question: the nature of the relationship between two persons and the nature of the perceptual measure. Before reporting the specific experiments, it may be well to discuss briefly these two aspects in a more general way.

There are clearly many different kinds of relationships between two individuals which might be expected to affect their perceptions of each other. Broadly speaking, we can distinguish between the influences of the affective elements in the relationship and those due more directly to the degree of familiarity between the two people involved. While this distinction is quite clear on the theoretical level, in practical experimentation it is often difficult or impossible to separate these two influences. People who are very familiar with one another are very likely to have an affective relationship as well, while on the other hand it is difficult to find cases in which two individuals have an affective relationship not accompanied by a high degree of familiarity. In the studies reported in this chapter, no attempt will be made to separate these two factors operating on the interpersonal situation. Rather, we shall simply attempt to obtain

* This chapter was prepared by Bernard Seidenberg and is based on data collected by William Ittelson, Erasmus L. Hoch, George Kaufer, and Arthur Wilner.

objective, verifiable measures of interpersonal relationships which can subsequently be compared with measured differences in perception.

In general, there are three procedures whereby such objectively determined differences in interpersonal relationships can be obtained. Since we have used all three of these sources in our experimentation, it may be worth-while to point out some of the advantages and disadvantages of each. The first and most convenient procedure is simply to decide on an a priori basis what the relationship is. It can be assumed that individuals with particular objective relationships with each other will have these objective relationships reflected in some way in their interpersonal relationships. For example, parents and children, husband and wife, can be cited as relationships which are almost certain to be accompanied by strong affective elements. In experimenting in a hospital setting authority figures such as doctors and nurses can also be expected to have affective qualities for the patients on an a priori basis. Also in this general category, one might include the self as an object of perception. The advantage of obtaining the measure of interpersonal relationship in this way is primarily its simplicity and speed. It also has the advantage of interfering least with the conditions of the interpersonal relationship. The chief disadvantage of such an approach lies in the fact that while one can be relatively certain that a particular individual is important for another individual, we cannot on an a priori basis know quantitatively just how important, nor can we always be sure of the direction of the affect.

The second procedure we have used for obtaining measures of interpersonal relationships is by direct observation. That is, we can observe our subject in his interactions with other people and on the basis of his observed behavior make inferences as to the nature of the interpersonal relationship. The advantages of this approach lie in its providing somewhat more information than can be obtained simply on an a priori basis while still offering relatively little direct interference with the relationship being studied. Of course, along with this advantage comes the problem of insuring the opportunity for observation and the added difficulty that the overt behavior of the subject may not necessarily reflect his underlying feelings.

A third approach which can be used is the most direct one. We can simply ask the person what he feels about someone else. This can be done in a variety of ways; for example, through clinical interviewing or through sociometric ratings. In many cases this is the only way in which the needed information can be obtained. Of course, it is always subject to the limitations of awareness, even when the subject is consciously trying to provide correct information.

As indicated earlier, all three of these approaches have been used in the studies reported in this chapter and elsewhere in this volume. Wherever the self enters as an object of perception the a priori assumption about the nature of the relationship is clear. In addition, one of the studies reported below makes a priori assumptions about the significance of the relationship between patients and therapists in the group therapy situation. Reliance on observed behavior as a measure of interpersonal relationship is used primarily in the first study to be reported, while the second study relies on sociometric data.

Having obtained the measure of interpersonal relationship, the next methodological problem is the determination of the most appropriate perceptual measure. Certainly, the results obtained hinge closely on the use of a measure which is, in fact, sensitive to the relationships involved. As a general principle, it would probably be better to use a live person rather than a representation of a person as a stimulus object. Certainly, we might expect any interpersonal factors which may be operating to manifest themselves most strongly when the subject is face to face with the actual living object of his perceptions. On the other hand, this is, except in rare cases, methodologically difficult to accomplish. In the studies reported here, representations of individuals,—specifically, photographs,—were used.

Within these limitations of stimulus material, a measure is required which is sensitive enough to reflect minimal effects produced by the interpersonal relationship and which gives a definite measure of some apparent physical characteristic or property of the person being viewed. There are a number of possible procedures which could be used for such a study. For example, a straightforward constancy experiment could be tried, in which size comparisons would be obtained for photographs of different people. The subject might be asked to select a white card the same size as a photograph. The assumption would be that the affective relationship between the subject and the person whose photograph he is viewing would influence the size of the card selected. This procedure was not used in the studies reported here but is mentioned because it offers interesting possibilities and will be pursued in the future. One important advantage of this procedure is that it would permit the use of actual people; for example, the subject might adjust a post to be the same height as the person he is viewing.

Another possible procedure mentioned here for the sake of completeness lies in the utilization of perceptual conflicts. The general features of such studies would consist of providing the observer with contrasting sets of cues. If he were to utilize one set of cues, the person he is observing will have one set of apparent physical characteristics; on the other hand, if he utilizes the other set of cues, the person he is observing will appear to have a different set of physical characteristics. The assumptions underlying such a procedure in studies of person perception is that the particular mode of resolution of the conflict will be influenced by the significance of the person being viewed to the observer. For example, if one set of cues makes the observed individual appear physically distorted, it might be assumed that the amount of distortion actually apparent to the observer will depend upon his relationship to the person he is viewing. This procedure is, in fact, utilized in a number of studies using the aniseikonic glasses as well as studies employing the technique of binocular rivalry.

The third possible experimental approach is the one actually utilized in the studies recorded in this chapter. It consists of obtaining distance settings on the Thereness-Thatness Table.

Experiment No. 1:

GROUP THERAPY STUDY

The specific hypothesis of this study is that observable differences in the interpersonal relationships between members of a therapy group are related to differences in the distance settings of photographs of the various members of the group.

The value of selecting a therapy group as a source of both subjects and significant persons lies in the fact that the interpersonal relationships tend to be quite intense and at the same time they are readily observable by the therapist. It should, however, be noted that a possible drawback to use of a therapy group for such a study lies in the very nature of group therapy itself. One of the major characteristics of a well-functioning therapy group is, almost by definition, that it is in a state of continuous change. Relationships can change quite rapidly and information gathered at one time may not be relevant at a later time. In recognition of this fact, the entire procedure utilized in this study was carried out within one week, with the actual perceptual measures being made on a single day.

Procedure

The group chosen was well-established and stable, consisting of eleven members and two therapists. For each member of the group there was designated the other person in the group whom he most liked and the other person whom he least liked. These choices were made by pooling independent judgments of the two therapists; there was almost complete agreement between them and the few differences were resolved. The possibility, of course, remains that they may have been in error in some of the cases. This procedure was nevertheless preferred to a sociometric measure in the group therapy situation. In addition to the inherent disadvantages of socio-metric measure, it was feared that forcing each person to make a conscious choice among the other group members might in itself alter the structure of the group, as well as possibly influencing the perceptual settings by calling the explicit attention of the subject to the affective relationship between himself and the person whose photograph he was viewing.

Photographs of the head and shoulders of all the group members and of the two therapists were taken and printed in a standard size (3 by 3 inches).

These together with a photograph of a playing card gave the following stimulus objects presented to each subject:

1. a ¾ size playing card
2. a photograph of his most liked group member
3. a photograph of his least liked group member
4. a photograph of therapist A
5. a photograph of therapist B
6. a photograph of himself

Stimulus objects 1, 4, and 5 were the same for each subject, while 2 and 3 varied from subject to subject. Six, of course, was different for each subject.

The playing card was used to provide a neutral, familiar object for all subjects. However, after the data had been collected, it was realized that the playing card represented, in reality, a different order of stimulus which could not be compared directly to the responses to the other stimuli. The photograph of the least liked person was substituted as a neutral stimulus for reasons given in the following section.

The stimulus objects were presented to each group member, one at a time, with the playing card always appearing first and the self photograph always last. The order of presentation of the remaining stimuli was varied from person to person.

Each subject was asked to make distance settings of each photograph so that it appeared as far away from him as the third post from him on the Thereness-Thatness Table.

Two settings were made for each stimulus, one starting for an initial near position and one from an initial far position. The mean of these two settings was used, resulting in six scores for each subject.

Results

If every subject could be expected to react to emotional involvement in the same way, the analysis would be clear-cut. We would simply look for differences in the mean settings for the entire group for each of the six photographs. However, there is ample theoretical and experimental evidence to suggest that this is probably not the case; that positive emotional involvement may lead to a tendency to approach in one person and to a tendency to avoid in another. Since we have no a priori reason to suppose that our group contained a predominance of individuals with one or the other tendency, we would have to predict for the group no differences in mean settings since the opposing tendencies would cancel each other out.

However, while these considerations apply to the group, we can still expect each individual's settings to be related to emotional involvement, either increasing or decreasing depending on the particular individual's tendency to approach or avoid. If this turns out to be the case, it can be shown for the group by two measures.

First, we would expect the settings for all of the six objects to be intercorrelated. This would mean that an individual who tends to approach one object tends to approach all, and vice versa.

Second, if the settings are correlated as above, then we would expect variances increasing with increasing emotional involvement. This would mean that those subjects who tend to make large settings with neutral objects will make still larger settings with emotionally involved objects, and vice versa.

Therefore, if all settings are intercorrelated and the variances increase in the order of emotional involvement as assumed above (i.e., playing card, least liked, most liked, therapists, and self), we can assert that the hypothesis that the degree of emotional involvement with an individual will influence the size-distance perception of a photograph of that individual has been substantiated, and that the way in which this influence shows itself is by accentuating the individual's usual way of perceiving emotionally neutral objects.

TABLE 1

Mean Settings and Variances for Each Stimulus

	PC	LL	ML	T_1	T_2	S
Mean	161	147	147	148	146	152
Variance	841	1024	1369	1444	1444	1849

Table 1 presents the mean settings and variances for each of the six stimulus objects. The mean settings are almost identical with the exception of that for the playing card and none of the differences between means approaches anything like statistical significance. This finding is in accordance with the prediction that there are no differences in these mean settings since the opposing tendencies to approach or avoid can be expected to cancel each other out for group data.

The variances also do not present any statistically significant differences. However, they do fall in exactly the order predicted by the hypothesis: a strongly suggestive finding.

Table 2 presents the rank-order correlations between the various objects used. All of these are significant at better than the 5% level

TABLE 2

Rank-Order Intercorrelations of Settings of Stimuli

	ML	T_1	T_2	S	PC
LL	.86	.90	.97	.84	.78
ML	—	.92	.87	.87	.63
T_1	—	—	.96	.89	.74
T_2	—	—	—	.83	.82
S	—	—	—	—	.54

with the exception of the correlation between self and playing card.

There is another, perhaps more direct, method for determining if the reaction to emotional stimuli involves an intensification of the idiosyncratic placement of neutral stimuli by the individual. If such intensification does in fact occur, when the mean settings of all stimuli for each subject are ranked across subjects with rank 1 being given to the closest mean and rank n to the furthest mean, the difference between the placement of the neutral stimulus and the mean ranked first should tend toward a higher positive value (indicating that the emotional stimuli have been placed closer than the neutral stimulus) while the difference between the neutral stimulus and the mean ranked n should tend toward higher negative values (indicating that the emotional stimuli have been placed further than the neutral stimulus). If the differences between the the neutral settings and the mean of all settings are then ranked, with rank 1 being given to the highest positive difference, a significant positive correlation would confirm that response to emotional stimuli involves an intensification of the idiosyncratic response to neutral stimuli.

In the present instance, it was realized after the study was done that the playing card did not in fact represent a neutral stimulus of the same order as the emotional stimuli. While the playing card is probably a relatively neutral stimulus, it is a different type of object in that it possesses a very specific familiar size and is therefore not so apt a neutral stimulus as would be a photograph of a human face of relatively neutral valence for the subject involved.

It was then decided to use as the neutral stimulus the least liked other member of the group for each subject as chosen by the therapists. This procedure is somewhat justified by the lower variance of the settings of the least liked picture and by the possibility that the therapists selected for each subject the other person in the group with whom he interacted least rather than that person whom he most disliked.

A rank-order correlation was performed, as described above, between the ranked means of all stimuli including the least liked picture (but excepting the playing card) and the rank-order of the difference between the placement of the least liked picture and the mean of all settings. The r obtained was .50 which is just short of significance at the 5% level with N = 11.

The results of this exploratory study, while not strictly statistically significant, suggest the following:

1. The affective relationship between the observer and a photograph of a person seems to manifest itself not in any difference in mean settings but rather in terms of the variability of the settings.

2. There is some evidence that the greater the affective involvement between the subject and the photographed person, the greater the perceptual effect. This effect is again in terms of setting variance rather than in terms of differences in mean settings and would seem to operate so that the greater the affective involvement, the greater the setting variance.

3. Finally, the direction of the perceptual effect is not the same for all subjects; but neither is it random. Rather, the perceptual effect seems related to the subject's characteristic mode of perceiving in the experimental situation (e.g., whether he characteristically "approaches" or "avoids" the object of perception). At the present time, it would appear that the direction of the perceptual effect involves an intensification of the subject's characteristic perceptual mode in the experimental situation.

Experiment No. 2

SIZE PERCEPTION AND INTERPERSONAL ATTITUDES IN PSYCHIATRIC PATIENTS

The purpose of this study was to explore some of the aspects of perception of stimuli selected on the basis of the emotional attitudes of patients in their interpersonal interactions on a ward. Also, a more refined neutral stimulus is used and the suggestions gleaned from the data of the previous study are subjected to a more rigorous test.

The general hypothesis to be tested is that there is a relationship between a person's emotional attitude toward another person and his perception of that other person. This general hypothesis gives rise to two more specific alternative hypotheses regarding the effect of emotionality on the quality of the response. The hypotheses which were tested are:

1a. Perception is related differentially to positively and negatively toned affective stimuli, i.e., the visual perception of liked, disliked, and neutrally valent figures differs significantly.

1b. Perception is related in the same way to both positively and negatively toned affective stimuli, i.e., the visual perception of liked and disliked figures, although differing from the perception of neutrally valent figures, do not differ significantly from each other.

2. It is also hypothesized that the relationship between the perception of a stimulus and the perceiver's emotional attitude toward the stimulus depends on the intensity of the affect involved in the emotional attitude (rather than the direction of the affect).

3. Finally, it is hypothesized that the relationship between attitudes toward a person and the perception of him is a function of the perceiver's characteristic perceptual mode. Perception of nonvalent stimuli will vary among individuals. This variation defines idiosyncratic perceptual functioning, and the perception of emotion-evoking stimuli reflects an accentuation of the idiosyncratic perceptual functioning.

Procedure

All patients on two open neuropsychiatric wards were asked to fill out a sociometric questionnaire which required that they name the ten patients they liked best and the ten patients they liked least. All patients were then photographed. On the basis of the sociometric response, there was selected for each experimental subject that patient which he designated as most liked, as fourth most liked, as least liked, and as fourth least liked. From among the patients whom he had designated as neither liked nor disliked, one was randomly selected to serve as an indifferent person for that subject.

Each subject was presented with photographs of the five patients whom he had designated in the above categories, and was asked to set each photograph to a certain fixed point (the third pole from him) on the "thereness-thatness" apparatus of the Ames demonstrations. The distances from the subject to the settings in centimeters constitute the raw data to be analyzed in this study.

A factor which had to be controlled was the possibility that subjective emotional states might be derived from immediate physiognomic impressions of the photographs used. Therefore, a control group consisting of persons from outside the hospital was also used. A control subject was randomly paired with each experimental subject and was asked to make placements using the same five photographs to which the experimental group responded.

Results

In Table 3 are presented the mean settings and the variances of both the experimental and control groups for photographs of the neutral (N), most liked (ML), fourth most liked (4ML), least liked (LL), and fourth least liked (4LL) persons.

TABLE 3

Mean Settings and Variances in Centimeters of Neutral (N), Most Liked (ML), Fourth Most Liked (4ML), Least Liked (LL), and Fourth Least Liked (4LL) Photographs for Experimental and Control Groups

	Experimental Group		Control Group	
	Mean	Variance	Mean	Variance
N	114.5	777.8	119.5	1313.0
ML	118.6	1007.6	124.0	1230.7
4ML	115.3	831.0	121.3	1194.1
4LL	114.3	830.1	121.8	1654.2
LL	119.4	1027.9	120.2	1229.0

To test the alternative hypotheses set forth above, 1a and 1b, t tests were performed on the means and variances of the N, ML, and LL photographs.

The results are presented in Table 4.

TABLE 4

t Tests * between Means and Variances of Settings of N, ML, and LL Photographs for Experimental Group

	Mean	p	Variance	p
N and ML	1.63	.20 > p > .10	1.59	.20 > p > .10
N and LL	2.00	.10 > p > .05	1.79	.20 > p > .10
LL and ML	.31	p > .50	.12	p > .70

* Two-tailed tests.

None of the differences required for acceptance of Hypothesis 1a is significant at the 5% level. However, most importantly, there is no difference between the ML and LL photographs in either the mean or the variance.

There is much stronger, albeit not conclusive, evidence in support of Hypothesis 1b. The differences between the ML and the N photographs and the differences between the LL and the N photographs approach the 5% level in the case of both the means and the variances. Furthermore, as required, the differences in both means and variances between the LL and ML stimuli are such that the means and variances of both may be considered identical.

The rejection of Hypothesis 1a and the tentative acceptance of Hypothesis 1b implies that both LL and ML photographs are reacted to similarly and may be considered together in subsequent analyses. To test Hypothesis 2, it is assumed that ML and LL photographs involve equal affective intensities irrespective of direction, that 4ML and 4LL photographs involve equal but lesser affective intensities and that the N photographs involve the least amount of affective intensity, theoretically zero.

Table 5 presents means and variances for the N, 4ML + 4LL, and ML + LL settings combined as indicated. For the experimental

TABLE 5

Means and Variances of Settings for Photographs Arranged
in Order of Increasing Affect

	N	4ML+4LL	ML+LL
Experimental			
Mean	114.5	114.8	119.0
Variance	777.8	830.6	1017.8
Control			
Mean	119.5	121.6	122.1
Variance	1313.0	1424.2	1229.9

group there is a slight progression in the means from the N through the ML + LL photographs, with an even more pronounced progression in the variances. In the case of the control group the progression in means is approximately of the same order as that of the experimental group, but the variances do not proceed in a regular manner. On the basis of this data, it is tentatively concluded that the perception of a stimulus depends, in part, on the intensity of the affect involved in the emotional attitude toward that stimulus.

Hypothesis 3 predicts an intensification of the individual's idiosyncratic mode of perceiving when confronted with affective stimuli. One way of demonstrating this effect is to correlate the settings for all the stimuli. High correlations indicate that each subject sets the stimuli presented to him in a consistent manner. A high correlation coupled with increasing variances as the affective intensity of the stimuli increases indicates that while the intrasubject consistency remains high, there is some change in the manner of response to the more affective stimuli. An inspection of Table 6, which contains the

TABLE 6

Rank-Order Intercorrelations of the Settings of the Various Stimuli *

	N	LL	ML	4LL	4ML
Control Group					
N	—	.93	.92	.89	.91
LL		—	.92	.85	.86
ML			—	.89	.89
4LL				—	.92
4ML					—
Experimental Group					
N	—	.89	.88	.93	.90
LL		—	.88	.89	.88
ML			—	.88	.87
4LL				—	.91
4ML					—

* All correlations are significant beyond the 1% level of confidence.

intercorrelations of responses to the different stimuli, and of Tables 1 and 5, which contain both separate and combined variances, indicates that this is the case.

Another, and perhaps more direct method, is to dichotomize the sample on the basis of the distance settings of the neutral stimulus and to determine if those patients who set the neutral figure near set the emotional figures still nearer, more so than could be expected by chance; and whether those who set the neutral figure further away set the emotional figures still further. A chi square analysis was performed using this scheme which yielded a chi square of 1.95, with $.20 > p > .10$. While the p is not significant at the 5% level, there is at least some tendency for this effect to take place.

Finally, the method used in the previous section of obtaining the correlation between the means of all stimuli and the discrepancies between the neutral placement and the mean of all placements yields a $r = .69$ for the experimental group. The correlation for the control group is .09. Since the two groups differ primarily in terms of the emotional meaning of the pictures for each group, it would seem that the significant correlation obtained in the case of the experimental group indicates an intensification of the idiosyncratic perceptual modes on the part of the members of the experimental group in response to heightened emotional stimuli. This effect does not occur among the members of the control group.

In order to determine the effects of the physiognomic properties of the photographs used, the ranks of the differences between the neutral photographs and the means of all settings of the control and experimental groups were correlated. Since the effect of emotionality of stimuli has already been demonstrated, a high positive correlation would indicate that both experimental and control subjects reacted similarly to the photographs. In such a case, with the control subjects not knowing the photographed persons, similarity of reaction would have to be attributed to the physiognomic qualities of the photographs. The r obtained is .38, which is significant at the 5% level. While this indicates a certain commonality of response between the experimental and control groups attributable to the effects of the photographs per se, the correlation between the mean of all settings and the difference between the neutral setting and the mean for the control group is only $-.09$. Thus, while there was some reaction on the part of the control group to the physiognomic aspects of the photographs used, there was no systematic intensification of response such as was found in the case of the experimental group for whom the stimuli possessed more affective meaning.

The results of this study confirm, generally, the findings of the initial exploratory study. In terms of the experimental framework used, perception of emotional stimuli manifests itself through differential variability of response rather than through differential mean placement of objects. Furthermore, the weight of evidence supports the view that perception is related similarly to both positively and negatively toned affective stimuli as opposed to neutral stimuli.

There is strong suggestive evidence, too, that the relationship between the emotional attitude toward a stimulus and the perception of the stimulus depends on the degree of affect involved. Thus, there is greater variability in the settings of greatly affective stimuli as compared to less affective stimuli.

Finally, particularly in the second study, there is strong evidence that the mode of perception of affective stimuli, while varying among individuals, involves an intensification of the individual's characteristic mode of perceiving.

· 6 ·

Small Group Interaction and Perceptual Changes in a Perceptual Conflict Situation *

Two major areas of experimentation have been emphasized in the study of visual perception. One has shed light on the more structural, physiological aspects of perception; the other, the "new look," has emphasized the influence of motives and personality variables. Research in the latter area indicates that group interaction, the organization or structure of the situation, as well as the attitudes and personality attributes of subjects, influence visual perception. It has been found, for example, that presentation of the group norm to the members of the group affects individual judgments. Individuals seem to modify their own perceptual experience in order to conform to the group norm (Bovard, 1951). One might say that in some situations we do not perceive only that which is our own particularly sensory experience, rather we unconsciously modify our own experience in the direction of some consensually validated perception. In almost all of these studies there seems to be an important problem that has escaped investigation, namely, the actual verbal interaction process and the content of the discussion that leads to such consensual validation of perceptual experience on the part of the members of a group.

Though there are many researchers working in the area of verbal

* This chapter was prepared by Gerald J. McCarty and represents a condensation of a doctoral dissertation entitled "Small Group Interaction and Perceptual Changes" submitted to the Graduate School of Arts and Sciences of the Catholic University of America.

interaction, their work has been aimed mostly at methods of analysis of such interaction. In reviewing the literature, it appears that only a few studies have attempted to relate such analysis of verbal interaction to other behavior. Martin (1954) indirectly considered interpersonal verbalization when, as a measure of intolerance of ambiguity, he counted the number of questions asked in an interpersonal situation. Bovard (1951) used the amount of interaction between group members as a control or definition of group-centered vs. leader-centered groups. It would contribute a great deal to our understanding of perceptual behavior if we knew more about how it is related to attitudes, the structure of a situation, and the structure of the group. It would be of interest, at the same time, to find out how small group verbal interaction behavior involved in reaching a consensual agreement regarding perceptual experience is related to those same independent variables. Such a study, combining all these elements, might offer evidence suggestive of further research on the relationship between these two dependent variables, i.e., perceptual behavior and small group verbal interaction behavior.

THE PRESENT STUDY

It is the problem in this study to investigate further the variables of visual perceptual behavior and small group verbal interaction as they are related to the independent variables of attitude, structure of the situation, and structure of the group. The first question is whether or not "perceptual rigidity" as measured by the amount of initial distortion perceived on the Aniseikonic Lens Demonstration is related to authoritarianism as measured by the F scale? Secondly, is perceptual change in a small group interaction related to personality attitudes, the structure of the group, or the organization or structure of the situation? Thirdly, is the effectiveness of meeting the demands of the situation as measured in terms of the co-operativeness of the verbal interaction process in a small group, related to the attitudes of the individuals in the group, the pairing of subjects in terms of attitudes, or the structure of the situation? Finally, are rigidity and intolerance of ambiguity reflected in the verbalizations of authoritarians as a technique of meeting the need to reach agreement on inconsistent or incompatible experiences? Conversely, are flexibility and tolerance of ambiguity reflected in the verbalizations of equalitarians as a technique of meeting this same need?

The following hypotheses were tested:

1. If rigidity and intolerance of ambiguity are generalized traits in authoritarian individuals, they should be reflected in perceptual measures that are correlated with personality rigidity and intolerance of ambiguity. The authoritarians, therefore, show less perceived apparent distortion initially than equalitarians.

2. Changes in the amount of apparent distortion perceived on the Aniseikonic Lens Demonstration are related to the organization of a small group situation rather than to personality orientation (as defined by the F scale), or to homogeneity or heterogeneity of personality orientation among the members of a small group. Primarily, there is a greater magnitude of change in perceptions and more people changing towards a decrease in perceived distortion (moving toward a group norm) in a permissive, group-centered, less-structured situation than in a more-structured, authoritarian situation.

3. Differences in the amount of co-operative interaction in a small group interaction are related to the organization of the small group situation rather than to personality orientation or to homogeneity or heterogeneity of partners. There is a greater amount of co-operative interaction in the less-structured, permissive situation than in the more-structured authoritarian one.

4. Differences in the techniques of dealing with a situation which demands agreement on what are discovered to be incompatibilities are related to the personality orientation of the subject. Specifically, authoritarians should show a greater reliance on selectiveness and distortion as techniques of reducing incompatibilities in a permissive interaction situation than will equalitarians. Equalitarians, since they are flexible, tolerant of ambiguity, and permissive, should show a greater reliance on ambiguity as a technique of reducing incompatibilities in a permissive interaction situation than will authoritarians.

METHOD

Subjects

Sixty subjects were used in the experiment, all female nurses and volunteer workers, with an age range of 20-60 years. The mean age was 33.05 and the standard deviation was 10.08. Differences between "authoritarian" and "equalitarian" individuals are most demonstrable in the extreme ends of the distribution of F scale scores (Adorno, *et al.*, 1950). On the basis of the scores on this scale, previously given to 131 subjects, an experimental population of 30 authoritarians and

30 equalitarian subjects was selected from the upper and lower 29 per cent of the distribution. The mean age for the authoritarian subjects was 35.27, with a standard deviation of 11.20, and the mean age for the equalitarians was 30.83, with a standard deviation of 8.23. A test of significance showed that there was no significant difference between the mean ages of the authoritarian and equalitarian subjects.

The subjects were grouped into three types of pairs of subjects. One group consisted of pairs of two authoritarian individuals, another of pairs of two equalitarians. These groups were designated as the AA group, AE group and EE group, respectively. Since testing was to be done in pairs, each pair was matched for age, education level, occupation, and supervisory experience, to rule out any variance that might be introduced by intrapair differences in these variables.

Design

The design of the experiment included one perceptual measure replicated at three different times, and two interaction situations with the aniseikonic lenses and Leaf Room Demonstration as stimulus. The experimental testing time for each pair was approximately 30 minutes. The procedure was as follows: Introduction to the laboratory, instructions for the Aniseikonic Lens Demonstration, initial perceptual measure, less-structured action period, interim perceptual measure, more-structured interaction period, and final perceptual measure.

Perceptual Measure. The subjects were first given a general introduction to some of the other Ames Demonstrations in the laboratory (e.g., rotating trapezoid, distorted rooms), as an orientation to the equipment. They were given standard instructions to the Aniseikonic Lens Demonstration and were told that the glasses would give a way of measuring what they saw when they relied on binocular cues, past experience, and their own way of seeing things. The room, the experimenter indicated, was just a cube lined with leaves, but the glasses, which as they could see were identical, would distort the room and change its shape. Following this the glasses were put on the subjects by the experimenter so that each subject had the opposite apparent distortion to his partner. This fact was unknown to the subjects.

A full description of the Aniseikonic Lens Demonstration, including procedural details, has been given by Ittelson (1952). The glasses produce distortions in binocular disparity without significantly affecting any other aspect of the retinal images. Most observers experience greater apparent distortion in viewing environments with relatively few monocular depth indications and the least apparent distortion in environments in which there are many monocular indicators. According to Ittelson, "Two size lenses that produce different magnifications along the same or different axes combine to form a pair of aniseikonic or unequal-size image glasses." (1952, p. 53) The two types used in this experiment were the Ex-cycle (oblique meridians out at the top) and the In-cycle (oblique meridians in at the top). The Leaf Room was used since it provides an environment with a minimum of monocular depth cues. The glasses are worn in the same manner as any other pair of spectacles. They may be, and in some cases were, worn over the observer's regular glasses. For each of the 30 pairs, one subject viewed the room through the Ex-cycle lenses and the other viewed it through the In-cycle lenses.

In order to procure objective measurements of initial, interim, and final perceptual distortion experienced, each subject, independent of her partner and without either being aware of the other's response, was required to set a movable bar parallel to the juncture of one of the side walls and the back wall. The amount of apparent distortion experienced was then recorded by the experimenter, in terms of degrees from the vertical, on a protractor attached to the device with which the subject rotated the bar. For each of the three occasions of measurements, two settings were made by each subject. The mean setting for each subject, on each occasion, was used to get a stable, accurate measure of the amount of apparent distortion perceived. As a matter of computational convenience, the scores of subjects wearing In-cycle lenses which were recorded in terms of degrees of deviation above 90 degrees were reflected to the equivalent deviation below 90 degrees. There is no evidence that the amount of apparent distortion perceived changes as a function of time. If the glasses are worn constantly for a few days, there is some compensation or adjustment to the apparent distortion. However, in order to rule out the effect of time on perceptual change, ten control subjects were put through the identical procedure of perceptual measurement over the same period of time as the experimental subjects. They were not allowed to discuss the perceptual experience. The findings based on these control subjects are reported later along with the presentation of the experimental results.

The Two Interaction Periods. Following their initial judgments of amount of distortion perceived, each pair of subjects was given a period of free interaction with permissive instructions. This will be referred to as the "Less-Structured" situation. Instructions were as follows:

> Your instructions are to discuss together *what* you see, *how* you see it, all of your perceptual experiences, reactions (emotional or whatever) and any associations to the room; you are to try to reach agreement on *what* you see, *how* you see it, and these reactions and associations. Since you are different people you may not see some things the same way. You may expect some such differences but your instructions are to try to reach agreement on as many points as you can. You have seven minutes and you may use all the time in whatever way you wish to fulfill these instructions.

After seven minutes the interim settings were made. Then the "More-Structured" interaction period was introduced. The experimenter became authoritarian and in a very directive manner controlled what the subjects discussed, saying, Okay!! enough of the bantering about!!! I want you to reach some agreement here!!! I'll mention several things I want you to discuss and on which I want you to come to some agreement. Then he read a list of monocular and binocular cues (approximately 50/50). The list was the same for all subjects even though some of the items may already have been discussed during the Less-Structured situation. As he read off each item the subjects were told to talk it over and come to some agreement. Following this period, the final perceptual measure was obtained. Both discussions were tape recorded, later transcribed, and used as the basis for scoring the interaction process and the content.

Measure of Co-operativeness of Interaction Process. There are many methods reported in the literature to enable the experimenter to measure different aspects of interaction process. Since none of these methods was suitable to a test of our hypothesis concerning co-operativeness of interaction, a method was developed modeled along the lines of Bales' Interaction Analysis (1950). Co-operative interaction was defined as any verbalization which tends to facilitate, foster, or integrate mutual understanding, co-operation, and compromise. Unco-operative interaction was defined as any verbalization which tends to impair, prevent, inhibit, or disintegrate mutual understanding, co-operation, and compromise.

Ten judges were given the task of judging, independently, five categories of interaction process modified from Bales in terms of the extent to which they fitted a seven-point scale of co-operativeness as defined above. Next, they were given the task of judging five other categories of interaction process, modified as above, independently, in terms of the extent to which they fitted a seven-point scale of unco-operativeness as defined above. Since the judges' ratings indicated that each subcategory could be used as a measure of co-operative or unco-operative interaction, a manual was drawn up composed of these categories. The manual was used by the experimenter to score all protocols and by an independent judge to check the reliability of a sample of the total protocol population. The reliability data are presented in the original publication (McCarty, 1956).

Content Scoring. The experimental situation was designed with the instructions giving a "set" to agree on *what* was seen, and *how* it was seen, etc. Any communication not including a reference to perceptual cues under this set of instructions leaves the speaker's position unrevealed, obscure, or ambiguous to the degree that the cues for perceptual experiences are not verbalized. Thus the content may or may not be vague or equivocal in itself, but the criterion used was whether it contained reference to a perceptual cue. Any communication based on an objective perceptual cue, but which failed to include any direct mention of this cue, was scored as *ambiguity*. For example, in reference to monocular cues such as varicolored leaves, the subject might say, "Yes, mm hmm, it is pretty," with no direct reference to *what* is pretty; i.e., what elicited or cued this comment. Or in reference to binocular cues such as the direction of slant of the walls, ceiling or floor, the subject might say, "The walls slope," with no reference to the direction of slope, i.e., the cue which determines *how* he sees it.

Any communication referring only to perceptual experiences or cues that are compatible, i.e., seen the same by both subjects because they are not modified by the lenses, were scored as *selective*, that is, accepting only compatible and overlooking incompatible percepts. To the degree that the discussion is saturated with such communications it is selective. Thus direct references to a discussion of monocular cues in the room were scored as selective. A long drawn-out discussion of the color of the leaves, or the bar used to make the perceptual settings, or the construction of the room, e.g., "It's made of chicken wire, and red and gold leaves, etc.," was scored as selectivity.

Any communications that are inconsistent with the objective perceptual cues known to be present for the subject, or based on non-mutual experience, were called *distortions*. The degree to which communications are saturated with distortions is an indication or measure, then, of the amount of unrealistic or shallow appraisal of the situation. For example, with respect to binocular aspects of the room seen as objectively different by both subjects, one subject might say, "Yes, I see the room same as you said, exactly." Or with respect to some experience that is not mutual (from one subject's childhood), the subject might say, "Reminds me of a little hut we had when I was five, don't you think?" and the other subject might respond, "Yes." Both of these would be distortions as defined. In the first example the subject concurs in something, or indicates agreement on something, that is not *what* he sees objectively. In the second example both subjects co-operate in a fraud. The first subject attempts to elicit agreement on something the other has no basis for judging, and the second subject agrees or goes along with the fraud.

The meanings of these three categories are mutually exclusive by nature of their operational definitions. Since the scoring of these three categories relied only on the presence of an objective cue reference, and since the scoring was an objective counting method and not a value analysis, only one scorer was used.

RESULTS

For the sake of clarity the statistical analysis of the perceptual measure will be presented first, and that of the interaction process and content second and third respectively.

The first hypothesis stated that authoritarians perceive less apparent distortion initially than the equalitarians. This was based on findings that initial magnitude of distortion is related to rigidity and intolerance of ambiguity. These traits have been used to describe the authoritarian individual. The data on the 60 subjects, 30 authoritarians (A) and 30 equalitarians (E), based on the magnitude of the initial distortion as measured by the mean of the first two selsyn settings are presented in Table 1.

The t of .41 between the mean initial setting of the A subjects and the mean of the E subjects shows that there is no significant difference between the two types of subjects with respect to the amount of apparent distortion initially perceived, on the Aniseikonic Lens Demonstration. Hypothesis 1, therefore, is not supported.

TABLE 1

Means, Sigmas, and t Tests of Significance between A Subjects and
E Subjects on Initial Perceptual Measure

	A Ss	E Ss
M	75.55 *	76.17 *
S.D.	6.30	5.07
t	.41	
p	n.s.	

* Units are in degrees.

In Table 2, part (a), the t values indicating the significance of the
difference of the observed perceptual change from the hypothetical
no change or zero change are significant for the ten control subjects
in both the time period comparable to the Less-Structured interaction situation and the time period comparable to the More-Structured interaction situation. Perceptual change in the Less-Structured
situation was measured in terms of any differences between the
mean of the two initial settings and the mean of the two interim
settings on the selsyn for each subject. Similarly, change in the
More-Structured situation was measured in terms of any difference
between the mean of the two interim settings and the two final settings on the selsyn for each subject. The significant t of 2.99 (.02
level of confidence) for the Less-Structured situation and the t of
3.05 (.02 level for the More-Structured situation) give highly re-

TABLE 2

(a) Means, Standard Deviations, and t's for Control Subjects between Observed
Change and Zero Change on Perceptual Measure for Less- and More-Structural
Interaction Situations. (b) Identical Statistics on Experimental Subjects. (c) "t"
between Experimental and Control Subjects for Both Less-Structured and More-
Structured Situations

	(a) Controls (n = 10)		(b) Experimentals (n = 60)		(c) t between Experimentals and Controls	
	L.S.	M.S.	L.S.	M.S.	"t"	P
M	.80	.65	3.13	2.13		
S.D.	.84	.67	2.96	3.21		
t	2.99	3.05	8.20	5.18	L.S. 5.01	.0001
p	.02	.02	.0001	.0001	M.S. 3.20	.01

liable evidence that the aniseikonic distortion does vary purely as a function of time.

The same analysis of the data of the 60 subjects in the experimental population for both interaction situations show t's in Table 2, part (b) significant at greater than the .001 level of confidence. It is obvious that the experimental subjects show significant changes in the amount of distortion perceived. The question remains whether or not it is a function of time alone or of their verbal interaction. Part (c) of Table 2 gives the t value indicating the significance of the difference between control and experimental subjects on the perceptual change variable. For the Less-Structural interaction period the t of 5.01 is significant at greater than the .001 level of confidence, and for the More-Structured situation the t of 3.20 at greater than the .01 level. Since the only difference between the control and experimental subjects was that the latter interacted verbally with respect to the Leaf Room and the former did not, this is interpreted to mean that though time alone results in variation of the amount of distortion experienced, interaction between observers regarding the perceptual experience affects it to a much greater extent.

We may now proceed to Hypothesis 2, which states that the changes in the amount of apparent distortion perceived are related to the organization of a small group situation. Perceptual change, in this case, is measured as outlined above. Is such change related to a situation difference or to differences in personality orientation or to grouping of personalities as differentiated by the F scale? The summary of the analysis of variance computed on the experimental subjects' perceptual change scores is presented in Table 3. This analysis was done on only 57 of the 60 subjects. The scores of one

TABLE 3

Analysis of Variance on 57 Subjects on the Perceptual Change Variable

Source	Var.	df	Var. Est.	F	p
Between Situations	23.53	1	23.53	7.77	.01
Between Groups	8.54	2	4.27	1.40	n.s.
Interaction	0.68	2	0.34	0.11	n.s.
Individ. Diff.	327.26	108	3.03		
Total	360.01	113			

subject were so eccentric that she could be considered as not typical of the population under study, at least with respect to this particular analysis. In order to equalize the N's for the three groups the subject showing the most extreme eccentricity from each other group was dropped.

The F of 7.77, significant at greater than the .01 level of confidence for between situations variance (Less-Structured/More Structured) is significant and indicates that there is a greater amount of perceptual change in the permissive, Less-Structured situation than in the More-Structured situation. The analysis also reveals that differences between subjects (as measured by the F scale) or differences in partner groupings do not result in significant differences in the amount of perceptual change.

The chi square indicating the significance of the difference between the possible alternatives of decreased distortion, increased distortion, and no change in perceptual judgment for 59 subjects (excluding the same eccentric subject as in the analysis of variance) and the two interaction periods, is 11.68. With 2 degrees of freedom, this value is significant at greater than the .01 level of confidence. An analysis of the computation shows that the value of 2.68, the sum of the values for the Less-Structured and the More-Structured periods on the decrease in perceived distortion, is not quite significant at the .05 level of confidence. In view of the over-all significance of the table, the value strongly indicates a trend for more people to decrease the amount of distortion perceived whether the situation be Less-Structured or More-Structured. The sum of the values of the Less-Structured and More-Structured situations on the increase in perceived distortion is 8.56 and is significant at the .02 level of confidence, indicating that fewer people show an increase in apparent distortion perceived in the Less-Structured situation and more people show an increase in perceived distortion in the More-Structured period than may be expected by chance. The value of .44, the sum of the individual cells for the no-change category, is, of course, not significant. Thus we may say that fewer individuals show no change in their perceptual judgments in either situation than may be expected by chance.

For further interpretation it was necessary to break down the direction of change even more. The original paper published on this research considered the direction of change in apparent distortion for each interaction situation individually (McCarty, 1956). The Less-Structured interaction period shows a chi square of 43.09, significant at the .001 level of confidence. This was interpreted to mean more individuals were showing a change towards decreased apparent distortion, fewer showing an increase in perceived distortion, and fewer showing no change than may be expected by chance. In the More-Structured situation there are more individuals changing toward a decrease in perceived distortion, more showing an increase in perceived distortion, and fewer showing no change in perceptual judgment, than would be expected by chance (chi square of 19.69, significant at the .001 level of confidence).

Stated simply, this means that there are fewer people showing no change in their perceptual experience than would be expected by chance in either the Less-Structured or the More-Structured situations. This is further confirmation of the finding that just the opportunity for interaction results in perceptual change. Of those who change, the tendency is for more to show a decrease in the amount of perceived distortion (i.e., to see the room as more square than a perception based purely on the retinal image as supplied by the lenses). This holds for both types of situation. However, an analysis of the values in the original computation diagrams (McCarty, 1956) shows that more individuals perform in this manner in the Less-Structured situation than in the More-Structured situation than chance expectancy. The evidence confirms Hypothesis 2 with respect to the direction of change on the perceptual measures.

Hypothesis 3 stated that a Less-Structured situation results in a greater amount of co-operative interaction than does a More-Structured authoritarian one. Each subject could interact an unspecified number of times, and since their scores were then based on different Ns, percentages of co-operative interaction were computed for each period. The scoring method used was highly reliable (McCarty, 1956). The medians of the distributions of co-operative interaction scores for all 60 subjects for the Less-Structured and the More-Structured interaction periods were computed. On the basis of a dichotomy of above the median or below the median, chi squares were computed between the three groups (AA, AE, EE) for each situation separately. The chi squares based on the co-operative interaction variable between the three groups for each of the two interaction situations were not significant. This indicates that none of the three groups shows a significantly greater amount of co-operative interaction than the others in either the Less-Structured or More-Structured situations. Since the groups were made up to test for differences caused either by authoritarianism or by homogeneity or heterogeneity of partners, we can conclude that neither of these independent variables significantly affects the amount of co-operative interaction. In order to check whether or not there were differences in the amount of co-operative interaction caused by the difference in the two situations, the t between the mean per cents of co-operative interaction in the two periods was computed and is presented in Table 4.

TABLE 4

Difference in Co-operative Interaction Variable (in Percentage) between
Less-Structured and More-Structured Periods for all 60 Subjects

	L.S.	M.S.
M	74	53
S.D.	3	3
t	7.00	
p	.0001	

In order to compute this t value, the correlation between Less-Structured and More-Structured situations for the co-operative interaction variable was necessary. This was computed as a Phi co-efficient, or estimate of the Pearson product-moment correlation. Phi, or Phi corrected for dichotomized variates, was .45, which is significant at the .01 level of confidence. The nonsignificant chi squares and the t of 7.00, significant at the .001 level of confidence, confirm Hypothesis 3 with respect to differences in the amount of co-operative interaction being related to the organization of the situation rather than to personality differences or homogeneity of subjects in a group.

The last hypothesis, 4, related to differences between the two types of subjects (A or E). Do they differ with regard to the use of different techniques of reaching agreement (since agreement is demanded by the instructions) on experiences that are not mutually compatible? Is some defensive rigidity reflected in the verbal interaction of the authoritarian subjects as opposed to the equalitarian subjects? Is a greater flexibility as measured by toleration of ambiguity reflected in the interaction of equalitarian subjects as opposed to the authoritarians?

Again, percentage scores were computed for each subject on the three content variables (ambiguity, selection, and distortion), in the same manner as they were computed for the co-operative interaction variable. However, since the More-Structured situation, by definition, ruled out any use of these techniques, scores could only be computed for the Less-Structured situation. The median for the 60 subjects was obtained on each variable. A chi square was computed by a 2×3 table between the three groups on the basis of the dichotomy of above or below the median. Table 5 gives the re-

TABLE 5

Chi Squares on the Content Variables between the Three Groups of Subjects

	χ^2	df	p
Ambiguity	1.75	2	n.s.
Selection	1.22	2	n.s.
Distortion	6.58 *	2	.05

* Corrected for continuity.

sults of this computation for the ambiguity, selection, and distortion variables.

The values of the chi square for ambiguity and selection are not significant and we may conclude that there is no difference between A subjects and E subjects or between homogeneity and heterogeneity of partners for either of these variables. With respect to the distortion variable, Table 5 shows a significant difference. It is not immediately clear whether this difference is caused by differences in personality orientation of the subjects or by homogeneity or lack of homogeneity of partners in a pair. For this reason, a further chi square was computed between types of subjects (A or E) and the dichotomy of above or below the median. The resultant was a chi square of 2.20, which is not significant. We may conclude that the differences in use of distortion are related to partner grouping rather than to personality orientation alone.

An analysis of the comptuation diagram used in arriving at this significant chi square shows that the nonhomogeneous pairing AE (χ^2 sum = 3.29) and the homogeneous AA pairing (χ^2 sum = .00) contribute equally to the significant value, but the EE pairing (χ^2 sum = .00) contributes nothing to it (McCarty, 1956). In this respect only does authoritarianism contribute to a greater amount of distortion or unrealistic appraisal of the situation. More of those in the AA group are above and fewer below the median than would be expected by chance. There are fewer in the AE group above the median and more below, than would be expected by chance.

An analysis of the mean percentages of occurrence of each of these variables, for all 60 subjects, indicates that selection was the most frequently used technique (Mean % = 31), ambiguity was second (Mean % = 25.3), and distortion was the least used technique (Mean % = 5). It is suggested that better measures of differences in content techniques may result in further clarification of the part authoritarianism plays in small group verbal interaction behavior.

DISCUSSION

Becker's study (1954), relating the degree of distortion perceived to perceptual and personality rigidity, and the study by Martin (1954), relating the same to a measure of toleration of ambiguity, were both based on aniseikonic distortion of "normal" environments. The assumption is that previous experience with the field makes it difficult for the rigid person to experience distortion. Though in the present study a field free from monocular depth cues was used, it is felt that the results are comparable. If resistance to experiencing the distortion in a normal environment is related to a generalized rigidity and intolerance of ambiguity and not to a situationally dependent type of rigidity that is meaningful only with an operational subscript, then these traits should also influence perceptions in the less stable environment. Since the two groups of subjects showed no real difference on this measure, serious doubt is cast on the claim of a generalized rigidity (Rokeach, 1948) and intolerance of ambiguity (O'Connor, 1952). The results obtained in the present study suggest further confirmation of the study by Pitcher and Stacey (1954), who conclude that Einstellung rigidity is not a measure of a generalized trait. It would seem that rigidity must have an operational subscript in the area of visual perception as well as in the area of problem solving.

We find that interaction among subjects regarding their perceptual experiences results in a greater amount of change in their perceptual judgments than if there is no interaction. This finding is, of course, not surprising when one considers the studies such as Bovard's (1951), in which presentation of the group norm resulted in later judgments of an objective perceptual stimulus modified in the direction of the group norm. In the present experiment, the interaction of the two subjects regarding their perceptual experiences with the inevitable communication of the incompatibility of some of their

individual experiences, along with the set to agree, evidently resulted in modification of their individual perceptual experience.

The fact that subjects do show differences in the amount of apparent distortion perceived in the two different situations seems
to be evidence of some flexibility with respect to their perceptual
experiences. If any rigidity is evidenced in their perceptual processes
as measured, it seems to be situationally dependent. Such a finding
lends support to the findings of Brown (1953) and his hypothesis
of a situationally dependent or defensive rigidity. Even in this case,
though, such rigidity would not be associated with authoritarianism.
Both A subjects and E subjects, whether interacting with subjects
of like attitude or opposite attitude, show this situationally dependent perceptual rigidity or resistance as indicated by less change in
their perceptual judgments in a More-Structured situation than in
a Less-Structured one. In order to discuss this fully we must also
consider the direction of change in their perceptual judgments. A
permissive, Less-Structured situation results in more individuals
changing toward a decrease in perceived distortion (moving toward
a group norm). A More-Structured situation results in fewer people
changing toward the group norm than in the Less-Structured situation and more moving away or showing an increase in perceived
distortion than in the Less-Structured situation.

Since our Less-Structured situation approximates what has been
defined in previous studies as a group-centered situation and our
More-Structured situation approximates what has been called a
leader-centered situation, our findings confirm the fact that the
former results in greater modification of judgments regarding an
objective perceptual stimulus. They also confirm the finding that
the group-centered type of situation results in greater movement
toward the group norm than the leader-centered type of situation.

Of interest, however, is the question of how the verbal behavior
of the subjects varies with the different conditions of the experiment
and inferentially how this verbal behavior is related to the perceptual
behavior. The finding that there is a greater amount of co-operative
interaction in a permissive Less-Structured situation coincides with
Lippitt's conclusion that more constructive work products result
from the greater freedom and permissiveness of a Less-Structured
or group-centered interaction (1940). Constructiveness could be
compared to co-operativeness and compromise in the present study
since the instructions gave the set to reach agreement. We might say

that compromising and co-operating is more facilitated by the permissiveness of the situation. Such compromising, then, results in modification of the individual perceptual experiences so that some norm or agreement is reached with respect to compatible perceptual experiences. In the More-Structured situation, however, the interference, as indicated by the decrease in co-operative interaction, is also reflected in a decrease in the magnitude of change in perceptual judgments and a tendency for more people to revert toward their original perceptual judgment.

Measures of the verbal techniques of handling the incompatibilities that arise in the discussion add little information about differences in the personality orientation of the subjects. Both types of subjects used ambiguity and selection to an equal extent. With respect to distortion we find that the nonhomogeneous mixture of partners tends to reduce or prevent reliance on distortion. With the homogeneous authoritarian pairing there is more of a tendency to engage in this type of fraud. This seems to be the result of the fact that both partners are authoritarian subjects, since there is no difference between A and E subjects, considered independent of pairing. At least in the Less-Structured situation where these techniques were measured, it seems that not enough threat is aroused to bring about a defensive rigidity in verbalization that can be related solely to authoritarianism. Perhaps this would be observed in a More-Structured interaction situation, but the techniques of measurement developed for this study are of no help in revealing this. The findings suggest that verbal rigidity of this type may be more dependent on situations and the homogeneity of personality attitudes of the members of the group than on attitudes alone. This would be a tenable hypothesis in view of the finding that there is less co-operativeness in a More-Structured situation, for both equalitarians and authoritarians.

Correlates of Perceptual Change:
C. Stress

· 7 ·

Stress and Flicker Fusion *

It has been observed in clinical and experimental situations that psychological stress and anxiety may produce marked changes in perceptual functioning. The present research is concerned with the study of a single visual phenomenon, flicker fusion threshold, and its relationship to anxiety level.

The term "flicker fusion threshold" will be abbreviated FFT in this discussion. FFT refers to the frequency of an intermittent light stimulus at which the perception of flicker changes to the perception of a steady light. This threshold is also known in the literature as "critical fusion frequency (CFF)," and "flicker fusion frequency (FFF)."

The scientific study of FFT has a long and interesting history. Investigators in many fields have shown that a relationship exists between this visual threshold and a myriad of experimental variables. The focus of attention has been primarily directed toward relating physiological stress factors to retinal reactivity and central nervous system excitability. Landis (1951), in offering an over-all perspective to these findings, suggested, "They indicate that any condition or agent which acts to decrease the available blood sugar and/or oxygen available to the retina or to the brain decreases CFF, whereas conditions increasing the efficiency of the vascular supply increase CFF."

The recent upsurge of interest in FFT arises from clinical research,

* This chapter was prepared by Robert A. Buhler and represents a condensation of a doctoral dissertation entitled "Flicker Fusion Threshold and Anxiety Level," submitted to Columbia University.

which suggests the potential usefulness of this measurement as an aid in establishing diagnoses and assessing prognoses in various types of pathological conditions. Although many of the studies are of an exploratory nature and lack experimental rigor, the findings are so unequivocally significant that the application of FFT as a clinical research tool continues with increasing impetus. In reviewing this work, Simonson and Brozek (1952) caution, "Further work and passage of time is needed before a comprehensive evaluation and balanced judgment concerning the validity and sensitivity of the FFT can be rendered."

Noting that FFT had successfully discriminated between normal subjects and patients exhibiting symptoms of abnormal metabolic states, Krugman (1947) designed a controlled experiment which attempted to evaluate the relationship between FFT and anxiety in two groups of subjects. The anxiety group consisted of Army Air Force combat crew returnees having an anxiety syndrome officially designated "operational fatigue." The anxiety group mean FFT was significantly lower (less sensitive to flicker) than the normal group mean. Krugman concluded, "Because of the relationship between FFF and anxiety reaction ('generalized fatigue') demonstrated in this study, it would be expected that the FFF scores of such patients would rise during the progress of successful therapy. Further research would seem to be indicated."

In another study, Ricciuti (1949) compared the mean FFT of four psychiatric groups and a normal group, but found no significant differences. His normal group had a nonsignificantly higher FFT than each of the psychiatric groups.

Gravely (1953) examined the FFT in two groups of neurotic patients and a normal group. Although the FFT failed to differentiate the groups at a significant level, the normal group mean was again higher than the means of the psychiatric groups.

In a recently reported study dealing with the effects of anxiety level on FFT, Goldstone (1953) found his high-anxiety subjects to have a significantly lower FFT than the low-anxiety subjects. The subjects were drawn from psychiatric and nonpsychiatric populations and selected on a basis of their responses to a symptom check list and ratings by a psychiatrist on an anxiety-tension scale. The results of this research supported Krugman's findings, and suggested that subjects with high anxiety and low anxiety may be differentiated by the ability to discriminate effectively a certain number of visual stimuli per unit of time.

The findings of the previous research studies are not altogether consistent. Krugman and Goldstone obtained significant differences between their anxiety and normal groups, whereas Riccuiti and Gravely failed to find a marked difference. Granger (1953) has pointed out that "these discrepancies may not be fundamental, owing to differences in experimental procedures between the various investigations."

In all studies, however, the normal or nonanxious group has obtained a higher FFT than the anxious or pathological group. This finding in itself supports clinical observation that, in general, the anxious individual makes poorer discriminations and performs less efficiently than the nonanxious individual.

THEORETICAL IMPLICATIONS

Changes in FFT may be interpreted on both physiological and psychological levels. However, it was beyond the scope of the present experiment to provide a test of either interpretation or to make a crucial decision between them.

Physiological Interpretation

The research literature reviewed by Simonson and Brozek (1952) indicated that FFT is lowered by altered metabolic processes, decreased supply of blood sugar and oxygen, and fatigue of the central nervous system. The effect of anxiety on bodily functioning is known to vary according to constitutional predisposition as well as to the status and chronicity of the anxiety. Since it was not possible to determine the nature of hormone balance or automatic nervous system activity from the types of observations and tests conducted in the present investigation, the findings will not be discussed with reference to specific physiological consideration.

Psychological Interpretation

Pullen and Stagner (1953) have theorized, within a perceptual framework, that the normal personality is characterized by perceptual processes which are alert to changing stimuli, and response sequences which are oriented to these external stimuli. They then reasoned, from experimental evidence, that perception always depends upon a balance of two complex systems: "(a) System R, the system of perceptual response tendencies which are closely oriented to reality, and: (b) System W, the system of perceptual response

tendencies which are oriented away from the external stimulus."
Applying this theoretical structure to FFT measurements, it would
appear that a lowered threshold indicates the dominance of the W
(withdrawal) System over the R (reality) system.

In Klein's (1951) scheme of perceptual attitudes, the lowered
FFT represents a need to stabilize an unsteady field and reflects an
intolerance for the unstable or equivocal. He has suggested that this
perceptual need or attitude is expressed in terms of constriction and
enslavement to form on the Rorschach, and also is reflected in the
ease with which this phi phenomenon is experienced.

The studies already reviewed point to the usefulness of theoretical
models in understanding how the dynamics of psychological processes may be related to perceptual performance on a "contentless"
task such as flicker fusion. Although the findings are somewhat dis-
crepant, there nevertheless appears to be strong suggestive evidence
that anxious people tend to give up the flicker perception too
quickly, as if to gain stability from an unchanging stable field
(fusion). This perceptual attitude leads to a lowering of FFT and
is a response tendency oriented away from the external stimulus.

THE PRESENT EXPERIMENT

Three serious shortcomings or limitations have been evident in
studies of FFT which the present investigation attempted to correct.
They are: (a) the lack of control over many variables which are
now known to affect FFT significantly; (b) the cross-sectional study
of individuals that precluded the evaluation of changes of FFT
with changes in anxiety; (c) defining anxiety in terms of nosology
or psychiatric classification.

Control of Relevant Variables

Recent research has shown that the following factors and conditions may exert an influence on FFT, and should be controlled
either by eliminating their influence or by holding them constant:
smoking, drugs, alcoholic intake, exercise, fatigue, age, time of day
tested, oral temperature, structure of instructions, rate of frequency
acceleration, and all physical factors in the room and experimental
apparatus. It was felt that the careful application of rigorous controls was of the utmost importance, for the accuracy of the findings
would be greatly enhanced if contamination from extraneous factors
were held to a minimum.

Measurement of Change in Anxiety Level

Since the previous studies evaluated FFT on the basis of a cross-sectional analysis of groups of subjects, it is not clear what the relationships are between changes in FFT and changes in anxiety level. For example, it has not been shown whether the anxious subjects have a changed FFT when their anxiety symptoms subside. The experimental procedures have not allowed for such an assessment. One may speculate that some constitutional factor which predisposed the individual to symptom ownership was responsible for the low FFT, and that this somatic factor is operant in that individual whether or not he has anxiety symptoms or a psychiatric diagnosis. In approaching this problem, it was decided to assign the role of an independent variable to "anxiety level," and to evaluate its influence on FFT by longitudinal testing of experimental and control subjects. This type of experimental design allowed for the evaluation of both change and status of all variables under consideration. Another advantage of a longitudinal procedure is that it minimized the importance of large individual differences in the reactions measured, for each subject served as his own control. Thus, a sharp focus on the relationship between FFT and anxiety level was gained by a closer adherence to a classical experimental methodology.

A longitudinal design also permitted the evaluation of the possible effect of practice on FFT. The literature on the reliability of FFT measurements indicates that practice does not change FFT significantly. However, since no other researcher has conducted an identical study, the question of FFT being practice-free in this investigation deserved consideration.

Criteria of Anxiety

It was considered advisable to define anxiety in terms of an individual's presence in a real-life stress situation rather than by the usual criteria of symptoms or psychiatric diagnosis. The situation used was one in which the very psychobiological existence of the individual was threatened. May (1950) has written that "anxiety is the apprehension cued off by a threat to some value which the individual holds essential to his existence as a personality." In this research the value threatened was the continuation of life, which was endangered by surgical procedures scheduled to take place 24 hours after the experimental testing.

As an extra refinement, two additional measures of anxiety were employed: (1) systolic blood pressure; (2) self-rating on an anxiety inventory. (The self-rating anxiety inventory and systolic blood pressure are hereinafter abbreviated "S-I" and "BP.") These measurements were intended to verify the assumption that the preoperative situation was more stressful than the postoperative situation and also to provide physiological and psychological indices of anxiety level which could then be related to FFT.

Bernstein (1951) also used a group of minor surgical patients in his study of the validation of the alleged Rorschach signs of anxiety. He found significant differences in both psychological (Rorschach) and physiological (systolic blood pressure) indicators of anxiety. The differences were in the predicted directions both for surgical (preoperative and postoperative) and nonsurgical groups.

In summary, the present experiment attempts to clarify the relationship between FFT and anxiety. It was felt that a longitudinal study of changes in anxiety in experimental and control subjects would provide an appropriate experimental design for evaluating the relationship between FFT and anxiety level.

Experimental Hypotheses

Five specific hypotheses will be tested:

1. The experimental group mean FFT is significantly lower preoperatively than postoperatively.

2. The experimental group mean blood pressure and self-inventory scores are significantly higher before surgery than after surgery.

3. The control group means show no significant difference in FFT, blood pressure, and self-inventory score from test to retest.

4. Before surgery, the mean FFT, blood pressure, and self-inventory score of the experimental group differ significantly from the corresponding means of the control group; after surgery, no significant differences exist between the respective means of the experimental and control groups.

5. In the presurgical testing of the experimental group, the correlations between FFT and blood pressure and between FFT and self-inventory score are negative, while the correlation between blood pressure and self-inventory score is positive.

METHOD

The research design employed in this study conforms to the traditional experimental approach. It uses a psychophysical measurement (FFT) to evaluate the effects of a single variable (anxiety), in a highly controlled setting.

Assumptions made concerning the independent variable, anxiety level, are as follows: (a) Surgical patients will have a higher level of anxiety preoperatively than postoperatively. (b) Control group subjects will show no appreciable change in anxiety level from test to retest provided intervening stresses are minimal. A rationale for definite anxiety in terms of real-life stress was offered earlier.

Subjects

Two groups of subjects selected for study are hereafter referred to as the experimental (surgical) group (E) and the control (employee) group (C). The experimental group consisted of thirty presurgical patients examined (E-I) 24 hours prior to minor surgical procedures, and re-examined (E-II) after recovery from surgery had been ascertained. The postsurgical testing was conducted just prior to the patient's discharge from the hospital.

The control group was composed of 30 hospital employees who were tested (C-I) and then retested (C-II) at approximately a one-week interval.

A comparison of the experimental and control group means and ranges in respect to age (at last birthday), education (last year completed), testing interval (in days), and oral temperature (in degrees Fahrenheit), is presented in Table 1. An inspection of these data reveals that there were no marked group differences and that the groups were similar enough so that they may be considered homogeneous regarding these specific measurements.

TABLE 1

Comparison of the Experimental and Control Group—Means and Range in Respect to Age, Education, Interval, and Temperature

Group	Age (years)	Education (years)	Interval (days)	Temperature (degrees)	
Experimental				Preoper.	Postoper.
Mean	28.9	11.7	7.4	98.53	98.50
Range	21-39	5-16	5-17	97.6-99.1	97.7-99.4
Control				Test	Retest
Mean	30.5	12.1	7.6	98.46	98.39
Range	21-40	8-19	4-18	97.9-99.1	97.8-99.0

Self-Inventory Scale

In an effort to tap conscious feelings of discomfort, a self-rating inventory of anxiety was developed by the author. The test items were phrased in the present tense and pertained to manifest anxiety as it is reflected in various mental and somatic symptoms. The items were similar to those which appeared most frequently on six well-known health questionnaires and adjustment inventories. In a small validating study, a 20-item scale significantly differentiated a group of 10 patients from a group of 10 hospital employees at the .05 level. Five items appeared somewhat ambiguous and were not fully understood by many of the subjects. These items were eliminated and the difference between the group means increased to the .02 level. The revised 15-item self-rating inventory remained without further change and was administered to all subjects in this study. It is interesting to note that Ebaugh (1948) lists most of these items as symptoms in a table of spontaneous complaints offered by patients with anxiety reactions.

Selection Criteria

To control a number of extraneous factors known to affect FFT, all subjects in both the experimental and control groups were required to meet the following criteria:

Age................. 21-40, age in years at last birthday
Vision............... 20/20, natural or corrected, measured by Snellen Chart
Sedation............. no sedation during the twenty-four-hour period prior to testing
Alcoholic intake...... no alcohol during the twenty-four-hour period prior to testing
Sleep................ at least six hours sleep the night before testing
Exercise............. no exercise the morning of testing
Smoking............. no smoking during the one-hour period prior to testing
Pain................. no severe pain at the time of testing
Psychiatric history.... no history of a diagnosis of or treatment for nervous or mental illness
Temperature......... oral temperature within 97.6-99.6 degrees Fahrenheit
Time................. All testing done between 1-2 P.M.
Intervening stress..... no major intervening stress in the control group
Type of operation..... minor surgery in pathological conditions which have no additional systemic involvement; no blood transfusions; discharge must follow this operation
Complications........ no major postoperative complications

Apparatus

Krugman (1947) gave an explicit and systematic description of the apparatus and experimental conditions used in his study. The present experiment attempted to follow his design in all possible respects.

The apparatus used to measure FFT was a General Radio Company "Strobotac," Model 631-A, which produces a variable oscillating light with a range of 600 to 14,500 cycles per minute. The accuracy of this instrument is claimed by the manufacturer to be within one per cent.

Following Krugman's design, the apparatus and room were modified in the following manner:

1. The 5-inch diameter of the light source and reflector was reduced to 1¾ inches by placing an opaque cardboard mask in front of the apparatus. A circle of 1¾ inches was cut out of the mask.

2. A single sheet of "Eagle-A Coupon Bond paper of 100% rag content" was pasted to the back of the cardboard mask and served as a translucent screen for the light source.

3. A fixation point on the mask was provided by drawing a white cross with an axis ⅝ inch long which intersected at a point 2 inches below the center of the light stimulus.

4. Each subject was seated in such a manner that, when his chin was properly situated on the adjustable chin rest, his eyes were level with the center of the stimulus light and 24 inches distant. A 5 degree angle of vision was assured by this arrangement when the subject fixated on the cross 2 inches below the center of the stimulus light. All testing was with binocular vision.

5. A 50-watt, G.E. Mazda Lamp, located in the center of the ceiling and 9 feet from the floor, provided the light present during the testing period. The amount of light falling on the subject's eyes during the FFT determination, as measured by a photovolt meter, was .10 foot-candle.

6. Auditory cues emanating from the Strobotac vibrator were effectively screened by a 12-inch Hunter fan mounted on the wall 6 feet from the subject.

7. The test room was 9 feet high by 10 feet wide and 20 feet long. Black-out curtains were used at the window. The apparatus was placed 7 feet from the center of the room and equidistant from either side.

Procedure

The following procedure was used invariably in the solicitation and testing of each subject:

1. When first approached to enlist his participation in the study, each subject was told only that the investigation was concerned

with the development of a new visual test. After the subject had consented to participate, a testing appointment was scheduled. At this time he was asked not to smoke for one hour prior to the testing time. Since only one prospective subject refused to participate in the study, a bias introduced by using only candidates who were willing to co-operate was avoided.

2. When the subject appeared at the testing room as scheduled, his eyes were tested with the Snellen Chart for 20/20 vision.

3. Following a brief interview, the criteria sheet was checked and completed. The preoperative patients were asked how they felt about the forthcoming surgery and their remarks were recorded. The control group subjects were questioned about intervening stresses at the retest period.

4. Oral temperature was next obtained and noted.

5. The systolic blood pressure recorded was the average of two readings taken at this time.

6. The subject then filled out the self-inventory.

7. The subject was seated facing the apparatus. A three-minute period was then devoted to adapting the subject to the illumination level of the room.

8. During the light-adaptation period the following instructions were read to the subject: "You will shortly see a flickering light. I want you to keep your eyes on the cross and tell me when the light appears to stop flickering and become steady. Remember, keep staring at the cross and say *now* when the light appears steady."

9. Ten determinations of FFT were taken. Each threshold determination was separated by a 15-second rest period. During this period a shield was placed between the light stimulus and the subject's eyes. The subject's FFT was the average of the ten determinations expressed in cycles per second.

10. A base frequency of 2,000 cycles per minute was used. The acceleration of the frequency of the light stimulus was controlled by a hand-operated dial. The rate of acceleration was checked three times during the course of the study and it closely approximated 1.5 cycles per second.

RESULTS

The statistical treatment of the data was guided primarily by the experimental hypotheses. Therefore, the analyses of results are presented in the order of the specific hypotheses. Statistical decision procedures are based on critical regions of size .05.

Hypothesis 1

The experimental group mean FFT is significantly lower preoperatively than postoperatively.

Hypothesis 2

The experimental group mean blood pressure and self-inventory score are significantly higher before than after surgery.

Table 2 shows a comparison of the preoperative and postoperative means of the experimental group. As hypothesized, the experimental

TABLE 2

Comparison of the Experimental Group Means
Before (E-I) and After (E-II) Surgery

Measure	Preoper.		Postoper.			
	Mean	SD	Mean	SD	t	P
FFT	43.33	1.69	44.64	2.06	6.89	<.01
Blood Pressure	132.0	13.73	122.7	9.18	4.94	<.01
Self-Inventory	33.5	10.81	30.9	9.57	2.95	<.01

group mean FFT is significantly lower preoperatively (E-I), during the stress period, than postoperatively (E-II). Also, as predicted, the blood pressure readings and self-inventory scores were significantly higher during the preoperative stress period. All mean differences were significant at better than the .01 level.

Hypothesis 3

The control group shows no significant differences in FFT, blood pressure, and self-inventory score from test to retest.

A comparison of the control group test (C-I) and retest (C-II) means is presented in Table 3. As hypothesized, there are no signifi-

TABLE 3

Comparison of the Control Group Means
Test (C-I) and Retest (C-II)

Measure	Test		Retest			
	Mean	SD	Mean	SD	t	P
FFT	45.11	1.92	45.00	1.99	.69	NS
Blood Pressure	123.4	10.04	122.0	8.24	1.69	NS
Self-Inventory	29.1	8.14	28.8	8.83	.35	NS

cant differences between the means of all three measures. The importance of these results will be discussed later in relation to practice effects and test reliability.

Hypothesis 4

Before surgery, the mean FFT, blood pressure, and self-inventory scores of the experimental group differ significantly from the corresponding means of the control group; after surgery, no significant differences exist between the respective means of the experimental and control groups.

Since there were no significant differences between the test and retest means of the control group, it was decided to combine them for a comparison of the differences between the presurgical (E-I) and control (C-I, -II) groups and postsurgical (E-II) and control (C-I, -II) groups. However, in order to combine the control group measures, it had to be demonstrated that there were no significant differences in the variances.

Neither FFT nor self-inventory scores showed significant differences in their variances from test to retest. It was decided, therefore, to combine the test-retest measurements of each of these variables in the control group. However, the variances of blood pressure differed significantly (.05 level) from test to retest; therefore, the combining of these measurements was not undertaken.

The results presented in Tables 4 and 5 confirm Hypothesis 4. As predicted, there are significant differences between the means

TABLE 4

Comparison of the Experimental Group Preoperative (E-I) Means and
the Combined Control (C-I, -II) Group Means

	Preoper.		Test-Retest			
Measure	Mean	SD	Mean	SD	t	P
FFT	43.33	1.69	45.05	1.94	4.12	>.01
Blood Pressure	132.0	13.73	123.4	10.04	3.20	>.01
Self-Inventory	33.5	10.81	29.0	8.42	2.17	>.05

of the preoperative (E-I) and control (C-II) groups with respect to blood pressure, self-inventory score, and FFT, and no significant differences between the respective means of the postoperative (E-II) and control (C-I, -II) groups.

TABLE 5

Comparison of the Experimental Group Postoperative (E-II) Means and
the Combined Control (C-I, -II) Group Means

Measure	Postoper.		Test-Retest			
	Mean	SD	Mean	SD	t	P
FFT	44.64	2.06	45.05	1.94	.93	NS
Blood Pressure	122.7	9.18	122.0	8.24	.26	NS
Self-Inventory	30.9	9.57	29.0	8.42	.96	NS

Hypothesis 5

In the presurgical testing of the experimental group, the correlations between FFT and blood pressure and between FFT and self-inventory score are negative, while the correlation between blood pressure and self-inventory score is positive.

In testing this hypothesis, product-moment correlations were used. The only significant relationship is the negative correlation between the preoperative (E-I) FFT and blood pressure. This relationship was predicted. A low positive correlation is observed between FFT and self-inventory score. Self-inventory score and blood pressure, interestingly, have a negative but nonsignificant relationship in three of four instances.

In all four testing situations, the highest correlations are those between blood pressure and FFT. In each case the relationship is a negative one, but only in the preoperative situation does the correlation reach a significant level.

Tables 6 and 7 present the correlations for the experimental (E-I, E-II) and control (C-I, C-II) measurements.

TABLE 6

Correlations of the Experimental Group Presurgical (E-I)
and Postsurgical (E-II) Measurements

	Preoper.		Postoper.	
	S-I	FFT	S-I	FFT
BP	−.23	−.37	−.10	−.35
S-I		.10		.12

TABLE 7

Correlations of the Control Group Test (C-I) and Retest (C-II) Measurements

	Test		Retest	
	S-I	FFT	S-I	FFT
BP	−.17	−.19	.03	−.25
S-I	.09			.09

DISCUSSION

The results of the present study offer clear confirmatory evidence to support the findings of Krugman (1947) and Goldstone (1953). The sensitivity of FFT to anxiety level is demonstrated by its significant lowering in the experimental group during the subjects' stress period (presurgery) and its elevation to a level comparable to that of the control group upon the subjects' removal from the stress situation (postsurgery). The direction of change of FFT is markedly consistent, having occurred in 27 of the 30 experimental subjects.

The intraindividual variability of FFT also appears to have been influenced by the stress situation. The preoperative variance is significantly higher than the postoperative variance. The control group shows no significant change in the intraindividual variability of FFT.

In assaying the value of FFT as a test of anxiety level, the preoperative (stress) thresholds were compared to the control (nonstress) thresholds. Designating 44.0 cycles per second as the critical cutoff point, 70% of the stress subjects and 23% of the nonstress subjects achieved an FFT at or below this frequency. The FFT is more efficient in differentiating stress from nonstress subjects than are blood pressure and self-inventory scores. Further standardization and cross-validation are necessary before the FFT measurements can be put to practical use as a diagnostic or screening device for the differentiation of anxious from nonanxious persons.

Misiak (1948), in his reliability study, suggested that the FFT is an inherent, stable physiological characteristic of the individual. The data presented here lend support to this assumption insofar as all other things remain the same. The stability is seen in the control group where an analysis of the test-retest FFT measurements revealed a high reliability (.93) and lack of practice effects. However, in the experimental group where the independent variable, stress, was introduced, large individual and group fluctuations in FFT were observed. The reliability coefficient for FFT was higher than those attained by blood pressure and self-inventory measurements.

Although the research design did not provide a crucial test of physiological or psychological interpretations of changes in FFT, the findings are consonant with the perceptual theories (Klein, 1951; Pullen & Stagner, 1953) discussed earlier. In terms of FFT, the perceptual models would seem to hold that the anxious person, being greatly preoccupied with the internal state of affairs, directs less attention to the external reality (flicker). Thus, because of his inner personal insecurity, he becomes intolerant of the unstable and ambiguous and seeks to resolve these conflicts.

The anxious subjects in this research showed a lowering of sensitivity to flicker (low FFT), resolving the ambiguity by organizing the unstable (flickering) field into a stable (fusion) field.

As a further check on the basic assumption that surgical patients are more anxious 24 hours before surgery than at a period after surgery but prior to hospital discharge, blood pressure and self-inventory scores of the experimental group were analyzed, pre-operatively and postoperatively. The assumptions were verified by the findings of significant differences in both the physiological (blood pressure) and psychological (self-inventory) indicators of anxiety, in the predicted directions, for the experimental and control groups.

In addition, the patients' pre- and postoperative statements concerning their feelings about the surgical procedures and general state of well-being were recorded. No attempt was made to quantify these statements. An inspection revealed that nearly 95% of the patients experienced some worry and concern during the preoperative period, and expressed relief postoperatively.

The only significant correlation among the measures of anxiety is between blood pressure and FFT. Both measures appear to be valid physiological correlates of anxiety. The intercorrelations of these two measures are the highest obtained in all four testing sessions. They are significant, however, only in the preoperative stress period, as hypothesized.

The failure of the self-inventory scores to correlate significantly with blood pressure and FFT may be explained on the basis of the common clinical observation that the anxious individual frequently is unwilling to admit to himself, as well as to others, the true extent of his inner feelings.

The FFT measurement seems to meet most of Eysenck's (1952) criteria for inclusion in a battery of tests for the objective evaluation of behavior. That the FFT is a simply obtained, objective, reliable measurement which is sensitive to anxiety level has been established. It appears that the research applications of FFT in the area of psychotherapy and psychopathology would be fruitful and would lead, perhaps, to further testable hypotheses concerning the generalization of perceptual attitudes and the relationships between personality and perception.

SUMMARY

The present investigation sought to determine the effects of psychological stress and anxiety on FFT.

The following groups were selected for study: (a) an experimental group of 30 surgical patients examined 24 hours preoperatively and re-examined postoperatively after recovery from surgery had been ascertained and prior to the patients' hospital discharge; (b) a control group of 30 hospital employees tested and then retested at approximately a one-week interval.

Assumptions made concerning the independent variable, anxiety level, were: (a) surgical patients have a higher level of anxiety preoperatively than postoperatively; (b) control group subjects show no appreciable change in anxiety level from test to retest provided intervening stresses are minimal.

Systolic blood pressure and score on a self-rating inventory of anxiety were used as additional measures of anxiety. These measures provided a check on the basic assumptions.

The experimental testing conditions were essentially those outlined by Krugman (1947). Additional controls over extraneous factors included the application of rigorous criteria for the selection of subjects.

The following conclusions were drawn:

1. FFT is a sensitive, reliable, and valid index of anxiety level.

2. Increases in psychological stress and anxiety are accompanied by a significant lowering of FFT and an increase in the intraindividual variability.

3. FFT has a potential usefulness as a screening device for the differentiation of anxious from nonanxious persons.

· 8 ·

The Effect of Anxiety on the Resolution
of Perceptual Conflict *

The purpose of this research was to investigate the relationship between anxiety and the resolution of a perceptual conflict. Although theoretical observations and experimental evidence have consistently supported the hypothesis that severe psychological stress influences perceptual functioning, there is considerable disagreement in the theoretical conceptions relating personality variables to perceptual behavior. The present study, therefore, was designed to clarify the theoretical interpretation of the relationship between emotional stress and perception.

There are at least two divergent schools of thought among those theorists who believe that anxiety has a predictable effect on perception. One point of view suggests that anxiety results in a greater reliance on past experiences and manifests itself in a resistance to perceptual change. Under normal conditions, individuals presumably are alert to changing stimuli. The introduction of anxiety reduces attention to external stimuli, thereby lessening the probability of appropriate changes in perceptual behavior.

An alternative view is exemplified by some learning theorists who interpret anxiety as a drive. From this point of view, responses associated with anxiety are learned as a consequence of anxiety reduction. There may be a striking contrast in the behavioral effects of anxiety in different individuals because of the particular mode of

* This chapter was prepared by Dorothy Block and represents a condensation of a doctoral dissertation submitted to Columbia University.

response which has been reinforced by anxiety reduction. Hence, a state of anxiety leads to an emphasis of the previously learned anxiety-reducing response, whatever it was.

Thus, this viewpoint emphasizes the drive-reducing value of perceptual behavior and individual differences resulting from specific learning experience, rather than the uniform resistance to perceptual change explicit in the first set of expectations.

It should be pointed out that these two views, both of which involve a predictable generalized effect of anxiety on perception, are not necessarily antithetical. The two response tendencies of resistance to perceptual change and accentuation of the usual mode of perceiving may occur simultaneously under anxiety.

In addition to these two views about the predictable effect of anxiety, an alternative view suggests that the effect of anxiety is the disorganization and disruption of the individual's perceptions as manifested in erratic performance. In other words, perceptual performance in an acutely anxious state bears no predictable relation to perceptual functioning in a less anxious state.

EXPERIMENTAL HYPOTHESES

In order to evaluate the theoretical interpretations of the effect of anxiety on perception, several alternative hypotheses, each based on a particular theory, were tested. If anxiety results in perceptual rigidity, constriction of perceptual behavior, and persistence of perceptual behavior in spite of environmental changes, it seems reasonable to predict that there is a positive relationship between anxiety and resistance to perceptual change. On the other hand, the theoretical view that perceptual behavior under conditions of emotional stress depends primarily on previously learned perceptual responses suggests the hypothesis that there is a positive relationship between anxiety and accentuation of the individual's typical mode of perceiving. Furthermore, if there is a positive relationship between anxiety and resistance to perceptual change as well as accentuation of the individual's typical mode of perceiving, it is hypothesized that under conditions of anxiety, there is a positive relation between accentuation of the typical mode of perceiving and increased resistance to perceptual change. Finally, if the consequence of anxiety is the disorganization and disruption of perceptual behavior, the correlation between scores on a perceptual task under an anxious and a nonanxious condition is lower than the correlation between scores under two nonanxious conditions.

In summary, the following hypotheses were tested:

1. There is a positive relationship between anxiety and resistance to perceptual change.

2. There is a positive relationship between anxiety and the accentuation of the individual's typical mode of perceiving.

3. Under conditions of anxiety, there is a positive relationship between accentuation of the typical mode of perceiving and increased resistance to perceptual change.

4. The correlation between perceptual scores is lower for subjects under anxious and nonanxious conditions than the correlation for subjects tested twice under nonanxious conditions.

METHOD

The present experiment was concerned with the effect of situational anxiety on the time required for the resolution of a perceptual conflict. The assumptions made concerning the independent variable, anxiety level, were that surgical patients have a higher level of anxiety preoperatively than postoperatively, and that control group subjects show no significant change in anxiety level from test to retest provided there are no intervening stresses.

A group of surgical patients and a comparable group of hospital employees were tested and retested with the same measures. The experimental group of surgical patients was tested preoperatively, presumably under the condition of stress induced by the forthcoming operation and retested postoperatively when the threat of the operation presumably had been reduced. The control group of hospital employees was tested and retested under conditions of no apparent or consistent stress. The "Test" refers to the anxiety situation, whereas the "Retest" refers to the nonstress situation. Two measures of anxiety, namely, systolic blood pressure and self-ratings on an anxiety inventory, were employed to verify the assumption that the presurgical situation was more stressful than the postsurgical situation, and also to provide both physiological and psychological indices of anxiety level. The use of aniseikonic lenses for viewing the Leaf Room constituted the perceptual conflict induced. The measure used was the time taken by the individual to resolve this conflict, defined as the time to reach and maintain a stable perception in relation to the magnitude of distortion experienced.

Subjects

The experimental subjects were 19 nonpsychiatric male, minor surgical patients selected from the presurgical ward of the East Orange Veterans Administration Hospital. These patients were examined 24 hours prior to minor surgical procedures and examined after successful recovery from surgery. No subject who was under the influence of drugs was included.

The control subjects consisted of 25 male hospital employees. The groups were equated for age and education. Table 1 presents the

TABLE 1

Characteristics of Experimental and Control Groups

Characteristic	Experimental	Control
Mean Age	31.42	32.80
Standard Deviation of Age	6.83	5.69
Range of Age	20-42	24-44
Mean Education	11.08	11.76
Standard Deviation of Education	2.48	1.80
Range of Education	7-16	8-16
Mean Days between Test and Retest	9.26	8.04
Standard Deviation of Days between Test and Retest	4.73	3.24
Range of Days between Test and Retest	4-21	3-16

group means, standard deviations, and ranges for these variables as well as the average and range of time between Test and Retest for both groups. An inspection of these data reveals that there were no marked differences and that the groups were sufficiently similar so that they may be considered homogeneous with regard to age, education, and time between Test and Retest.

Apparatus

The experiment was performed in the Perception Laboratory of the hospital, which contained modifications of the Ames demonstrations. The Leaf Room was the setting for the experimental introduction of the perceptual conflict to be resolved. Covering the surface of the three walls and ceiling of the room was wire mesh through which oak leaves of uniform size and color were interwoven. The floor was covered with leaves as well. In the center of the wall opposite to the doorway where the individual was seated, was a white rod which he could manipulate to a 180 degree angle by use of the selsyn situated at his side.

Axis-90 aniseikonic lenses were used to induce a perceptual conflict in the Leaf Room. According to Ames:

> The development of aniseikonic or size lenses provided . . . means by which sharply defined dioptric image patterns of various types could be precisely altered in size and shape by known amounts, thus permitting a more thorough investigation than had heretofore been possible of the relation between the dimensions of the uniocular stimulus-patterns and binocular spatial appearances. (1952, p. 17.)

The lenses used altered the relationship between the stimulus patterns received by the two eyes so that the individual experienced the back wall of the room as slanted either to the right or to the left depending upon whether the aniseikonic lens was worn over the right or the left eye.

Ames has also emphasized the role of the observer in the perception of the aniseikonic illusion:

> Apparently, all persons with normal binocular vision have similar visual experiences when wearing the same size lenses in the same environmental conditions, the magnitude of the effects being directly related to the magnitude of the distortion produced by the size lenses . . . The rapidity with which the abnormal appearances develop varies with different observers. Some experience the effects immediately, others with more or less delay. In view of the unequivocal and most marked, one might say, dramatic nature of these anomalous appearances, it might be expected that looking through the above described glasses should produce similar anomalous appearances under all conditions. Actually, however, this is not the case. The nature and degree of the anomalous appearances that are experienced depend not only upon the particular environmental conditions, but also upon the observer. (1952, p. 37.)

Of further importance is the notion that if there are factors in the environment which produce predominantly monocular stimulus-patterns, such as an ordinary room, no illusion will be experienced; rather, the room appears substantially normal. Thus, the function of the Leaf Room is to reduce monocular cues to a minimum. The use of aniseikonic lenses in the present experiment was to exaggerate the conflict between the individual's immediate sensory impressions and the tendency to preserve and keep constant his past perception of the external world.

A stop watch was used for the purpose of recording from the

selsyn the magnitude of perceptual distortion at five-second intervals for a period of three minutes.

Buhler's (1954) Self-Rating Manifest Anxiety Inventory was used. The subjects rated themselves on each of 15 items. Each point on the six-point continuum represented a score of one. Therefore, the higher the score, the greater the degree of anxiety reported as experienced consciously by the individual.

A sphygmomanometer was used to measure systolic blood pressure. The mean of two successive readings was considered representative of the subject's systolic blood pressure at the time of testing. Both blood pressure and the self-ratings were obtained in both groups in both testing sessions.

Procedure

The subjects were seen individually. When the subject was brought into the perception laboratory, he was given a short introduction to the effect that he was going to be administered a new test of vision which had been tried at other Veterans Administration hospitals.

Experimental subjects were asked how they felt about the forthcoming surgery, and their remarks were recorded. Firstly, each subject was asked to record the self-ratings on Buhler's Manifest Anxiety Inventory. Secondly, each subject's blood pressure was recorded twice. Subjects were then shown the Leaf Room.

The Leaf Room lights and the general illumination in the perception laboratory were left on. The subject was seated facing into the Leaf Room, wearing his own glasses, if any, but not the aniseikonic glasses.

The subject was shown the selsyn and instructed as follows: "This knob moves the white rod over there. Turn it a few times to get the feel of it."

The experimenter then explained the task to the subject in the following way:

> Do you see the back wall? The four edges of that wall make a square. I would like you to set the rod so that it is lined up with the top edge of the back wall. Just for practice, let's do that a few times.

Four settings of this kind were taken. The experimenter set the rod 17 degrees to the right and left, and then 25 degrees to the right and left. The subject each time set the rod parallel. The experimenter recorded the subject's settings. The mean of his four settings was used as the horizontal reference value for each subject.

The experimenter then showed the aniseikonic glasses to the subject and gave the following instructions:

> Now I'm going to ask you to do the same thing while you are wearing these glasses. These glasses may make the room appear to change shape while you are looking at it; whatever it does, I would like you to keep the rod always lined up with the top edge of the back wall. If that edge seems to move, you move the rod with it just as fast or as slow as it moves. Is that clear?

The experimenter than set the rod to the subject's horizontal reference value and had him repeat the setting with the glasses reversed. The subject was required to make four settings in all.

The same procedure was followed in both sessions. Control subjects were questioned about any intervening stresses at the retest period.

The magnitude of distortion was recorded from the selsyn at five-second intervals for a period of three minutes. From these readings, the measure of time taken to achieve stability with respect to the changed perception of the Leaf Room was derived and used in the analysis of the data.

RESULTS

Table 2 contains the medians, semi-interquartile ranges, and ranges on all measures considered in this experiment.

Four alternative hypotheses concerning the effect of anxiety on the resolution of a perceptual conflict were tested.

TABLE 2

Characteristics of Experimental and Control Groups for Perceptual, Anxiety Inventory, and Blood Pressure Measures on Test and Retest

Measures	Median		Q		Range	
	Test	Retest	Test	Retest	Test	Retest
Experimental Group (N = 19)						
Perceptual Scores	25	12	4.25	8.73	5-119	5-50
Anxiety Inventory Scores	33	32	7.38	8.25	17-68	15-47
Blood Pressure Scores	139	129	2.16	2.97	128-149	111-140
Control Group (N = 25)						
Perceptual Scores	12	9	5.25	3.16	5-34	5-29
Anxiety Inventory Scores	26	24	7.31	7.41	15-38	15-50
Blood Pressure Scores	129	130	4.06	5.31	120-162	117-154

The first hypothesis stated that there is a positive relationship between anxiety and resistance to perceptual change. This hypothesis was tested by two methods. First, to test the hypothesis that the nonanxious perceptual performances of both groups are not significantly different from each other, members of the experimental and control groups were tested in a nonanxiety situation. For the Retest, the subjects' perceptual scores, which consisted of the time taken to resolve the perceptual conflict, in both groups were combined and ranked without regard to group. The median rank was found, and a chi square test was performed to determine whether the difference in distribution of rank for the experimental and control groups in the nonanxious situation was statistically significant. The ranks above the median were considered "fast" resolutions to the perceptual conflict, while those below were defined as "slow" or more resistant to perceptual change. Table 3 presents the distribution of

TABLE 3

Distribution of Subjects' Perceptual Scores on Retest

Group	Above Median	Below Median
Experimental	8	11
Control	14	11

Chi square = .83.

ranks above and below the median on the Retest. Since the distributions of the control and experimental subjects for the nonanxious condition are not significantly different from each other, the null hypothesis could not be rejected.

The identical statistical procedures were followed for the anxiety situation. Table 4 presents the distribution of perceptual scores

TABLE 4

Distribution of Subjects' Perceptual Scores on Test

Group	Above Median	Below Median
Experimental	4	15
Control	18	7

Chi square = 11.21.

above and below the median of the Test. The chi square value obtained shows that the distributions of the control and experimental subjects for the anxious condition are significantly different from each other beyond the .01 level.

In the second method by which the first hypothesis was tested, the differences between the time taken to resolve the perceptual conflict on the Test and Retest for all subjects were ranked with sign taken into account. A chi square test was performed to determine whether there is a relationship between being above or below the median and experimental or control group status. Table 5 presents

TABLE 5

Distribution of Differences between Perceptual Scores on Test and Retest

Group	Above Median	Below Median
Experimental	16	3
Control	6	19

Chi square = 15.65.

the distributions of scores above and below the median of the differences between Test and Retest perceptual scores. The chi square value obtained shows that the distributions of the control and experimental subjects are significantly different from each other beyond the .01 level. Thus, the hypothesis that there is a positive relationship between anxiety and resistance to perceptual change was supported.

The second hypothesis stated that there is a positive relationship between anxiety and the accentuation of the individual's typical mode of perceiving. Since the Retest was presumed to represent the individual's typical mode of perceiving, the experimental subjects were ranked from fastest to slowest on the basis of their perceptual scores on the Retest. The median score was found, and subjects whose scores were above the median were considered "slow." Each subject's score on the Retest was compared with his score on the Test. A plus value was given if a subject's score moved further in the same direction in the anxiety situation, while a minus value was given if his score remained the same in both the anxiety and non-anxiety situations. Support of the hypothesis would be indicated by a proportion of plus values greater than that expected by chance. Table 6 presents the distribution of scores which were accentuated

TABLE 6

Distribution of Scores Accentuated and Reversed on Test

Group	Reversed Direction	Same Direction
Experimental	9	9

Chi square = 0.

and reversed under anxious conditions. A chi square value of zero was obtained, indicating there is no relationship between anxiety and the accentuation of the individual's typical mode of perceiving. While the chi square test of the hypothesis is by no means the most powerful available, examination of the distribution of changes by inspection indicates a chance character that would warrant no further testing.

The third hypothesis stated that there is a positive relationship between accentuation of the typical mode of perceiving and increased resistance to perceptual change. In order for this hypothesis to be supported, it is necessary that the first two hypotheses be supported. Since the second hypothesis was not supported, it follows that the third hypothesis is not supported.

Assuming that anxiety disorganizes perceptual performances, the correlation between presurgical and postsurgical perceptual scores should be lower for the experimental subjects than for the control subjects. Rank-order correlation coefficients were computed between the Test and Retest performances for both groups. There is no significant difference between the *rho* of .57 for the experimental group and the *rho* of .79 for the control group. Therefore, this hypothesis was not supported. These indices of relationship, however, indicate a rather high degree of reliability over time in the perceptual performance of subjects.

DISCUSSION

This experiment derived from the conflict between two theoretical views concerning the effect of anxiety on perception. The first view predicted the unilateral effect of resistance to perceptual change, whereas the second emphasized the drive-reducing value of perceptual behavior and the individual differences resulting from specific learning experiences. The results of this study clearly favor the superiority of the former theoretical view over the latter.

Within this frame of reference, these findings are relevant to the transactional theory of perception which states: "Perception is a process by which an individual attributes to his immediate environment the significance which he has found from previous experience to have furthered his purposes." (Allport, 1955, p. 280.) According to Kilpatrick:

> By perception, then, is meant that part of the transactional process which is an implicit awareness of the probable significance for action of present impingements from the environment, based on assumptions related to the same or similar impingements from the environment. By assumption is meant that generally unconscious aspect of the transactional process which may be described as a weighted average of past experience in dealing with these portions of the impingements from the environment to which it is related. Assumptions function as probabilities which are built up by action, checked by action, and modified by action as the consequences of these actions are registered in relation to purposes. Taken altogether, our assumptions form our "assumptive world" which we bring to every occasion and on which our perceptions are based; therefore, the only world we know is determined by our assumptions. (1952, p. 89.)

Allport's summary of transactionalism is as follows:

> We thus hold on to certain presumptive aspects and relinquish others; and we perceive in accordance with these assumptive emphases. These indications to which we cling are said to be the ones which on the basis of experience, have the greatest "prognostic reliability" with respect to our own potential action in the situation. (Allport, 1955, p. 277.)

In other words, the theoretical view of the transactionalists is that an individual perceives as he "assumes," and that each individual accumulates certain assumptions about the world in which he lives on the basis of his past experience. In this experiment, it was assumed that the expectancy of the individual looking into the Leaf Room was that the room was rectangular. Similarly, past experiences of all individuals have indicated that walls and ceilings join at right angles. The individual was placed in a situation of perceptual conflict by the introduction of aniseikonic lenses which altered the usual relation of the dioptric images on the respective retinas. The conflict was one in which the immediate sensory impressions gave the visual illusion of tilt while past experience and learning with regard to the nature of rooms was in the opposite direction. In other words, there was a tendency to preserve the perception of the room as the individual had experienced rooms in the past. Although there were individual differences in the speed with which the illusion was seen, the time delay under conditions of anxiety was greater for all subjects, indicating that under stress the tendency to preserve the familiar world is greater than under normal conditions. While all subjects eventually responded to the objective perceptual distortion, in a state of anxiety the immediate reliance was on the reality as it had been commonly perceived in the past and not on the reality of the immediate situation. These results are in keeping with the concept of need for perceptual stability demonstrated by other experimenters.

The question arises as to the absence in these results of a positive relationship between anxiety and the individual's typical mode of perceiving. If assumptions about the objective world may be thought of as "sets," then personality characteristics are reflected by individual differences in assumptions or sets. According to Allport, "There are differences in (as well as universal aspects in) the assumptions (and hence in the perceptions) of different persons, because of difference in past experiences." (1955, p. 279.) It is likely that the present experiment involved an emphasis on the universal aspects of assumptions and perceptions. It may be said generally that all people have had similar past experience with regard to the physical nature of rooms. The fact that the second hypothesis was not supported does not disprove the drive-reducing value of perceptual behavior and the emphasis on individual differences resulting from individual learning experiences, but rather points to the need for adequate evaluation of experimental stimuli in order to evaluate the ensuing perceptions appropriately. Further experimentation is necessary in order to indicate whether there is an exaggeration of individual differences under conditions of anxiety in the perception of a stimulus in relation to which past experience has resulted in a greater initial variability of assumption than the present stimulus situation.

The view that the effect of anxiety is the disorganization and disruption of the individual's perceptions as manifested in erratic performance was not supported by the present experimental findings. It is likely that the anxiety level dealt with in this experiment, while severe enough to affect perceptual functioning, was not of sufficient intensity to result in totally disordered behavior. The degree of anxiety experienced by experimental subjects was probably not of "catastrophic" dimensions in Goldstein's (1939) terms; thus, the integrity of the self was not seriously threatened and consistency of perceptual performance was maintained.

One question raised by the results is the evaluation of stress or anxiety. Anxiety, in this experiment, was defined in terms of the individual's presence in a real-life stress situation. Caution is advised against equating this criterion of anxiety with the usual criteria of symptoms or psychiatric diagnoses and drawing generalizations on that basis. This study did not attempt to stimulate anxiety above and beyond that which was inherent in acting as a subject in an experimental situation during the 24 hours prior to undergoing surgical procedures. The implications drawn are that the effect of anxiety on perception should be evaluated in relation both to the criterion and source of anxiety and the stimuli to be perceived.

The results further suggest that anxiety inventory ratings are not as useful and consistent an index of anxiety as a physiological index such as blood pressure, which seemed to tap the same function as that sampled by the experimental condition.

The results also suggest the care with which the pressure and expression of anxiety must be evaluated. In this study, the physiological change induced through sympathetic nerve activity was a measurable, physical expression of anxiety which could not be consciously withheld. The results indicated that under presurgical conditions, systolic blood pressure measurements are significantly higher than under nonanxious conditions. This is in keeping with May's discussion of the physical expressions of anxiety and fear: "The peripheral blood vessels are constricted (and the blood pressure thereby raised) to maintain arterial pressure for the emergency needs." (1950, p. 62.) Inspection of the subjects' responses to an open-ended question, "How do you feel about the operation you're having tomorrow?" indicated the presence of anxiety in preoperative patients. However, the subjects' lack of awareness of that which they were revealing about themselves should be emphasized. The anxiety scale, which involved communicating in writing to the experimenter the presence of symptoms betraying anxiety, did not differentiate between presurgical and control subjects. Since Buhler used similar subjects and found significant differences between the experimental and control groups in ratings on the anxiety scale, the question arises as to why the present study did not find such differences. The experimenter's subjective observation was that these male surgery patients were reluctant to acknowledge to a female examiner the severity of their anxiety. If this observation is valid, a fruitful investigation would be to explore the accuracy of self-ratings on an anxiety inventory in relation to the various aspects of the interpersonal relationship between a subject and an experimenter.

Further exploration may clarify the effect of anxiety on the perception of interpersonal relationships more generally. For example, a practical question to be raised is whether anxious surgery patients tend to perceive their physicians in line with their past experiences in relation to authority figures or in correspondence to the reality of the specific authority in the new situation. If their perception in the immediate situation is distorted, what role does this distortion play in generating further anxiety?

Generally, this study clarifies the role anxiety plays in perception. It points to further research in understanding the expectations and assumptions of the individual, the role anxiety manifests in distorting his perceptions, and consequently to the need to develop therapeutic measures to alleviate this anxiety and thereby permit a more adequate and constructive evaluation of ongoing stimuli. Within the specific experimental context, there are implications for the application of these general ideas to the management of presurgical cases.

This study demonstrates the usefulness of the aniseikonic phenomenon as a perceptual situation in experimental research. Previous experimental research has indicated the usefulness of relating personality factors to the aniseikonic phenomenon. Becker (1952) found that individuals who took a longer time to report distortion while looking through aniseikonic lenses revealed more rigidity on personality measures than those who took a shorter time to see the effect. The results of Martin's study (1954) supported the hypothesis that people who took a long time to see the aniseikonic illusion were intolerant of ambiguity in interpersonal situations. Thus, the evidence points to the continual exploration of the methodological utility of this kind of perceptual situation in the further study of personality functioning.

SUMMARY

The present experiment was concerned with the effect of anxiety on the speed of resolution of a perceptual conflict. Several alternative hypotheses were tested. The first hypothesis stated that there is a positive relationship between anxiety and resistance to perceptual change; a second hypothesis stated that there is a positive relationship between anxiety and the accentuation of the individual's typical mode of perceiving, and a third hypothesis stated that under conditions of anxiety, there is a positive relationship between accentuation of the typical mode of perceiving and increased resistance to perceptual change. In addition to these hypotheses concerning the predictable effect on anxiety, an alternative hypothesis stated that the correlation between perceptual scores is lower for subjects under anxious and nonanxious conditions than the correlation for subjects tested twice under nonanxious conditions.

Nineteen nonpsychiatric male, minor surgical patients were tested and retested from 4 to 21 days after surgery. Twenty-five control subjects were equated for age, education, and testing interval with the experimental group and were tested and retested between 3 and 16 days later. Self-ratings on Buhler's Manifest Anxiety Inventory, systolic blood pressure measurements, and a measure of the speed with which the distortion induced by aniseikonic lenses in the Leaf Room was perceived, were obtained.

The hypothesis that there is a positive relationship between anxiety and resistance to perceptual change was supported. The hypothesis that there is a positive relationship between anxiety and the accentuation of the individual's typical mode of perceiving was not supported. The hypothesis that under conditions of anxiety, there is a positive relationship between accentuation of the typical mode of perceiving and increased resistance to perceptual change was not supported. The hypothesis that the correlation between perceptual scores is lower for subjects under anxious and nonanxious conditions than the correlation for subjects tested twice under nonanxious conditions was not supported.

The results suggest that under a real-life stress situation, when a stimulus with which people have had similar past experiences is altered, there is a reliance on perceptions which have grown out of past experience which manifests itself in a retarded reaction to the change in the immediate external reality.

The data suggest further research in which the source of the anxiety and the individual's past experience with the stimuli presented are experimentally controlled and varied.

· 9 ·

The Effect of Experimentally Induced Stress on Perceptual Measures [*]

The major hypothesis in this research is that psychologically oriented stresses produce demonstrable changes in the results of perceptual tasks when compared with the results on the same tasks performed before the introduction of stress. This study undertakes to measure the effects of experimentally induced stress upon distance judgment, aniseikonic distortion, and a variation of flicker fusion (Double-Flash Generator). Three different methods to induce stress are utilized: stylus maze with shock; mirror drawing with shock; and a mixed letter-and-digit attention test with distraction.

The following aspects of the problem are considered:

1. What is the effect of the stressors (stylus maze, mirror drawing, and attention test) upon distance judgment (Thereness-Thatness Table)?

A particular aspect of the above-mentioned question that is investigated is whether the stressors have a different effect on the setting of a familiar stimulus than on the setting of an unfamiliar stimulus.

2. What is the effect of the stressors upon the threshold between fusion and discrimination as measured with the Double-Flash Generator?

[*] This chapter was prepared by Ammon C. Roth, Jr., and represents a condensation of a doctoral dissertation entitled "Effects of Experimentally Induced Stress on Certain Measures of Perceptual Organization" and submitted to the Temple University Graduate School.

3. What is the effect of the stressors on both the extent of distortion and the time to reach maximum distortion produced by aniseikonic glasses as measured in the Leaf Room?

4. How do the stressors compare with each other in their effects upon the dependent variables?

5. What is the nature of the correlations between the Leaf Room performance and the fusion-discrimination threshold?

6. Are there any sex differences in the effect of stress on the dependent variables?

A survey of the present literature on stress and its perceptual effects would seem to indicate that, although there is general evidence for the statement that stress produces changes in the perceptual abilities of the individual, there is still a need for experimental work which will define the nature and conditions of such changes in terms of specific types of stress and specific perceptual tasks. It is for such a purpose that the present research has been undertaken.

METHOD

The Experimental Design

The design utilized in this experiment consisted of prestress and poststress exposures to one or two of the three perceptual tasks.

Although it might have been desirable, for purposes of analysis, to expose all subjects to the three dependent variables, this was not feasible for several reasons. First, the elapsed time per subject would have approximated two hours. In the pilot work preceding this study, it was found that this amount of time placed undesirable emphasis on fatigue effects and also brought about a loss of interest which made it difficult to motivate the subject to want to do his best on the final trials. Another problem which would have been accentuated by using all three dependent variables for each subject was the deterioration of the effects of stress during the time necessary to administer the three perceptual tasks in the final trials. Even though this deterioration could have been spread equally over the three dependent variables by an appropriate temporal alternation sequence, the very spreading of this effect would have weakened the net effect on each of the perceptual tasks.

For the reasons just given, it was decided to use two groups of equal number and to present the Thereness-Thatness Table task to one group and the Double-Flash and Leaf Room tasks to the other.

This particular pairing of the Double-Flash and Leaf Room was not a matter of chance. Rather, it was felt that the Thereness-Thatness Table should be the single task because the time required to complete it was not imposed by the instructions but by the individual approach taken by each subject. The Double-Flash was used with the Leaf Room to afford an opportunity to compare the results on these two different types of visual perception.

In the experimental sequence utilizing two perceptual tasks, the Double-Flash was presented first in both initial and final trials because of the existing information on the characteristics of CFF. That is, although the fusion-discrimination threshold has been shown to be sensitive to changes involving the CNS, these effects tend to undergo diminution soon after the condition bringing about the changes has been removed. Thus, in order to obtain the maximum effect of the experimentally induced stress on the fusion-discrimination threshold measured by the Double-Flash apparatus, this perceptual measure was performed before the Leaf Room in the sequence of the experimental conditions.

The subjects were divided into eight equal groups. For groups A, B, C, and D, the Table was used as the dependent variable and for groups E, F, G, and H, both the Double-Flash and the Leaf Room served as dependent variables. The experimental variable for groups A and E was the maze stressor; for groups B and F, the mirror-drawing stressor; for groups C and G, the digit-letter attention stressor; and groups D and H were controls. The subjects were assigned to the various groups with the aid of a table of random numbers. Each group contained ten males and ten females.

Subjects

The subjects in the present research were 160 college students of whom 80 were males and 80 were females.

In the selection of the subjects, it was decided to use those who had not progressed beyond the introductory course in psychology. The main reason for this decision lay in the hope of ruling out as much as possible significant sophistication in psychological experimentation.

The age range of the subjects was from 17 to 31 years. The mean age of the female subjects was 19.60 years and that of the male subjects was 21.80 years. The median age for females was 19.27 years and the median age for males was 21.08 years. The nature of this age differential was in keeping with the usual college situation in which a larger percentage of males exceed the average college age than do females.

Apparatus

Thereness-Thatness Table. This instrument is a modification of one of the Ames demonstrations.

There were two stimuli used in this study. A playing card (the five of spades), which was reduced to two-thirds the usual size, served as a "familiar" stimulus. A photograph of greatly magnified white, bubble-like plastic forms in a bluish-green background was cut to the same size as the "familiar" stimulus and served as an "unfamiliar" stimulus. It is called the ambiguous stimulus throughout the paper. Each stimulus was mounted on a rod which slipped into a base fastened to the stimulus cart.

Double-Flash Generator. The significant difference incorporated in this fusion instrument compared to the conventional CFF apparatus is that the flashes constituting the basis for a judgment of fusion or discrimination are presented in such a manner that there is not the usual cumulative retinal effect. Stimulus pairs were initiated automatically every 2½ seconds. The flash duration was in the order of 50 microseconds.

Leaf Room. The Leaf Room situation with aniseikonic lenses is described elsewhere in this volume (Chapter 2).

Stylus Maze Stressor. The instrumentation consists of a stylus maze pattern containing twelve cul-de-sacs cut into one aluminum plate which is bolted onto another aluminum plate. The risers which hold the plate apart are about ¼ inch high. A stylus is used which fits into the track and can be withdrawn from the maze only at the starting point and the goal because the diameter of the screw head forming the tip of the stylus is larger than is the width of the track.

The maze and the stylus are both connected to a Gorrell and Gorrell "Ene-volt" which is capable of emitting a continuously perceived shock of a wide range of intensities. This shock is initiated when the experimenter applies pressure to a toggle switch, the movement of which cannot be detected by the blindfolded subject.

Mirror-Drawing Stressor. A regular Stoelting mirror-drawing apparatus was used with a pattern devised by the writer to maximize difficulty in completing the tracing. The subject wears a pair of electrode pads strapped to his free hand and attached to the "Ene-volt" described above.

Digit-Letter Stressor. This task was modified from a Wittenborn attention test. The subject wears earphones (with tips inserted in the ears) attached to a tape recorder which plays back the instructions while the subject is filling in the test form. The recording was prepared at 7½ feet per second but is played during the experiment at 3¾ feet per second.

Procedure

Thereness-Thatness Table. Having adjusted the chair so that the individual was comfortable in the chin rest and aware of the knob which operated the stimulus cart, the experimenter informed the subject that he would be given a few minutes to adjust to the darkness. The laboratory was light-proofed and so, with the exception of the lighted poles and the stimulus cart, the room was in total darkness. The subject was then given the following instructions:

> Move the knob in either direction so that you get the feeling of how it moves. . . . By turning the knob I want you to set the card so that it is the same distance away from you as is the fourth pole away from you. You may move it in or out as much as you wish until you are satisfied that it is the same distance from you as is the fourth pole. When you are satisfied, tell me by saying "Now!"

For the first trial the stimulus was placed at the "far point," about 310 centimeters, and for the second trial, at the "near point," about 110 centimeters. This sequence was repeated three times and the first two trials were discarded in the analysis because they served as orientation trials.

Every subject was presented with the playing card for the full six trials, and then with the ambiguous stimulus for six more trials. Following the completion of these trials, the subject was given either one of the stressors or the control period, depending on the group to which he had been previously assigned. When the stressor or control period was ended the subject came back to the table with the comment from the experimenter: "Well, let's try this again." During these final trials the orientation trials were not given. Rather the sequence followed in the initial trials was repeated twice with the playing card again being used first.

No information as to quality of performance was given to any subject at the conclusion of the initial or final trials. Such information was requested by relatively few subjects but many volunteered self-evaluations which were generally uncomplimentary.

Double-Flash Generator. After the chair was adjusted so that the subject was comfortable with his chin on the rest the following instructions were given:

> You will see two flashes in close succession. Watch the flashes carefully and when you no longer see two flashes but see only one flash, say "Now!" (When the fusion point was reached the experimenter continued.) This time we will begin with one flash. Watch it carefully and when you see more than a single flash, say "Now!"

This sequence was performed three times. The first two trials were discarded in the analysis since they served as orientation trials. Care was exercised to vary the number of times each interval was presented in the six trials. It was felt that this would minimize the possibility that the subject might say "now" after allowing a certain uniform amount of time to elapse following the experimenter's instructions to watch the light in each of the trials.

Trials leading to fusion started with 86 milliseconds separating the flashes, while trials leading to discrimination started with a 10 millisecond interval. Time between pairs of flashes was 2½ seconds. It was found in the pilot work that this interval between pairs allowed the subject to ready himself for the next pair of flashes without engendering undesired restlessness.

At the conclusion of the six trials, the subject went immediately to the Leaf Room. When he had concluded the Leaf Room, he performed one of the stressors or the control situation and then came back to the Double-Flash. Before starting the final trials on the Double-Flash, the experimenter said, "Well, let's try this one again." In the final trials, the sequence of the initial trials was repeated twice since no orientation was deemed necessary.

Leaf Room. Each subject who was measured on the Leaf Room came to it after completing the Double-Flash Generator in both initial and final trials. The subject was seated and was told to move the dial until the rod appeared parallel to the ceiling line. This process was repeated four times. The average setting over these four trials was taken as the individual's horizontal reference point for ascertaining the ensuing degree of distortion. That is, in the trials with the aniseikonic lenses, the average obtained as just described was used as the starting position.

After the subject fastened the glasses in place, the experimenter gave the following instructions:

> After I ask you to open your eyes I want you, by turning the knob on that dial, to keep the rod parallel with the top edge of the far wall of

the room. That is, I want you at all times to keep the rod lined up with the line made by the ceiling and the wall of the room on which the rod is attached. You may move the knob as much as you wish, but keep that rod always lined up with the ceiling line until I tell you to stop. All right, put your hand on the dial and open your eyes.

As soon as the subject opened his eyes the experimenter started a stop watch and recorded the dial readings after 5, 10, 15, and 20 seconds, and at 10-second intervals thereafter until one minute had elapsed. This was used as the orientation trial. If the subject did not seem to understand what he was expected to do, the instructions were repeated and elaborated, in response to his questions, before the four initial trials began.

In the first of the initial trials, the dial readings were recorded as in the orientation trial, but the recording was continued for a full three minutes. The glasses were then reversed and the process repeated. This alternation proceeded until the four trials were completed. Between the trials, while the rod was being returned to the starting position and the glasses were being reversed, the subject closed his eyes. This was done so that the individual could not ascertain the degree of distortion which he had perceived for each trial by noting the displacement of the rod from the horizontal after the glasses had been removed.

When the subject returned to the Leaf Room for the final trials he was not given the orientation minute. The same order was used in the final trials as in the initial trials.

Before outlining the procedures involved in the stressors, it seems appropriate to mention the type of stress induction each of the methods was felt to provide. The *stylus maze* was used to produce a feeling of failure to master a learning situation with externally orientated reinforcement in the form of electric shock. The *mirror drawing* provided a basis for failure and accompanying frustration through inability to perform a seemingly simple task bolstered not only by a shock pattern but also by the comments of disappointment from the experimenter. The *digit-letter* test induced stress by setting up a difficult pattern of directions (but seemingly within the expected comprehensibility of college students) and then distracting the subject as he tried to carry out these instructions.

Stylus Maze Stressor. The stylus maze was covered as it lay before the subject. He was given the following instructions:

The next part of the experiment is a test of learning. You will learn the maze beneath the covering. In order to make it a little easier for you we will allow you to look at it for a few seconds before you put on the blindfold (The subject was given five seconds to look at the pattern and the beginning and end were pointed out). Now as you progress in the maze, if you should make too many errors or go too slowly, or a combination of these two, you will receive an electric shock through the stylus you are holding in your hand. Before we start I would like to measure your resistance (The voltage was regulated until the subject showed a consistent muscular withdrawal without complaining of pain). All right, you may begin.

In order to increase the stress potential of this task, the shocks were not administered in relation to success and failure in the maze. Rather, they were given on a predetermined schedule which was independent of the individual's performance. During the first minute, three shocks were presented; during the second minute, one; during the third minute, five; during the fourth minute, four; and during the fifth minute, six. At the end of five minutes the subject was asked to stop and was told: "You seem to be having some difficulty, so we will give you another chance to look at the maze." Following a five-second visual impression of the maze another five-minute period was begun in which the same shock pattern used in the first five minutes was employed. Whenever the goal was reached, the subject's hand was placed, with the stylus, back into the starting box with the simple statement: "Try it again."

At the conclusion of the second five-minute session, the announcement, "We will come back and try this again," was made. The subject was then seated for the final trials on the perceptual task or tasks.

Mirror-Drawing Stressor. The subject, after being seated before the apparatus, was given the following instructions:

This is a test of skill and co-ordination. Your task will be to trace with a pencil a line right through the middle of the space formed by the two printed lines. You start here at the arrow and go to the goal. There are two things that are important in this task: one is speed; the other is accuracy. Do not sacrifice the one for the other. . . . Are you right- or left-handed? (Whichever hand was mentioned the subject was asked to extend the other.) The purpose of the electrodes (this was said as the experimenter attached the pads) is this—as we go along in this test, if you are making too many errors or going too slowly, or a combination of these two, you will receive a shock through this apparatus. Before we start I want to get a measure of your resistance. (The voltage was regulated until muscular reactions were seen to be involuntary without producing a complaint of pain.) Line up your pencil with the arrow. Begin!

The 4 by 4-inch electrodes containing cotton pads soaked in water were strapped to the individual's free hand with a great show of care and precision and no attempt was made to hide the "Ene-volt" which was to supply the shock. To heighten the stress potential of this task even more, the subject was given an automatic pencil in which the lead tended to retract even with normal pressure. As the pencil pressure increased with increased concentration on the part of the subject, the number of times the pencil had to be removed from the paper to adjust the lead also increased.

As with the stylus maze stressor, the shock pattern used in the mirror drawing was independent of the subject's performances. During the first minute, no shocks were administered; during the second minute, four were given; and during the third minute, six. If the subject had not finished the first pattern by this time, he was given a second pattern and asked to start at the beginning. The experimenter made the comment: "Well, that certainly wasn't a good performance, let's try another one." During the second three-minute period the shocks were administered in a two, one, two sequence. After a similar derogatory comment was made, a third pattern was presented. In the final four-minute period, the shocks were given in a three, five, four, six sequence.

Since even a subject who finished the pattern before a designated time period had elapsed was not able to draw a straight line, the comments indicating disappointment were not entirely unrealistic. At no time was praise given to any subject during this ten-minute stress period. When the stressor was completed the subject was told: "Well, we'll have to go back to this again." He was then seated to perform the final trials on the perceptual measure or measures.

Digit-Letter Stressor. The subject was seated at a table and the following instructions were given:

The next part of the experiment will be a test on how well you can follow instructions and how well you can work with a distraction. Listen carefully to the instructions that I am going to read. I will read them only once and then you will begin the task. If you don't understand the instructions or want to clear up any point you may refer to the instruction booklet there in front of you as often as you wish after the test begins. However, each time you refer to the directions, you will press the bar on this counter so that we have a record of how many times you had to refer to the instructions. Listen carefully, I will read them only once.

By mixing digits and letters, six-item series have been prepared. A series may contain an equal number of digits and letters; it may contain more letters than digits, or it may contain more digits than letters. The digits may be any of the numbers from one to nine. The letters will be taken from the group A, B, C, D, and E. There is an answer line for each series. In each answer line there is a space reserved for each item of the series. The directions as to how and when you are to mark the answer spaces will now be given. (The answer sheet was shown to the individual for a few seconds at this time, but it was put away while the following paragraphs were read verbatim.)

If a digit is larger than the one preceding it in the series, mark the answer space for this digit plus. If a digit is smaller than the one preceding it in the series, mark the answer space minus.

If a letter is one occurring later in the alphabet than the letter just preceding it in the series, mark the answer space for this letter plus. If a letter occurs earlier in the alphabet than the letter just preceding it in the series, mark the answer space minus.

If the first item in the series is a letter followed by a digit, mark the answer space for that digit plus. If the first item in the series is a digit followed by a letter, mark the answer space for that letter minus. You will never mark the first answer space since the item occupying that position will never be preceded in the series.

Work as rapidly as possible, since your score will be determined by how many series you have finished and how many series you have correct in the time limit.

You have exactly ten minutes. Plug in your earphones and begin.

Again in this stressor, as in the mirror drawing, the pencil with the easily retracting lead was utilized to penalize concentration which translated itself into pencil pressure. As the subject worked through the ten-minute period, he heard the same instructions just quoted being repeated over and over—but at half speed. If he showed signs of finishing the fifty series before the ten minutes had elapsed, another sheet was placed in clear view. In this way no subject was able to nurture the feeling that he had completed what was expected of him.

At the completion of the stressor period, the experimenter made the comment: "We will come back to this again." The subject was then seated for the final trials in the perceptual variable or variables.

After the final trials on the perceptual measure or measures, each subject returned to the stressor to which he previously had been exposed. He was allowed to work at it for approximately two minutes without shock or distraction and was complimented on his improvement. If the latter was not evident, he was given additional time and the difficulty of the task was emphasized rather than the individual's ineptness.

Control Period. Members of the control groups were seated in comfortable chairs, after the initial perceptual measure had been completed, and told to relax for ten minutes. It was felt that almost any activity which could have been assigned to these groups would have had a potential stress-producing effect for some. Therefore, it was decided that allowing the subjects to sit quietly while the experimenter moved to another part of the laboratory (though still in view of the subject) was the least questionable activity to interject at this point in the experiment.

The experimenter attempted to make it possible for every subject to leave the experiment without feeling frustrated or upset by a lack of knowledge of the purpose of the experiment or by his individual performance. The possibility for the experimenter to achieve the proper departure attitude in the subjects was greatly enhanced by the presence in the laboratory of other Ames demonstrations. The distorted rooms and rotating trapezoid attracted the attention of most as the laboratory was entered and these subjects were generally quite interested in having these pieces of apparatus explained before they left. All subjects were requested, with emphasis, not to discuss the experiment with anyone excepting those who had already served as subjects.

RESULTS

The analysis of data involved a total of eight pairs of measures based on the three dependent variables. The Thereness-Thatness Table yielded the following measures for each subject: (a) the average of the four settings in centimeters of the playing card stimulus for both initial and final trials; (b) the average of the four settings in centimeters of the ambiguous stimulus for both initial and final trials; (c) a variability index, which was obtained by dividing the mean deviation of the four settings by the average setting and multiplying the quotient by 1000, for the playing card for both initial and final trials; (d) a variability index for the ambiguous stimulus for both initial and final trials. These measures permitted an investigation of the effects of experimentally-induced stress on both the magnitude of distance judgments based on the size cue and the consistency of these judgments.

Only one pair of measures was considered necessary on the Double-Flash Generator. This consisted of the average of the two millisecond intervals between flashes at the point of the fusion judgment and the two millisecond intervals at the point of the discrimination judgment of flashes—for both initial and final trials. The conversion of dial readings to millisecond equivalents was done with a calibration graph.

Because of the factors involved in the task, three pairs of measures were taken from the Leaf Room data. Thus, it was possible to investigate the effects of stress on the time necessary to resolve a perceptual conflict, on the extent of resolution, and on a combined time and extent measure. The data obtained for these purposes were as follows: (a) the combined time and extent measures consisting of the average deflections based on the deflections recorded at each of the 20 times readings (see Procedure); (b) the time measures consisting of the time in seconds necessary to reach 80% of the maximum average of deflection; and (c) the extent measures consisting of the averages of the three greatest deflections obtained over the 20 time readings.

Bartlett's Test of homogeneity of variance, performed on the eight measures, offered no evidence to refute the assumption that the stressor groups were drawn from a common population as far as the variance was concerned. The same statement pertains to the assumption that the sexes were drawn from a common population with regard to variance, with the exception of the "average of the three greatest deflections on the Leaf Room" measure, where a χ^2 with a P = .03 was obtained.

With the exception of the "average centimeter settings for ambiguous stimulus on Thereness-Thatness measure," where the null hypothesis for the stressor groups was refuted at the .04 level, the analyses of variance of initial scores on all measures explored in the study failed to support a rejection of the assumption that the stressor groups and the sex groups were drawn from a common population insofar as mean performance on these measures was concerned. The analysis of variance indicated no significant interaction effect of stressor groups and sexes in any of the initial scores on the eight measures.

The covariance technique revealed statistically significant differences between the mirror-drawing stressor and control group and between the digit-letter stressor group and control group on the average setting for the playing card on the Thereness-Thatness Table measure for the adjusted final means (Tables 1 and 2). In both instances, the average settings of the control group are larger (significant beyond the .01 level) than the average settings of the stressor groups.

TABLE 1

Summary of Means and Beta Weight for Average Settings on
Thereness-Thatness for Playing Card

Group	$\overline{\overline{Y}}$ (final)	$b_{y \cdot x}$	$\overline{X}$ (initial)	Gen'l $\overline{\overline{X}}$	Group $\overline{X}$ − Gen'l $\overline{X}$	Adjusted $\overline{Y}$
			For the Stressor Groups			
A	168.6		159.2		1.8	166.7
B	145.8	1.0298	147.4	157.4	−10.0	156.1
C	150.7		152.6		−4.8	155.6
D	188.9		170.3		12.9	175.6
			For Sexes			
Male	160.3	1.0298	156.5	157.4	−.9	161.2
Female	166.7		158.2		.8	165.9

TABLE 2

Comparisons of Adjusted Final Means among the Four Groups for
Average Settings on Thereness-Thatness for Playing Card

Groups	B (156.1)	C (155.6)	D (175.6) control
A (166.7) Maze	10.6	11.1	8.9
B (156.1) Mirror-drawing		.5	19.5 *
C (155.6) Digit-letter			20.0 *

Numbers appearing in parentheses are adjusted final means. Numbers in body of table are differences between adjusted final means.

* .01 > P > .001.

Analyses of covariance on the fusion-discrimination threshold data showed that, following stress, each of the three stressor groups had thresholds higher than the control group and that these differences were statistically significant beyond the .001 level of confidence. (Tables 3 and 4.) On the same data, a significant sex difference (P = .02) was obtained indicating a greater interval between flashes at the fusion-discrimination threshold for females than for males.

TABLE 3

Summary of Means and Beta Weight for Fusion-Discrimination
Threshold on Double-Flash Generator

Group	$\overline{Y}$ (final)	$b_{y \cdot x}$	$\overline{X}$ (initial)	Gen'l $\overline{X}$	Group $\overline{X}$ − Gen'l $\overline{X}$	Adjusted $\overline{Y}$
			For the Stressor Groups			
E	61.03		53.05		−.66	61.62
F	60.91	.8896	55.07	53.71	1.36	59.70
G	59.51		53.58		−.13	59.63
H	53.29		53.13		−.58	53.81
			For Sexes			
Males	57.19	.8896	53.25	53.71	−.46	57.60
Females	60.18		54.16		.45	59.75

Sex Difference = 2.15. P = .02.

TABLE 4

Comparisons of Adjusted Final Means among the Four Groups for
Fusion-Discrimination Threshold on Double-Flash Generator

Groups	F (59.70)	G (59.63)	H (53.81) Control
E (61.62) Maze	1.92	1.99	7.81 *
F (59.70) Mirror-drawing		.07	5.89 *
G (59.63) Digit-letter			5.82 *

Numbers appearing in parentheses are adjusted final means. Numbers in body of table are differences between adjusted final means.
  * P <.001.

No significant differences between stressors or differences between sexes or interaction were found by the covariance technique on the average centimeter settings of the ambiguous stimulus on the Thereness-Thatness or for the variability indices on the Thereness-Thatness.

No significant differences between sexes or interaction were found for any of the three measures for the aniseikonic glasses. Table 5, however, indicates a trend which did not reach statistical significance in this study, but is consistent with the findings of other studies reported in this volume. For all three stressor groups, the distortion time is longer under stress, while the time for the control group decreases on the final trials.

TABLE 5

Summary of Means and Beta Weight for Time in Seconds to Reach 80% of Maximum Deflection in the Leaf Room

Group	$\overline{Y}$ (final)	$b_{y \cdot x}$	$\overline{X}$ (initial)	Gen'l $\overline{X}$	Group $\overline{X}$ − Gen'l $\overline{X}$	Adjusted $\overline{Y}$
			For the Stressor Groups			
E	31.3		25.2		−3.0	32.9
F	31.9	.5653	30.8	28.2	2.6	30.4
G	28.8		26.3		−1.9	29.9
H	23.5		30.5		2.3	22.2
			For Sexes			
Males	30.9	.5653	28.4	28.2	.2	30.8
Females	26.7		28.0		−.2	26.8

Product-moment correlations were computed between the fusion-discrimination thresholds on the Double-Flash Generator and each of the three measures on the Leaf Room. Statistically reliable but low correlations were obtained for the male subjects and for the combined subjects between the thresholds and the "average of the three greatest deflections" on the Leaf Room. A small reliable correlation was also obtained for the combined subjects between the thresholds and the "average deflections for the 20 time readings" on the Leaf Room.

Large reliable correlations were obtained for males, females, and combined sexes between initial average settings of the playing card and initial average settings of the ambiguous stimulus on the "thereness-thatness" apparatus.

DISCUSSION

The discussion of the results of the present investigation will be directed to the several questions raised earlier.

Problem One

It should be noted that the fourth pole (which was the reference pole used on the Thereness-Thatness Table) was 285 centimeters from the position of the subject. Since the playing card used was two-thirds the size of a normal playing card, one might assume that the expected setting would have been 190 centimeters. If we accept this expected setting as a reference point, then on the initial trials all groups set the playing card closer than the proportionate distance. In the final trials, the control group showed the greatest improvement (moved out toward the 190 centimeters mark), the maze group showed some improvement, and the mirror and digit-letter groups showed no improvement.

Even though the ambiguous stimulus was the same size as the playing card, all groups set it closer to themselves than they had the card on the initial trials. On the final trials all groups showed very slight improvement in the settings.

A possible explanation of these phenomena is found by referring to the work of Hastings (1952). Thus, we might speculate that all subjects felt somewhat insecure during the initial trials on the Table because of the uniqueness of the task and the fact that they were in almost complete darkness while making their judgments. The subjective reports gathered from the subjects at the conclusion of the experiment would certainly support such a statement. If, then, we make this assumption, Hastings' work indicates that insecure persons set stimuli closer to themselves than would normally be expected—thus the results on the initial trials. Following this speculation one step further, we would say that stress should accentuate insecurity. On the other hand, in the final trials when the subjects should be more acclimated to the task, we would expect the settings to be closer to the 190 centimeters mark than they were in the initial trials. This phenomenon did occur with the nonstressed control group for the playing card. Since stress would counteract the acclimation effect in the final trials, we would expect considerably less improvement with the stressor groups.

The same rationale can be applied to the ambiguous stimulus with the exception that the acclimation effect is not as likely to occur, since the subject has no familiarity through experience with this stimulus. In view of the fact that the subject has no size concept for the ambiguous stimulus, he probably is no less anxious about his settings in the final trials than he was in the initial trials. Again, the subjective reports of the subjects would support such a statement.

The correlations of .876 between initial settings of the playing card and the ambiguous stimulus indicates that the perceptual process involved is markedly similar for the two stimuli.

Problem Two

The most striking differences in the experiment were obtained between the experimental and control groups for the fusion-discrimination threshold. Since the thresholds in the experimental groups increased from initial to final trials, while the threshold in the control group remained the same, it may be stated that stress definitely interferes with the CNS mechanism involved in the perception of fusion and discrimination of intense visual flashes.

Problem Three

The results on the Leaf Room were both disappointing and enlightening. The stressors employed appeared to have no differentiating effects on the resolution of the perceptual conflict involved. This might have resulted for several reasons. First, the Leaf Room always was administered after the Double-Flash Generator. Therefore, the effects of the induced stress probably were diminished through temporal fading. Secondly, the Leaf Room necessitated a perceptual resolution in which personality factors undoubtedly play a major role. That is, the experimenter noted that a greater number of distinctly different approaches were utilized in handling this variable than in either of the other two.

A definite practice effect was obtained on the Leaf Room in the "average of the three greatest deflections" measure. The subjects reliably perceived the Room as more "normal" in the final trials than in the initial trials. This fact would suggest that noticeable CNS adjustments were made as a result of only two exposures to this novel situation. More research seems necessary using a series of trials and a more inclusive set of instructions.

Problem Four

On the Thereness-Thatness Table, for average settings of the playing card, the results indicate that the maze group average is not significantly different than the control group average. However, both the mirror group and the digit-letter group averages are significantly different (beyond the .01 level) from the control group average. In view of the proposed explanation offered for the Table results, the mirror and digit-letter stressors would appear to have been more effective than the maze stressor.

On the Double-Flash Generator, all these stressor groups yielded significantly different fusion-discrimination thresholds from the control group, but were not significantly different from each other. It would, therefore, appear that all three stressors were equally effective in this situation.

Problem Five

Though some of the correlations between the Leaf Room and the Double-Flash measures are significant, all are uniformly low. This would add support to the opinion that these two perceptual tasks involve different basic mechanisms. The fusion-discrimination threshold is probably not so dependent upon past experience and personality factors as is the resolution of the Leaf Room conflict. This would indicate that the fusion-discrimination threshold could be thought of as being more dependent upon the immediate condition of the subject as well as upon the nature of the physical stimulation (intensity of flash, duration of flash, area of retina stimulated, etc.), while the Leaf Room measures could involve a more complex perceptual organization dependent upon a larger amount of the experiential background of the subject. If this speculation is supported, then the fact that the same subject was not equally effective in handling these two perceptual tasks would be quite understandable and even expected.

Problem Six

A reliable sex difference was obtained in the fusion-discrimination threshold data. In this instance, the results indicated that the females were more adversely influenced in their perceptual efficiency than were the males. These findings, though provocative, seem hardly a sufficient basis for a generalized assumption of inferiority of the female in terms of resisting effects of stress in life adjustments.

SUMMARY AND CONCLUSIONS

This investigation sought to study the effects of experimentally induced stress on three measures of visual perception. The following served as dependent variables:

a) Thereness-Thatness Table. This task involved distance judgments using size as the primary cue. The subjects attempted to set two stimuli, in turn, equal to a target pole. The first stimulus was a playing card two-thirds the regular size; the second stimulus, called the "ambiguous," was a photographic magnification of plastic molecules.

b) Double-Flash Generator. This fusion-discrimination task required the subject to report whether he perceived one or two flashes from a pair of flashes produced electronically every 2½ seconds.

c) Leaf Room. This task involved a perceptual conflict in which the subject revealed the nature of the distortion produced in a cubical leaf-lined room by keeping a rod in the room always parallel to the perceived ceiling line. The subject viewed the room through aniseikonic glasses which produced a different retinal image in each eye.

Three different methods of stress-induction were utilized: a complex aluminum stylus maze with provision for electric shock which was administered on a predetermined schedule without regard to performance, although the subject thought it was related to errors he was making; a mirror-drawing task involving a difficult pattern which the subject traced while electric shocks, undetermined by his performance, were being administered; and a difficult attention task (digit-letter test) that was made more stressful through a distraction provided by playing back the instructions for the test at half speed through earphones. On all the stressors, exaggeration of movements, grimacing, and flushing helped to support the verbal reports as to the upsetting effects for most subjects.

The subjects were 80 male and 80 female college students who were volunteers gathered from the introductory psychology classes at Upsala College. The subjects were randomly divided into eight groups, each consisting of ten males and ten females. The Thereness-Thatness Table served as the dependent variable for four of the groups, while the Double-Flash Generator and the Leaf Room served as the dependent variables for the other four groups. A control group, whose members rested instead of performing a stress-inducing task, was utilized for each of the two dependent variable conditions. Each of the remaining six groups was exposed to one of the stressors. A sequence of two measurements were taken; an initial trial, and, after the application of the stress, a final trial. The results of these two trials were compared for stress effects.

Four measures on the Thereness-Thatness Table were analyzed: average settings in centimeters for both the playing card and the ambiguous stimulus, and variability indices for both stimuli. The fusion-discrimination threshold in milliseconds was the only measure used on the Double-Flash Generator. The Leaf Room yielded three measures: time in seconds to reach 80% of maximum distortion; the average of the three greatest distortions found in 20 time-recordings over a three-minute period; and the average of the 20 recordings of distortion (deflections on selsyn-dial controlling rod in Leaf Room).

The mirror-drawing and digit-letter stress groups showed a statistically significant lack of improvement in the final trials compared to the control group on the "average centimeter settings" measure for the playing card on the Thereness-Thatness Table. The stylus maze group showed improvement in the direction of the control group, but this difference was not significant when compared with the results of either the other two stress groups or the control group. No differences were obtained between the stress groups and the control groups with regard to the ambiguous stimulus for the "average centimeter setting" measure. The variability indices also failed to reveal significant changes.

All three groups showed a significant increase in the millisecond interval involved in the fusion-discrimination threshold on the Double-Flash Generator, while the control group showed no increase. The three stressors were approximately equal in effectiveness. A significant sex difference was noted in the direction of greater stress effects upon females than males for this variable.

No significant differences were found in any of the three Leaf Room measures, thus indicating that the stress utilized in the study was not sufficient to disrupt the complex perceptual resolution involved in this variable. All groups, including the control group, showed a significant practice effect on the "average of the three greatest distortions" measure in the Leaf Room.

Correlates of Perceptual Change:
D. Perceptual Consistency

· 10 ·

Perceptual Generalization
of an Avoidance Response*

Perceptual studies which emphasize the effects of motivational or need determinants on perception have, in the past ten years, generated a good deal of research, discussion, and controversy. However, since the initial impetus was given to research on this problem there have been significant changes in research approach and in emphasis. There is now a sufficiently large body of experimental data indicating that needs and motivation can influence perception. Hence, although there is still some controversy surrounding the relevancy and importance of this data, experimenters are no longer concerned with merely demonstrating the presence of this relationship. There has also been a growing attempt to incorporate these findings within the framework of a more inclusive personality theory instead of dealing with them as discrete behaviors. Perceptual vigilance and perceptual defense, for example, have now been defined within the context of both psychoanalytic theory and behavior theory. Finally, it has been increasingly evident that there is a need to define the controls and limitations within which it is possible to demonstrate the relationships between need and motivational variables and changes in perception. The pioneer studies in this field were taken to task for failing to control such factors as set and familiarity. Later, when these perceptual behaviors were analyzed from a learning theory approach, it became apparent that one could

* This chapter was prepared by Allen Raskin.

not assume, on an a priori basis, that everyone would demonstrate the same perceptual response to an affectively-toned stimulus.

The present research reflects this change in approach and grew out of a behavior theory analysis. The study was designed as a test of the hypothesis that once an instrumental act of approach or avoidance toward an unpleasant stimulus has been learned a subject will show consistency in the use of these learned responses on a variety of perceptual tasks.

A brief description of this theoretical position will high light controls necessary to test this hypothesis. If, in a previously neutral situation, we arouse pain, the autonomic and central portions of the response to pain become conditioned to the various perceptual cues in this situation. Those autonomic and central portions of the pain response which become conditioned to the previously neutral cues are commonly called "fear" or "anxiety." This "fear" becomes the basis for a learnable drive and a "threatening" or "emotional" stimulus is one which elicits the fear. The very association of a neutral cue with a fear reaction probably means that an individual is sensitized to that cue. Yet the fact that recognition of the cue-object brings pain could also lead to the avoidance of response.

However, once the approach or avoidance response is well established, the subject would be expected to show consistent evidence of this learning on a variety of perceptual tasks. An experimental demonstration of this consistency of perceptual response to an anxiety-arousing stimulus in a variety of perceptual tasks would help clarify and extend our thinking about the permanence of this type of response and the situations in which we can reasonably expect this response to manifest itself.

METHOD

Subjects

Thirty-two male employees at the Veterans Administration Hospital in East Orange comprised the experimental group. The only requirement for inclusion in the study was that they have 20/20 vision in both eyes with or without the use of corrective lenses.

Stimuli

The stimuli consisted of two simple Chinese characters. These were equated for size and discriminability.

Procedure

Each subject was seen for two sessions. In the first session the subject was run through the four perceptual tasks. The following is a brief description of these tasks in the order in which they were administered:

1. *Figure-drawing.* The subject was asked to draw the stimulus on a blank sheet of paper, from memory, after viewing the Chinese character for five seconds. Drawings were made of both Chinese characters.

2. *Distance Perception Test.* The subject was required to turn a dial which in turn moved the stimulus card, and was instructed to line this card up with a pole set 594 centimeters away from the subject. The pole was viewed binocularly whereas the stimulus was viewed monocularly. The subject was required to make two settings for each stimulus. At the first setting the experimenter placed the card 260 centimeters away from the subject and at the second setting the card was placed 600 centimeters away from the subject. A practice trial using a standard playing card as the stimulus preceded the trials with the Chinese characters in order to give the subject an opportunity to adapt to the darkness and to get some experience with the apparatus.

3. *Tactile Discrimination.* Using tactile cues the subject was required to make size estimations of the stimuli. The tactile cues consisted of sandpaper cutouts for each of the two stimuli. The ten cards containing the five different-sized cutouts for each stimulus were presented to the subject in random order. The subject had before him drawings of the five different-sized cutouts for each stimulus and each size was given an alphabetical designation. After feeling the sandpaper cutout with both hands through a curtain, the subject responded with the letter corresponding to the size on the card in front of him judged equal in size to the sandpaper cutout.

4. *Hidden Character Test.* The subject was required to find the simple Chinese character embedded in a series of complex Chinese characters. The subject was given one minute to encircle those complex characters on the sheet that contained the simple character. Two trials were run, one for each stimulus, and these were preceded by a practice trial using a different Chinese character.

Following the administration of the four perceptual tasks the subject was shown one of the simple Chinese characters and asked to tell the experimenter what the character "looked like" or "reminded him of." He was then asked if the character evoked pleasant, unpleasant, or neutral feelings. The subject's associations and expression of feeling toward the character were recorded for both Chinese characters.

At the beginning of the second session the subject was told that he would be subjected to some electric shock. Two electrodes were secured to the inner portion of his left wrist and he was seated in front of the shock apparatus. The subject was told to move a dial that controlled the amount of voltage until the pain became intolerable. The experimenter stood by the on-off switch and cut off the current when the subject indicated that he could not tolerate any more shock. This dial setting was recorded. The subject was then seated in front of the distance perception apparatus which was adopted for use in the conditioning or sensitizing series. The shock electrodes were again secured to his left wrist and the dial on the shock apparatus was set five points higher than his tolerance level. In cases where subjects had set very low tolerance levels the dial was set at a minimum reading of 20, which had been judged painful in pretesting with the apparatus. The subject was told to look straight ahead and that he would see the two stimuli presented independently. He was also told that immediately following the presentation of one of the Chinese characters he would sometimes, but not always, receive an electric shock, whereas he would never get an electric shock when the other Chinese character was shown. The experimenter than flashed each character singly, in random order, for 2 seconds. There were 40 presentations and the shock was administered 30 seconds after the presentation of the emotional character 13 of the 20 times that this character was shown. Hence both shock and emotional character were presented simultaneously for 1 minute and 30 seconds. It was decided to use intermittent rather than continuous conditioning to slow down the tendency for the effects of the conditioning to dissipate.

Following the conditioning or sensitization series subjects were again run through the four perceptual tasks. However, as the subject was already dark-adapted, it was decided to run the Distance Perception task first, followed by the Figure-Drawing, Tactile Discrimination, and Hidden Character Test in that order. The subject's associations and expressions of feeling tone toward the two stimuli were again requested and recorded.

The purpose of running a base line series on the four perceptual tasks prior to conditioning, followed by the test series after conditioning, was to have each subject act as his own control. Hence, any differences in his responses to the stimuli following training would be related to the conditioning series that intervened between the base line and test series. The results are based on comparisons of the differences between the subject's responses to the emotional character on the perceptual tasks prior to a following shock, with the differences between his responses to the neutral character prior to a following shock. It is reasonable then to assume that practice effects, if any, would be constant for both figures and would be cancelled out in our computations. Also controlled were any differential effects due to the physical and preferential value of either character by randomly making one character emotional for half our subjects and the other emotional for the other half. Thus it was possible to evaluate statistically what effects, if any, were due to the figures themselves irrespective of our conditioning process.

The measure of the subject's tolerance for the electric shock served two purposes. First, this measure was used as a means of administering a subjectively painful shock during the conditioning or sensitizing process. Secondly, this measure provided an estimate of the extent to which shock was viewed as traumatic by the subject.

The subject's associations and expressions of feeling tone toward the two Chinese characters, both prior to and following the conditioning series, were used to get some independent estimate of the effectiveness of the conditioning experience. It was assumed that because of the association of shock with one of the Chinese characters this character would become more unpleasant and this would be reflected in a change in associations and in feeling tone to this stimulus. There should not be a comparable change in associations and feeling tone toward the neutral character.

On the basis of the theoretical analysis and experimental design the following predictions were made:

1. Subjects who acquire a learned instrumental response of avoidance toward the shocked stimulus should draw this character smaller following shock on the figure-drawing task. Similarly these subjects should place this figure further away on the distance perception task, find fewer of these figures in the hidden character test, and estimate its size as smaller on the tactile discrimination task, following shock, as compared to the neutral character.

2. Subjects who learn to *approach* the shocked stimulus following shock should draw this character larger, on the figure-drawing task, in comparison with the neutral figure. Similarly, following

shock these subjects should place this figure closer on the distance perception task, find more of these characters on the hidden characters test, and estimate its size as larger on the tactile discrimination task, as compared to the neutral character.

3. The magnitude of the avoidance or approach responses on the four perceptual tasks will be greater in those subjects who show low tolerance for the electric shock as compared with those subjects who can tolerate more of the electric shock. This prediction is based on the assumption that subjects with low tolerance for the electric shock will show more anxiety and fear. Hence, in learning an avoidance or approach response, there will be greater drive reduction in this group as compared with the group with high shock tolerance.

RESULTS

The magnitude and direction (i.e., approach or avoidance) of a subject's responses on the four perceptual tasks were ranked and and the rankings for all four tasks resulted in a coefficient of concordance of 0.27. This is significant at the .05% level of confidence and indicates some tendency for consistency in perceptual response on a variety of perceptual tasks. However, there is sufficient intra-individual variability to make infeasible an accurate prediction of a subject's tendency to use an avoidance or approach response on one of the four perceptual tasks based on his use of one of these responses on another perceptual task.

There appeared to be a significantly greater tendency for all subjects to use an avoidance response on the four perceptual tasks. A chi square of 3.5 (corrected for continuity), based on the total number of avoidance responses compared with the total number of approach responses, was obtained which is significant at the .07% level. Also of interest is the chi square of 7.1 based on the total number of avoidance as compared with approach responses on the distance perception and figure-drawing tasks. This is significant at the .01% level, indicating a very strong tendency for subjects to use an avoidance response on these two measures.

A check was made to see whether this preponderance of avoidance responses was in any way related to figure differences irrespective of the conditioning process. There was no significant difference in the number of avoidance or approach responses for the two characters.

The subjects were ranked in terms of their tolerance for shock and divided into two groups of 16 each, one a high shock tolerance group and the other a low shock tolerance group. An extremely high tendency was noted for subjects in the low shock group to use an avoidance response on the distance perception task. Fourteen of the 16 subjects in this group used the avoidance response, and this figure yielded a chi square of 9.06, which is significant at better than the .01% level of confidence. Similarly, the total number of avoidance responses compared with approach responses in this low shock group resulted in a chi square of 4.14, which is significant at the .01% level of confidence. On the other hand, there was no significant difference in the use of avoidance or approach responses in the high shock group.

Two independent judges rated the subjects' associations and expressions of feeling tone to the two Chinese characters in terms of positive or negative references. Although there was fairly good agreement between the two judges on these ratings, there was not, as predicted, a significant increase in negative associations or feeling tone toward the emotional character after shock. The two judges rated 13 subjects and 15 subjects, respectively, as having changed associations in this direction. One judge rated 14 subjects as showing no change, while the other judge rated 15 subjects as showing no change. There also appeared to be a few individuals who showed more negative associations and feeling tone toward the neutral character following shock and no comparable change toward the emotional character. One judge placed four subjects in this group and the other placed three subjects in this group.

However, it is of interest to note that in the 12 cases where both judges agreed that the subjects either had shown no change in their associations and feeling tone following shock, or had shown more negative associations and negative feeling tone toward the neutral character following shock, there was a total of 31 avoidance responses on the four perceptual tasks as compared to 13 approach responses. This difference resulted in a chi square of 7.29, which is significant at better than the .01% level of confidence.

DISCUSSION

The results point out that although there is some tendency toward intraindividual consistency in the use of an avoidance or approach response on the four perceptual tasks, the intraindividual variability is too great to warrant using a subject's responses on one of these tests as a means for predicting his response to any of the three other perceptual tasks. A closer look at the results reveals that this variability may be due, in part, to a dissipation of the learned approach or avoidance response during the later stages of testing. This is suggested by the fact that on the two tasks immediately following the conditioning or sensitization process, i.e., the distance perception and figure-drawing tasks, there are significantly more avoidance responses than on the two later tasks, i.e., the tactile discrimination and hidden character tests. This hypothesis is also borne out by the striking number of avoidance responses which the low pain group shows on the distance perception task. The prediction was made that the low pain group would show a stronger learned response and the results seem to support this hypothesis. The fact that this response is so marked on the distance perception test and is also prominent to a lesser degree on the figure-drawing task, while dissipating markedly on the two remaining perceptual tasks, may be related to a lack of reinforcement of the learned response and a subsequent tendency for this response to be unlearned in the later stages of testing. This seems to be a more tenable hypothesis than the assumption that the nature of the perceptual tasks themselves may be responsible for the great number of avoidance responses on the distance perception and figure-drawing tasks. The latter hypothesis would not account for the differences in the use of avoidance responses on these tasks between the high and low pain groups.

The large total number of avoidance responses on all four perceptual tasks seems striking and is at variance with the expectation that normal subjects would probably show a greater number of approach responses since, presumably, they generally deal with anxiety and fear in a direct manner and use a minimum of repressive or suppressive techniques. However, when we examine the conditioning or sensitizing process we see that the subject finds that he can make no overt responses that will lessen the shock. He is forced to sit and attend to the stimuli. In this situation avoidance responses toward the shocked figure may, in reality, represent the most adaptive response he can make. A response that keeps the shocked figure further away and minimizes its size may be more adaptive than attempts to magnify the size of the stimulus associated with his pain. Thus, it is possible that the sensitization or conditioning procedure in the experimental design rather than previously learned perceptual responses was the important variable responsible for the large number of avoidance responses.

As reported, the results did not support the hypothesis that there is a significant increase in negative associations and feeling tone toward the emotional character following shock. This could mean that the conditioning or sensitization process failed to establish a conditional anxiety response in many of the subjects toward the stimulus associated with the electric shock. In the early stages of the experiment, the use of a physiological measure was attempted, i.e., blood pressure and GSR, as independent estimates of this relationship. However, this effort was abandoned because of deficiencies in the equipment. There are, on the other hand, a number of factors that suggest that subjects did associate the shocked stimulus as more unpleasant and that these associations may have some meaning that was not originally anticipated. There was universal agreement among the subjects that the shock was painful, although some were more disturbed by this shock than others. Further, the fact that approximately half the subjects did show a shift in associations to the emotional character in the predicted directions does suggest that within this group, at least, the shocked stimulus was now regarded as unpleasant. The problem remains of interpreting the fact that half the subjects either failed to show an increase in negative associations to both characters or showed a reversal phenomenon, i.e., more negative associations toward the neutral character. In discussing the results, it was indicated that in the 12 cases where both judges agreed that subjects manifested the above-mentioned behavior there were 31 avoidance and only 13 approach responses on the perceptual tasks. This difference is significant at beyond the .01% level of confidence. Hence, this group of 12 is apparently made up of individuals who are predominantly using avoidance to cope with perceptual tasks. Avoidance is, essentially, a suppressive or repressive reaction that could also manifest itself in the quality of verbal associations to the stimuli. In other words, the failure of this group to give negative associations to the emotional character after shock may be another manifestation of their attempt to deny and avoid the pain associated with this character. This is a purely speculative interpretation but it does fit with most conceptions of the individual who does use avoidance or repressive mechanisms to reduce anxiety.

The results of this study suggest the need for further research in evaluating the relationship between variables such as drive strength and variations in the settings in which a conditioned anxiety response is imposed on the subject with the magnitude and kind of perceptual response that a subject will learn. If accurate predictions are to be made about the appearance of this type of learning in a variety of perceptual tasks, more data is needed concerning the permanence of this learning over extended periods of time.

· 11 ·

Interrelationships between Personality, Skeleto-Muscular, and Perceptual Functioning*

Conceptualization of motor activity or motor responsiveness as a reflection of an individual's attitude toward the world is not new; yet, as Ascher (1949) has pointed out, motor behavior has been relatively neglected as an avenue for the study of personality functioning. In psychopathology there has been implicit, if not explicit, recognition of the manifestation of psychological conflicts in muscular immobilization or hyperactivity. Charcot's work on hysteria followed by that of Freud, Breuer, and others, as well as the recent work of Strauss and Griffith (1955) on the "pseudoreversibility of catatonic stupor," give convincing proof that disordered functioning of skeletal-musculature need not be associated with detectable physiological damage and can be associated with disturbances in . the relationship between the individual and his world. The expression of "normal" psychological defenses through this avenue which Reich (1945) has called the "characterological armor" of the individual seems a likely possibility. This study investigates individual differences in one specific example of skeletal-muscular activity, the Kohnstamm phenomenon, as a function of differences in personality constriction or spontaneity.

* This chapter is based on doctoral research by Rebecca Snyder at the University of Kansas under the direction of Martin Scheerer.

The Nature of the Kohnstamm Phenomenon

The Kohnstamm phenomenon is a "curious phenomenon of involuntary muscular contraction" (Salmon, 1914), which consists of an involuntary arm movement outward and upward away from the side of the body shortly after the cessation of a briefly sustained voluntary isometric muscular contraction of that same arm. It is readily elicited in some healthy people by having them place the back of their hand against a wall and then press outwardly as vigorously as possible for a period of from 5 to 25 seconds. The arm is extended stiffly, free of any contact with the body. When the subject steps away from the wall, drops the arm, and relaxes, the arm seems to lose its weight, and, unless obstructed, begins to float upward as if of its own accord or "as if it is being raised by a secret power." (Kohnstamm, 1915) It is accompanied by a peculiar feeling of detachment and momentary depersonalization. It is as if the subject were an observer watching a part of himself behaving in a manner alien to himself. So marked is the feeling of detachment and passivity, the feeling of being acted upon and having no control over that which is happening, that subjects frequently make such spontaneous comments as: "You don't move it up; you see it go up." "It's the oddest feeling; you don't feel it's a part of you; you don't feel your arm; it's as if you had puppet strings." There is a feeling of magic about it which is captured in the very title of Schwartz's article on this experience: "Le Phénomène du 'Bras qui se lève tout seul.'" (1924)

Individual Differences. Individual differences were mentioned as early as 1915 by Kohnstamm when he raised the question as to whether this phenomenon was manifested by all people. Pinkhof (1922), Salmon (1925), and Matthaei (1924), raised the same question. The *interindividual differences* which have been reported in the literature are of three kinds: (1) those associated with differences in chronological age; (2) those associated with differences in manner or relating to the environments, i.e., the hyperreactivity of the hysteric, the weak movement of the person with "dementia praecox," the absence of movement in the "negativistic" person; and (3) those associated with differences in the familiarity of the subjects with the phenomenon. *Intraindividual differences* have been described as occurring in association with hypnosis, alcoholic intake, and increased familiarity with the expectation of the outcome of relaxing. Matthaei (1924) observed that hypnosis and alcohol strengthened the phenomenon and that increased familiarity with respect to the expectations of the outcome helped some subjects in manifesting a post contraction reaction. The generalization with respect to the facilitating effect of the alcohol and hypnosis was made on the basis of studies on only one subject for each situation. The modification associated with increased familiarity with the expectations of the outcome apparently holds only for those initially not manifesting a reaction since both Matthaei (1924) and Pinkhof (1922) emphasized the deterrent effect of familiarity with the outcome on some subjects by their use of conscious control.

Salmon (1925) explicitly stated the developmental differences. He reported the Kohnstamm phenomenon as being more pronounced in young people than in the older age group. He indicated that there is least reactivity in the aged. While Allen (1936-37), Pereira (1925), and Schwartz (1924) do not explicitly state that children have more pronounced reactions, they describe the delight with which children in the schools of Brazil, England, and Canada amuse themselves with this "birdlike" experience and they do not mention any nonreacting children. The impression given is that the children experience it freely.

Salmon (1925), Allen (1936-37), and Kohnstamm (1915) are those who have reported differences in reactivity associated with individual differences in manner of relating to the environment. Kohnstamm believed that the postcontraction probably occurred in every healthy person. However, he described it as being absent in "negativistic people." Salmon spoke of the weakened response in old people or in apathetic individuals, e.g., "those having dementia praecox." He also spoke of the exaggerated responses in two hysterics where, once the phenomenon had been obtained, it was sufficient to ask the subjects to contract their deltoid muscles voluntarily to obtain the involuntary elevation of their arms. Allen (1936-37) described a case of exaggerated reaction in a "hypersensitive" individual in which "after a single application of the stimulus to the arm, the postcontraction was so strong that the body was itself bent sideways, the arm sprang to an almost vertical position and the post-contraction of the latter was repeated twice, but with much diminished amplitudes." (p. 306.)

Pinkhof (1922) and Matthaei (1924) both were impressed with the more pronounced reaction occurring in naïve subjects.

Matthaei and Kohnstamm believe this postcontraction to be a normal phenomenon, demonstrable in every healthy (physiologically intact) individual. However, it would appear from the data they present that they are arguing for the universal *potentialities* for experiencing the phenomenon provided the proper conditions can be created for each individual. This seems implicit in Matthaei's report of having elicited a Kohnstamm reaction in only 5 out of a total of 16 subjects until he demonstrated it for them. Subsequent to his demonstration of the phenomenon there were several of those initial nonreactors who now manifested a Kohnstamm reaction. There were some, however, who still gave no manifest reaction in spite of their knowledge of the outcome and the demonstration.

Pinkhof also appeared to favor the view that this phenomenon was present in everyone but that there were variations in the types of responses obtained. He observed that it worked best with people who were unfamiliar with it; that the focus of attention upon it weakens the phenomenon. Allen and O'Donoghue (1927) stressed the usefulness of distracting the attention of the subject away from the phenomenon so as to prevent voluntary control of the arm movement. Whisler (1931) may also have been demonstrating the effect of distracting the attention of the subject away from the phenomenon when he showed that the postcontraction effect could be augmented by simultaneously presenting pictures or playing records to the subject. It made no difference insofar as the postcontraction was concerned whether the subject's affective reaction to the pictures or records was one of pleasure or displeasure.

Salmon (1925) noted that certain individuals showed a marked postcontraction after comparatively little previous voluntary effort while others showed little or no postcontraction after great voluntary effort. Allen (1936-37) supported this observation from his own experiences. Forbes, Baird, and Hopkins (1926) found that of seven Harvard students tested for this phenomenon, one had no reaction, one reacted feebly, and the other five responded positively with regularity. They also cited the findings of an army medical officer who reported the Kohnstamm reaction as being present in about 70% of the subjects tested in his unit. Scheerer and Austrin (1945) elicited the phenomenon in 7 out of 27 uninformed, naïve subjects. When the subjects were informed of the reaction possibilities, the number of reactors increased. After watching a demonstration, a few more gave a positive Kohnstamm reaction. Only 3 out of 32 failed to give a positive reaction after the demonstration. This latter study highlights the methodological necessity for knowing the conditions under which the subjects are tested, among them the state of naïveté of the subjects with respect to the phenomenon being investigated.

Nature of the Problem

Many of the investigators laid stress upon the ease with which the Kohnstamm phenomenon can be blocked by voluntary control. Others recognized the increased or even "exaggerated" reactivity in conditions associated with the relaxation of inhibitory controls (e.g., after alcoholic intake as reported by Matthaei and in the cases of hysterics as observed by Salmon and Allen independently). These observations suggested that control factors—both conscious and unconscious—might play an important role in producing the individual differences found. This control factor hypothesis is consistent with the developmental changes reported. It may possibly reflect the broad aspect of control associated with adult socialization (i.e., the developed sense of personal responsibility as contrasted with the lesser degree of social control, the more carefree period of childhood). It is for these reasons that the focus of this study is on the possible "control operation" shown by those who give a Kohnstamm reaction and those who do not.

It is assumed that every neurologically intact individual would manifest a Kohnstamm reaction, provided he were completely relaxed in the Kohnstamm situation and devoid of inhibiting defensiveness. It is further assumed that the inhibitory control or the spontaneity reflected in Kohnstamm behavior is not a manner of reacting to stimulation which is idiosyncratic to this specific situation: that it reflects rather the individual's characteristic way of reacting to or interacting with the world, his way of "coming to terms with the environment" (Goldstein), his "coping mechanism" (Maslow), or his "characteristic cognitive attitude" or "cognitive style" (Klein). The hypotheses which follow describe some of the personality differences expected between those persons who do give a positive Kohnstamm reaction and those who do not under similar conditions.

Hypotheses

1. *The Hypotheses of "Inner Freedom."* It is hypothesized that the degree and quality of "inner freedom" is a factor in determining the presence or absence of Kohnstamm reactivity.

Inner freedom is conceived of as being an openness to the environment and its stimuli which is behaviorally manifested by a relatively uninhibited interaction with the environment. "Inner freedom" implies an individual's potentiality for voluntarily adopting a quasipassive attitude towards accepting stimuli both from the environment and from within himself, and yet does not mean apathy. It also implies a freedom to react in many different ways to the stimulus situation without much attempt to control direction, duration, or intensity of the reaction. A person with "inner freedom" would tend to have the potentiality for a broad range of experiences including the new and the strange. In addition he would have the potentiality for variegated responsiveness and assimilation of this experience. He would be able to respond without constriction even if the experience were one contradictory to repeated past experiences and apparently illogical. He would thus be expected to be a relatively flexible person, able to change old established habits with comparative ease. When this "inner freedom" begins to resemble "inner looseness," then we might get what might be called a too flexible person, i.e., a person unable to delay between impulse to action and action. This group might well be considered *undercontrollers* since they are not sufficiently governed by the nature of the situation in which they find themselves but are ubiquitous reactors to whatever stimuli impinge upon them. *Adequate controllers,* on the other hand, would have the impulsivity and spontaneity of the more mature person who is able to relinquish control when the conditions are such as to make such behavior appropriate. The range of "inner freedom" in which is found the "adequate controller," as well as the "undercontroller," would tend to be associated with a positive Kohnstamm reaction. As the degree of "inner freedom" decreases beyond the range of the "adequate controller," one would expect to find more and more negative Kohnstamm reactions. (This would be consistent with the increase of personality rigidity as defined by Cattell (1947), i.e., "personality rigidity" is "the ease with which old established habits may be changed in the presence of new demands.") Moreno's definition of "spontaneity" embodies comparable characteristics of "an adequate response to a present situation." (1953) The degree of "inner freedom" is expected to be directly related to the degree of spontaneity and inversely related to "personality rigidity."

2. *The Security Hypothesis:* It is hypothesized that the Kohnstamm reaction is influenced by factors which determine security

feelings in the individual. It is probable, from the results of pilot studies, that some of the individuals who do not give an arm elevation may be constricted because of fear of doing the wrong thing, of not conforming with the expectations of others and of being therefore rejected. They may be *insecure* people who are unable to surrender themselves freely to the environment unless they have first been convinced that their reactions, whatever they might be, would be acceptable to others: that if they revealed uniqueness, it would be respected and not lead to ostracism. Other Kohnstamm-negative subjects may be thought of as being quite *secure* with themselves but as characteristically adjusting with evidence of definite control and never able to drop all control in any situation. It is self-demands rather than other demands that these people need to satisfy. Such persons could be described as "overcontrollers" since they tend to manifest control operations unwarranted by the apparent demands of the objective situation.

The purpose of the present investigation is to explore some of the above described possible personality characteristics which may differentiate Kohnstamm reactors from Kohnstamm nonreactors; to examine whether the individual differences elicited in the Kohnstamm situation are reflections of broader coping mechanisms or are idiosyncratic to this situation. We are also interested in exploring the hypothesis of "inner freedom." For example, is it possible to differentiate the Kohnstamm reactors from nonreactors in such dimensions as (a) greater responsiveness (openness) to the environment, (b) greater freedom to experience the uncanny and the new and accept it even when at variance with one's knowledge of reality, (c) less hesitancy about taking chances and committing oneself when confronted with a poorly structured situation, (d) greater capacity for relaxing control, for surrendering oneself to the moment and reacting spontaneously, impulsively rather than compulsively, (e) less concern about the conventionality of one's reactions?

METHOD

The over-all plan of the study was to compare Kohnstamm-positive and Kohnstamm-negative reactors on some personality measures which are relevant to the personality differences subsumed under the hypotheses of "inner freedom" and "security."

The first problem of the study was therefore that of getting a Kohnstamm reactor group (K+) and a Kohnstamm nonreactor group (K−). Some investigators have reported that in some subjects there are intraindividual differences in Kohnstamm reactivity associated with differences in the degree of naïveté concerning the phenomenon. Pilot studies by the authors confirmed this finding. It was, therefore, considered essential to take into account the familiarity of the subject with the Kohnstamm phenomenon. Only those subjects who had no previous knowledge about the Kohnstamm phenomenon were used. They were asked not to discuss the experiments with anyone and this restriction was readily accepted. It seems reasonable to assume, therefore, that each subject's knowledge about the Kohnstamm phenomenon was limited to what he was told and shown in the experimental conditions. Thus, such differences as might be obtained between K+ and K− subjects could not be ascribed to preconceptions about the Kohnstamm phenomenon. The subjects were tested for Kohnstamm reactivity under several conditions designed to bring about progressively increasing degrees of relaxation of inhibitory controls, so that those subjects who were relatively free in their Kohnstamm reactivity might be differentiated from those who were not. The experimental variations used in this study were planned to reassure those subjects who may tend to increase control when they become afraid of being considered different from others, to induce optimally possible psychological relaxation in them and, if possible, to obtain a positive Kohnstamm reaction. The conditions were expected to foster relaxation by (a) increasing the cognitive clarity about the situation; (b) reducing anxiety through information about "normal" reactions and thus counteracting the possible threat of being considered deviant; (c) increasing the co-operative relationship between the subject and the experimenter. Since the subject's mode of reacting was always recognized by the experimenter as being consistent with that of some "normals," changes in Kohnstamm reactivity, when knowledge of another acceptable mode of behavior became available, might suggest the following: either the inability to respond spontaneously in a strange situation can change as the situation loses strangeness, or, when other socially accepted behavior reactions are mentioned an attempt at emulating those from whom one differs may occur, especially if there is some implication that the other behavior is more desirable behavior. Either interpretation could be compatible with an underlying feeling of insecurity. Thus, changes in Kohnstamm reactivity under more structured directions were considered as a possible indication of an underlying insecurity factor, and as a means of differentiating between the secure and insecure subjects. For some comparative purposes, only the secure subjects were to be used, i.e., those who did not change their Kohnstamm reactions under the varying conditions. The Kohnstamm-positive group was to be composed of those individuals who, prior to any knowledge about the types of "normal" reactions, manifested an arm-elevation of at least 45 degrees and continued, in the subsequent conditions, to have an arm-elevation no less than 45 degrees. The Kohnstamm-negative group was to be composed of those individuals who gave no arm-elevation under any of the conditions.

The standardized conditions of Kohnstamm stimulation follow.

Standardized Conditions of Kohnstamm Stimulation

Condition I—naïve state. The subject was completely naïve about the Kohnstamm phenomenon. If either spontaneously or in response to direct questioning he indicated he was not naïve, he was not used as one of the experimental subjects.

Condition II—informed about the possibility of something happening to his arm. This was an attempt at increasing the feeling of permissiveness and relaxation. The subjects were given this information prior to the voluntary contraction if they had *not* manifested postcontraction rise in their naïve state. They were told that some normal persons have something happen to the arm with which they have been pressing, once they relaxed. Those subjects who had manifested a postcontraction in Condition I were told that there were some normal persons who had nothing happen to their arm when they relaxed. Both groups were then asked to try again to see how they would now react. Subjects in both groups were thus given information indicating the normalcy of responses contrary to those initially given by them. In this way, it was believed that indications of suggestibility might be obtained.

Condition III—informed about arm-rise and given a demonstration. It was believed that verbal reassurances as to the normalcy of reacting with an upward arm movement and a demonstration of this by the examiner might lead to lessened control in those individuals who are concerned about the acceptability of their behavior and afraid of rejection. If a subject changed his reaction after this, it was inferred that his previous behavior was to some extent influenced by his own insecurity, his inability to allow himself to respond spontaneously in a new situation. The secure people would be expected to maintain their initial reaction despite information about and observations of the reaction opposite to that they had given. The subjects who had not shown a Kohnstamm reaction under the preceding two conditions were told that some normal persons had their arm rise once they relaxed. Then the experimenter demonstrated a positive reaction. Those subjects who had previously experienced the arm-rise were told that while some normals reacted as they had, there were others who did not manifest an arm-rise subsequent to the voluntary contraction but had their arm remain by their side.

Condition IV—informed that the Kohnstamm phenomenon is a reflex reaction. This was an attempt at further relaxing those subjects who had not yet manifested a postcontraction arm-rise by making it intellectually acceptable to them. Again this information was given in such a way as to make their own previous reaction also acceptable. To those who had not yet manifested an arm elevation emphasis was placed upon the fact this is a reflex phenomenon which is elicited in some normal persons. Again it was stated that there were some normals who did not give such a reaction. To those who had already given an arm-elevation emphasis was placed upon the fact that some normal people did not have an arm-elevation.

Apparatus Used for Eliciting the Kohnstamm Phenomenon. The apparatus consisted of a small scale, such as is used for weighing mail, which was attached to a sliding block. In this way, it could be readily moved up and down and the platform adjusted to the back of the hand of the subject being tested. When the subject pressed against the scale as requested the scale registering the pressure with which the subject was pressing was easily visible to both him and the examiner.

Personality Measures

The subjects' reactions to perceptual tasks of varying degrees of ambiguity and their self-evaluations as reflected in their responses to personality inventories were chosen as techniques of personality evaluation. The former were looked upon as tools for eliciting behavior which was characteristic of the subject's "control operations"; the latter was largely exploratory in nature and directed toward ascertaining whether there are any measurable personality differences in the ways in which the two groups of subjects perceive themselves. A brief interview so structured as to tap control factors was also given each subject.

1. *Aniseikonic Lenses Test.* One of the more recent techniques for studying individual differences consists of investigating an individual's perceptual experience when confronted with a world distorted in various ways by mirrors or prisms (Ames 1946, Becker 1954, Martin 1954, Werner & Wapner 1955). Aniseikonic lenses have been introduced into the laboratory as a technique for bringing about distortions in the visual field. These lenses were designed to produce a difference in the size of the image received in each eye. The particular lenses used in this study magnify the image in the horizontal meridian for one eye. The induced effect gives the image (e.g., a desk) the appearance of tipping to the right if the glasses are so worn as to have the lens increasing the size of the image over the right eye. Ames (1946) reported that the currently accepted theories of binocular vision did not account adequately for the appearance of objects through these lenses. They fail to explain individual differences obtained between persons who have no visual defects. Some subjects perceive the distortion readily, others take a longer time, while others do not experience it at all. For this last group, the original appearance of things is maintained. Becker (1954), Kaplan (1952), and Martin (1954) suggest that individual differences in experiencing the aniseikonic illusion are manifestations of personality differences, differences in personality rigidity when defined as "the ease with which old established habits may be changed in the presence of new demands" (Cattell, 1947).

A subject's reactions to the aniseikonic lenses were assumed to sample the broad way in which he would react to other situations which are new and unusual, i.e., are contradictory to his established concepts of the world of reality. When the aniseikonic lenses are worn, the subject experiences something alien to his knowledge of reality. He sees as tipping a desk which he knows to be level. This discrepancy between reality knowledge and visual input creates a conflict which must be coped with. The person who is hesitant about trusting his immediate sensory impressions when they are in conflict with the external world as he knows it to be, must deal with this discrepancy. He may tend to suppress his own immediate sensations in an attempt to preserve perceptual constancy and may also attempt to delay this response to information-input. Consequently, those tending to "deny" the new perception would be expected to take a longer time to report the illusion or in some way minimize the deviation from reality. The insecure person (i.e., the one who mistrusts his own experience) would be expected to react thus since he might be thought of as interpreting the strange perception as a peculiarity within himself and not report it until he has checked again and again to convince himself that it is there. This would be expected to be true of those persons not giving a Kohnstamm reaction in the naïve state since the Kohnstamm reaction can be viewed as an experience at odds with what one knows objective reality to be. It is "birdlike" and not "human-like" to look and feel as if one flies.

The Kohnstamm phenomenon and the aniseikonic illusion differ in that the former results in a feeling of change and transitoriness within the self while the latter is an experience of changed appearance of familiar objects in the environment. Changes in the conception of the body-image are probably more threatening to people than changes in the appearance of objects external to themselves. Thus, some persons may more readily experience changes external to themselves without being able to yield to such changes within their own bodies.

It was predicted that Kohnstamm-negative reactors would take longer to perceive the desk as tilting than Kohnstamm-positive reactors. They would tend to be less open to unusual experiences and more apt to be bound by past experiences.

2. *Rorschach Test.* The Rorschach test has found wide clinical application and empirical support as a technique for evaluating the "control operations" which an individual uses in dealing with his spontaneous impulses and environmental stimulation. There is considerable reluctance on the part of some psychologists to accept the specific meanings attributed to many of the scores obtained on the Rorschach test. It is also recognized that some Rorschach interpretations have very weak research foundations. However, there is an increasing volume of studies which attempt to validate certain aspects of Rorschach technique as an instrument for clinical assessment and for scientific exploration into personality.

Several of these validating studies have been concerned with Rorschach indices of "personality rigidity" or "personality constriction" as defined in the present research. One of the more carefully validated Rorschach indices of "personality constriction" that is currently available is Fisher's "personality rigidity score" (1950). This index has the advantage of treating the entire protocol rather than each determinant in isolation. This more nearly approaches the way in which the Rorschach is clinically interpreted. It is based upon a "variety of Rorschach signs which clinically have been found to characterize persons who are habitually constricted and who find it necessary to deal with the environment with an unusual amount of guarded caution" (Fisher, 1950, p. 9). Such signs were used as: limitation of the number of responses; limitation in the use of color; restriction of percepts to one class of objects; delayed reaction times; limitations in the use of shading; failure to turn the cards. The subject is penalized, i.e., given a rigidity score, only when his protocol shows what is considered to be excess rigidity or restrictiveness. It has been demonstrated that this measure of personality rigidity yields results which are significantly related to other measures of personality rigidity (Becker, 1954; Johnson & Stern, 1955).

In the present study the individual Rorschach variables which were thought of as possibly differentiating the Kohnstamm-positive subjects from the Kohnstamm-negative group were the following: R—total number of responses; RT—reaction time; T—total time spent with the cards; T/R—time per response; RT Chrom.—chromatic cards; Sum C—a weighted summation of the total number of color responses; F%—the percentage of responses determined only by form; Fc plus cF response—tactual shading responses; CF plus C—number of responses in which color plays the primary or only role; variety of determinants. These are commonly used indicators of constriction in Rorschach interpretations (Beck, 1950; Fisher, 1950; Klopfer & Kelley, 1946; Klopfer *et al.*, 1954; Rorschach, 1949). The Rorschach interpretations based upon them are hypotheses still in need of validation. For some, F%, RT, Total Time, T/R, and R, an explicit rationale exists in that exclusion of all but one aspect of a situation (form), delay in responding to a stimulus, withdrawal from a situation rapidly and giving few responses to it, are clinically seen as characteristics of the constricted person. For other of the variables, color and movement responses, the Rorschach hypotheses have been found clinically useful but experimentally uncertain. The particular rationale underlying their use here is the acceptance of passivity and immediacy of interaction with the environment as characteristics of the "color-perception" attitude (Schachtel, 1943) and the recognition of movement perception as a mode of reacting in which the subject contributes something of himself to the perceptual experience. Since FM, CF, and C have been found characteristic of a more immature type of responsivity, a less controlled manner of reacting, they seemed appropriate as comparative variables for our two groups. Johnson and Stern (1955) found R, M, T/R, and RT to differentiate between their "flexible" and "rigid" subjects at less than the 5% level; F%, CF plus C and Sum C did not differentiate. Becker (1954), on the other hand, found Sum C and the variety of determinants to be significantly related to "personality rigidity" while initial time and the total number of responses failed to reach the 5% level of significance. The latter two were, however, in the expected direction. Johnson and Stern did not analyze for the significance of the variety of the determinants used by the two groups.

On the basis of Rorschach hypotheses the following specific predictions were made concerning the differences in Rorschach performance and Kohnstamm reactivity. It was predicted that the Kohnstamm-positive subjects differ from the Kohnstamm-negative subjects in the following ways: (1) a greater number of responses; (2) a shorter reaction time; (3) a longer total time; (4) more time per response; (5) the use of a greater variety of determinants; (6) a lower F%; (7) a shorter reaction time to the chromatic cards; (8) more CF plus C responses; (9) a higher Sum C; (10) more cF plus Fc; (11) more M responses; (12) more FM responses; (13) a lower Fisher "personality rigidity score."

3. *Ambiguous Figure Test.* Eight photographs of pieces of regular knitting wool and cotton thread strongly suggestive of people and backgrounds were tested on a pilot group of subjects.* One of the eight photographs resulted in marked individual differences on this preliminary testing. In this photograph, the figures and the background are more ambiguous than on all of the other arrangements. The more cautious and constricted person, the one with a lesser degree of "inner freedom," has been viewed as being less ready to accept those experiences which contradict previously established facts (e.g., tilting desk). Therefore we expected him to be less ready to commit himself to ambiguously structured situations; to be more comfortable in reacting to that which he definitely knows; and, when that with which he is confronted deviates markedly from his past experience, to show reluctance in making a commitment of interpretation. The tendency to deal with the "sure" may lead to a concretistic type of response in which relationships between various aspects of the situation are neglected at the expense of distinct and obvious parts which can be isolated without inferring less obvious meaningful relationships. The aspects of these photographs which are definite are: (a) their very obvious state of being photographs;

---

* Peter Dorp, a photographer, is the creator of these doodles, which appeared in *Life Magazine*, February 8, 1954.

(b) the fact that they are composed of lines differing in width and shape; (c) that these lines are intertwined in some way; (d) that the lines comprising the background (those made of thread) are thinner than those in the foreground; (e) that these lines seem to be made of some sort of yarn or thread or even pipe cleaners. Perceptions of these facts do not open one to much possibility of being wrong. They simply describe what the stimulus offers. A perception of these doodles as figure and ground meaningfully related requires less caution and more freedom of reaction. It requires of the subject some active participation, something other than a mere mirroring of the stimulus. The more ambiguous the doodle, the greater the freedom required to integrate it.

It was predicted that the positive Kohnstamm subjects are more apt to perceive as people in action that doodle which preliminary studies proved to be most ambiguous. It was also predicted that the Kohnstamm-negative subjects are likely to resort to the concretistic type of description mentioned above until they had gained a background of experience which could serve them as a model. In the present study, this background of experience consisted of the presentation of the more definitely structured photographs in which the relationships between the parts and the nature of their interaction was so clearly depicted that there was little chance of misinterpretation. A further prediction was that the Kohnstamm-negative subjects not initially perceiving the ambiguous doodle as a swimmer and diver would need presentation of more well-structured doodles to create a set favoring such a perception than would the Kohnstamm-positive persons not initially perceiving the swimmer and diver.

The same sequence of doodles was presented to each subject:

1. ambiguous doodle (swimmer and diver)
2. mountain-climber
3. ambiguous doodle for second time
4. lovers holding hands
5. man taking snapshot of woman in front of Eiffel tower
6. ambiguous doodle for third time
7. skier
8. man reclining in hammock
9. cafe scene
10. family group
11. ambiguous doodle for fourth time

The first time that the ambiguous doodle was reported as a swimmer and diver was taken as a successful performance and further presentation of the doodles was considered unnecessary.

4. *Guilford-Martin Inventories.* Three of the Guilford-Martin inventories purporting to measure "personality traits" were used in the present study. Of the thirteen factors isolated and described by the originators of these inventories, four appeared to be directly related to some of the hypotheses concerning Kohnstamm reactivity. These factors (R, N, I, and Co) are defined by Guilford and Martin (1942) as follows:

R—(Rhathymia)—"a happy-go-lucky or carefree disposition, liveliness, and impulsiveness."

N—(Nervousness)—"jumpiness, jitteriness, and a tendency to be easily distracted, irritated, and annoyed."

I—(Inferiority Feelings)—"a lack of confidence, underevaluation of one's self, and feelings of inadequacy and inferiority."

Co—(Co-operativeness)—"a willingness to accept people and things as they are and a generally tolerant attitude."

On the basis of the hypotheses being investigated, it was expected that the Kohnstamm-positive subjects have higher R scores, N scores and Co scores (after conversions to C-scale). Such findings would be consistent with the expectation that Kohnstamm-positive subjects differ from Kohnstamm-negative ones in the following directions: more impulsive, less "nervous," and more open to their environment. One prediction with respect to I was made irrespective of the pattern of the interrelationships of the other scores, namely, that those subjects who change their Kohnstamm reactivity when given knowledge about the variations of "normal" reactions have a lower C-score than those who do not change. This would be consistent with the hypothesis that shifting reactivity is associated with feelings of insecurity and lack of self-confidence.

Subjects

Fifty students at the University of Kansas were tested for Kohnstamm reactivity; 25 were males and 25 females. All but five of them were in the age range 18 to 30. The five exceptions consisted of two subjects 35 years of age, one subject who was 40 years of age, one who was 45, and one who was 55. Some of the subjects were graduate students and others were undergraduates. The subjects were asked if they would be willing to co-operate in some research directed at investigating the relationship between personality characteristics and behavior. They had the option of refusing without suffering thereby. All subjects who presented themselves as willing were tested for Kohnstamm reactivity. Forty-one of the subjects were tested in all Conditions I through IV. Nine were started in Condition II and tested through Condition IV.

Procedure

In general, the following temporal order of experimentation was used.

First session—Condition I Kohnstamm, Aniseikonic Lenses, Condition I repeated.

Second session (within a few days after the first)—Condition II Kohnstamm, Ambiguous Figures, Condition II Kohnstamm repeated.

Third session—Condition III.

Fourth session—Condition III repeated.

Fifth session—Condition IV.

Sixth session—Condition IV repeated.

The Rorschach was given whenever a sufficiently long time interval was available, usually within the time period covering the other tests. On occasion, it was delayed until everything else had been completed. The Guilford STDCR Personality Inventory (1944) and the Guilford-Martin GAMIN (1943) and OAgCo (1943) Personal Inventories were given the subjects to fill out at their leisure and then return. All tests, including the Rorschach, were administered by the same person, thus controlling for possible differences in the reactions of the subjects which might be due to differences in the personality of examiners. This does not deny the influence of the examiner upon the subjects but affords some control for this factor.

Procedure for Testing Kohnstamm Reactivity. The subject was given the following instructions:

This is an experiment to determine the effect of muscular exertion on behavior. You wil place the back of your hand against this scale platform and press outward with as much force as you can muster. Notice the weight this registers and try to maintain constant the maximal pressure which you initially exert. In pressing, you will try to keep your arm as rigid as possible and free from all contact with your body. Please do not speak but concentrate upon the upper arm muscular effort. (At this point the examiner demonstrated the position to be taken.) When I say "go" you will stand and when I say "relax" you will let both arms drop down by your sides, turn sideways so that you are facing parallel to the wall against which the scale is resting and relax your arms completely. (The experimenter now demonstrated this.) Stand as still as possible and relaxed as possible until I tell-you to move. I will be timing you for 25 seconds. It will probably seem like one of the longest 25 second periods you have ever experienced.

The latter sentence was added after a few preliminary trials without it, because the subjects commented upon how exhausted their arms were becoming and decreased the pressure with which they were pressing. It was found that preparing them for the experience in this way resulted in their maintaining the pressure constant. After the instructions had been given, the subject was asked if he had any questions. If he commented spontaneously that he had done something similar to this in the past he was excluded. If he did not spontaneously mention having had previous experience with the phenomenon, he was asked whether he had ever done anything like this before. If his answer was "no," he was given a trial. If it was "yes," he was excluded. Even if he answered "no," he was again asked about any familiarity with this experience once he had given a positive reaction in any of the four conditions. Sometimes, the actual experience reawakened a memory of having previously done this when the instructions alone did not. When this occurred, the subject was also excluded.

Two measurements were recorded: (a) the pressure exerted by the subjects as registered in pounds on the scale, and (b) the degree of arm-elevation when such occurred. The height reached was measured by taking the angle from the vertical traversed by the arm. A glass-topped drawing pin was stuck into the wall at the level of the wrist at the end of the postcontraction rise and another at the level of the shoulder joint. The angle of elevation was then read off by means of a protractor. A stop watch was used for timing the duration of the voluntary contraction.

There were two reasons for having the subject concentrate upon maintaining a constant pressure by focusing upon the scale throughout the voluntary contraction. This was a means of assuring an isometric contraction, and it provided a simple distraction for the subject, thus preventing too much attention from being directed to the movements of the arm.

All subjects were tested under all Conditions in the sequence as given. In each of the Conditions the instructions as given before were the same except for the first sentence and the last sentence.

These were omitted after the subject's first trial in the naïve state. Two trials were made under each of the first two Conditions with at least 30 minutes elapsed-time between trials in order to avoid the oscillatory effect reported by Allen (1936-37). Allen found that repetition of the Kohnstamm phenomenon led to some augmentation or decrease of response if the successive trials were within 20 minutes of one another. Whether it was augmentation or inhibition which resulted depended upon the exact time interval between trials. While most subjects were also given two trials in Conditions III and IV there were some who were tested but once in these Conditions because of the time inconvenience to the subject.

A brief interview, conducted following the elicitation of the Kohnstamm reaction, was planned so as to yield additional information pertinent to the subject's attitude toward control as well as to establish his naïveté. It was conducted immediately after the subject's arm returned to its resting state, and the following questions were asked:

1. Did you ever hear about this before?
2. What did you hear about it?
3. Did you try it yourself before today?
4. Under what circumstances?
5. What happened when you tried it before?
6. How did you feel when your arm went up?
7. Were you surprised? (Asked only if the element of surprise were not spontaneously mentioned.)
8. Did you like the experience?
9. What was there about it that you found pleasant (or unpleasant, as the case might be)?

It was believed that the subject's experience of pleasure or displeasure and his elaboration of this would indicate his subjective reactions to control and lack of it; his hesitancy about giving it up and assuming for the moment a passive role.

Personality Measures

Procedure for aniseikonic lenses. After the subject had been tested for the Kohnstamm phenomenon in the naïve state, he was asked to stand behind a line on the floor three feet away from the desk he was to view. This was in keeping with the conditions used by Becker at Stanford (1954). On the desk—in the center—was a tennis ball. The following instructions were given to him:

Stand here and look at this desk. I'm going to have you put these glasses on in a second, and, as soon as you see anything unusual in the appearance of the desk I want you to tell me. I want you to look generally in this direction (center of desk), and try to take in the whole top in one view. Don't move your eyes around freely, but you may have to do some shifting of your glance to see the entire desk. Keep this movement at a minimum, however, and try to keep a general fixed focus which takes in the whole top of the desk. Report to me as soon as you see anything unusual happen. Say "now" or something like that. Keep your eyes closed once you have put on the glasses until I tell you to start. Remember, report to me as soon as you see any changes.

After the subject reported a distortion, a tilt or tipping of the desk, he was asked in which direction the desk was tilting. Then he was given time for the effect to stabilize and asked: "How much higher would you estimate one side to be than the other?" If the subject reported no illusion at the end of 90 seconds, the glasses were removed and after a rest of one minute the experiment was again repeated with one modification. He was now given some information with respect to anticipated reactions. He was told that some persons perceived a tilt after they had the glasses on for a while. He was told that there were individual differences, however, just as with the Kohnstamm reactivity; that some persons saw the table tilt only after wearing the glasses for a relatively long time, others perceived it quickly, while others never did perceive it.

These instructions differ from those used by Becker in one important respect. His subjects were told initially to let him know "as soon as you see the desk start to tip. . . . Report to me as soon as you can tell which way it has tipped." It was felt that by initially withholding any information concerning expected responses, the influence of suggestion was minimized. It is recognized that the mere wearing of glasses with such visible distortions (of one lens) may exercise suggestive influence in that this leads to the subject's expectation of visual changes. Moreover, the subjects in the present study were told to inform the investigators as soon as they *saw* anything unusual in the appearance of the desk. However, it is felt that by simply asking the subject to report any visual changes he observes, the factor of suggestion is fairly minimized and any report of tilt is of his own perception.

The experiment was repeated three times with one-minute intervals between each trial for subjects not perceiving a tilt at the end of 90 seconds. It was repeated five times for those perceiving a tilt; also with a one-minute interval between trials. Becker found that learning effects were minimal after the first two trials and, in keeping with his techniques for analysis (1954), an average of the last three was used for measuring the time delay.

Since astigmatism has a definite effect upon the perception of this illusion, those subjects who wore glasses were asked to keep them on while looking through the aniseikonic lenses. The subjects fitted the aniseikonic lenses either on top of their own glasses or underneath them depending upon the shape of their frames.

The purpose of the tennis ball was to help focus the attention of the subject upon the center of the desk and to increase the feeling of incredulity at seeing a tennis ball standing still in the center of a decline, as if defying gravity. This would make it more demanding for those who reject the novel to check again and again to be sure it is not they who are peculiar but the situation in which they find themselves.

Procedure for ambiguous figure test. When the subject appeared for the second experimental session, he was first tested for Kohnstamm reactivity under Condition II. Then the examiner said, "I'm going to show you a picture and I'd like you to tell me what it looks like to you." Figure 1 was then presented to the subject. Whatever the subject said was recorded verbatim. If the subject did not perceive this photograph as a swimmer and diver, he was presented with Figure 2 and asked, "What does this one look like to you?" Then the first figure was again presented and the subject was asked, "Do you see anything now other than that which you saw before?" Again his answer was recorded. If he still did not perceive Figure 1 as a swimmer and diver, he was shown Figures 3 and 4 in that sequence and asked what they looked like to him. Then he was again presented with Figure 1. If he still did not perceive it as a swimmer and diver, Figures 5, 6, 7, and 8 were presented before Figure 1 was shown again for the last time.

Procedure for administering and scoring the Rorschach test. The Rorschach cards were administered and scored in accordance with the Klopfer technique for administration and scoring (1946). Since Fisher's weightings for his "general personality rigidity scores" were based upon Beck's scorings and Fisher's score was among the indices used, the protocols were rescored for form accuracy level and shading by Beck's method (1950). All of the protocols were independently scored by two persons familiar with the Klopfer method of scoring; these were always the examiner and one other expert scorer. The "second" scorer had no knowledge of the hypotheses being tested or of the reactions of the subjects with respect to the presence or absence of a Kohnstamm reaction. This precaution was thought to control against any bias in scoring. In general, there was surprising agreement between the scorers as to the primary determinants, the only ones used in the comparisons made. If there were any differences of opinion concerning the scoring of a particular response, one of two methods was used for resolving the difference. In some cases a third person was asked to score the controversial response with no knowledge of the scoring of the other two scorers. That scoring was used for which there were two of the three in agreement. In no case was the third scoring at variance with both of the others. In other cases, both of the initial scorers discussed the basis for their scoring and the differences were resolved. Which method was used depended upon the proximity of the two scorers and the possibility of their meeting for a discussion. It was in cases where this was impractical that the third scorer was introduced into the situation.

Personality Inventories. The three personality inventories were given the subjects to fill out at their leisure. They were asked to read the instructions before leaving and clarify for themselves anything about the instructions that was unclear to them.

RESULTS

Kohnstamm Reactivity

Forty-one subjects were tested for Kohnstamm reactivity under each of the four standardized conditions.

Eleven of the 41 subjects gave a Kohnstamm reaction under Condition I, when completely naïve with respect to the phenomenon. One additional subject became Kohnstamm-positive in Condition II when given the information that some people have something happen to their arm when they relax. Five more subjects became Kohnstamm-positive after being told of the type of arm movement characterizing "normal" reactions and witnessing a demonstration of a positive reaction under Condition III; and the last four who became Kohnstamm-positive did so only after being given the additional information, in Condition IV, that this was a normal reflex reaction. Twenty subjects showed no Kohnstamm reactivity even after exposure to all four conditions. A test of the statistical significance of these findings was made by applying to the data Cochran's technique for the comparison of percentages in matched samples (1950). A chi square of 22.29 was obtained which is significant at less than the .001 level and indicates that the conditions have a statistically significant effect upon the manifestation of the Kohnstamm phenomenon.

Further analysis of the data in Table 1 indicated that a significant change in Kohnstamm reactivity was associated with Condition III. The data of Table 1 were reorganized as in Table 2 for this analysis.

Condition III was therefore taken as the cutoff point for separating the Kohnstamm-positive and Kohnstamm-negative groups. Those

TABLE 1

Kohnstamm Reactivity under the Four Standard Stimulus Conditions *

No. of Subjects Reacting under Conditions	Conditions			
	I	II	III	IV
11	+	+	+	+
1	0	+	+	+
5	0	0	+	+
4	0	0	0	+
20	0	0	0	0
41	11	12	17	21

* Positive Kohnstamm Reactivity: +. Negative Kohnstamm Reactivity: 0.

TABLE 2

The Number of Subjects Giving a Positive Kohnstamm Reaction Before Condition III and Maintaining Such a Reaction in Condition III, the Number of Subjects Giving a Negative Reaction Prior to Condition III and Shifting to a Positive Reaction in Condition III, and the Number of Subjects Giving a Negative Kohnstamm Reaction Both Prior to and in Condition III

Before Cond. III	Condition III		
	K pos.	K neg.	Totals
K pos.	12	0	12
K neg.	5	24	29
Totals	17	24	41

$\chi^2 = 3.20$; $z = 1.789$; $p = .036$.

subjects giving an arm-elevation prior to Condition III were considered to be Kohnstamm-positive subjects. All others were considered to be Kohnstamm-negative. The Kohnstamm-negative group was considered to consist of two possible subgroups, those who were probably insecure and in need of reassurance before being able to relax sufficiently to manifest a Kohnstamm reaction and those who were consistently Kohnstamm-negative—the probably secure group. It was this latter group that was used for most of the later comparisons.

Voluntary Contraction Pressure and Shifts in Kohnstamm Reactivity

The procedure for eliciting Kohnstamm reactivity necessitated voluntary pressure by the subjects against the scale platform (with the instruction to keep this pressure constant for the induction period). The question arises as to whether any relationship existed between Kohnstamm reactivity and the amount of pressure exerted by the subjects during the voluntary contraction operation. Inspection of the data suggested that there was no relationship between the presence or absence of a Kohnstamm reaction and the intensity of the pressure exerted during the voluntary contraction. Some subjects who exerted as little as 5 pounds of pressure during the voluntary contraction were among those who showed a high arm-elevation while others who had exerted as much as 23 pounds of pressure in the voluntary contraction gave no Kohnstamm reaction. Moreover, there were some subjects who manifested no arm-elevation when exerting relatively greater pressure than at times when they shifted their reaction to a positive one. A striking example of this is the subject who gave no reaction at one time when he exerted a pressure of 22.5 pounds in the voluntary contraction; yet, under a different Condition, gave a repetitive reaction in which his arm flew back and forth nine times consecutively after a voluntary contraction pressure of 19.5 pounds.

Interview Findings Pertinent to the Hypothesis of Control Factors Playing an Important Role in Kohnstamm Reactivity. The affective experiences which the subjects communicated verbally were considered indicative of their attitude toward "giving up control" or "keeping control." Some subjects enjoyed the experience; others found it interesting but not particularly enjoyable. It seemed threatening to some. One subject who did not feel comfortable with her response explained that she liked to feel that she was always in control of her situation and tried to maintain that. However, she was not always successful and when a lapse occurred, she felt quite unhappy about it. The Kohnstamm-positive reaction was experienced by her as a lapse of control.

Subjects who gave a Kohnstamm-positive reaction under Condition I characteristically could not believe that others sometimes had no arm-elevation, unless the nonreactors consciously inhibited their "natural response." No subject in this group changed his reaction as a result of the information given him. One subject verbalized her feelings about this quite freely. She commented that she did not see how people could prevent their arm from going up if they "would let it." This group as a whole seemed to ascribe the failure to experience the Kohnstamm reaction to the use of control. They appeared also to consider this a problem of the Kohnstamm nonreactors. They seemed confident of the appropriateness of their own reactions in this particular situation.

Those subjects who did not give a Kohnstamm reaction reacted in one of three ways when they were told in Condition III that there were some normal persons who had their arm-rise after they relaxed. (1) Some seemed sceptical about the validity of the statement. (2) Some wondered why their arm did not go up and seemed disturbed about the appropriateness of their reactions. (3) Others accepted the statement about the reactions of "some normals" as being different from their own without seeming to be disturbed by it.

Personality Assessment Results

The Aniseikonic Lens Situation. The distorting influence of the lenses tends to lead to the perception of the desk as tilting. If a report of "tilt" was not forthcoming within 90 seconds, the subject was rated a "nonreactor" (i.e., as not perceiving the tilt).

The responses of the Kohnstamm-positive and Kohnstamm-negative subjects to the initial naïve exposure are presented in Table 3 as the frequencies of "tilt perceivers" and "nonperceivers" within each group.

The z test of significance (a one-tail test appropriate to the present analysis since predictions were made in but one direction) was applied to the distribution of frequencies in Table 3. A value of 1.784, which is significant at less than the 5% level (P of .0375), was obtained. This is strongly suggestive of the presence of an interaction factor between the presence or absence of Kohnstamm reactivity and the reported perception of desk tilt or nontilt under the

TABLE 3

Number of Subjects in Each Group (Kohnstamm-Positive and Kohnstamm-Negative) Who Reported the Table Tilt and Those Not Reporting It within 90 Seconds

Group	Tilt	No Tilt	Totals
K pos.	10	2	12
K neg.	10	12	22
Totals	20	14	34

$z = 1.784 = P$: 0.0375.

naïve condition. The Kohnstamm reactors tend more readily to report tilt, whereas the nonreactors, under the naïve conditions, most often fail to report this phenomenon.

In the second trial with the aniseikonic lenses there were some persons who now perceived the illusion when initially they had not done so. This second trial is analogous to Condition III of Kohnstamm testing since the subjects were told of the possibility of seeing the table tilt. Those Kohnstamm-positive subjects who perceived no tilt when naïve concerning the aniseikonic illusion remained uninfluenced by the given information about it so that they did not perceive the tilt in the second trial. There were, on the other hand, five Kohnstamm-negative subjects who perceived the table tilt once they were told of the possibility of such an illusion, whereas they had not reported a tilt when naïve in the first trial.

Acquired information tended to influence the perception of tilt among subjects who were nonreactive to the Kohnstamm phenomenon.

That the newly acquired knowledge was followed by a change in the *perception* of the desk rather than just a change in readiness to *report* a perception of tilt was tested for to some extent by *not* telling the subject the expected direction of tilt and asking him to report this. The subjects were also questioned as to whether they had perceived the tilt in the initial presentation and not reported it because they doubted their own sensory experience or whether they had initially not perceived it. The subjects' responses were accepted at face value since there was no apparent reason for dissimulation. All five subjects who changed their responses to reporting "tilt" under the second situation reported that they had not perceived the tilt originally. They all gave a correct report of the direction of the apparent tilt. The hypothesis that the change was a simple response to suggestion based on the verbal information presented does not seem adequate to account for the correct, consistent report of the direction since the information contained no hints as to the direction of the tilt.

The Rorschach Findings. The Rorschach variables which were selected for study were those which are widely used as indices of "personality constriction" or those which appeared relevant to the aspects of sensitivity of openness to the environment and responsibility to it. The Mann-Whitney U Test was used for the statistical calculations since the normality of the distribution of the Rorschach variables is questionable and this test makes no assumptions concerning the type of distribution from which the data is derived.

Rorschachs were obtained on the 12 Kohnstamm-positive subjects as previously defined. Three of the Kohnstamm-negative subjects were not available for the test. The Kohnstamm-negative Rorschach findings are therefore based upon the results of the remaining 19 subjects tested. The data on which the determinations were made are given in Table 3 and Table 4. Table 4a gives the data for the Kohnstamm-positive subjects and Table 4b that for the Kohnstamm-negative ones.

The z value obtained by applying the Mann-Whitney Test to the data of Tables 4a and 4b are given in Table 5. The significance of the results is also given there.

From Table 4 it is seen that eight of the thirteen predictions made concerning Rorschach performances differentiate between the Kohnstamm-negative and Kohnstamm-positive groups as the 5% level of significance. These are R, Total Time, RT Chrom., Variety of Determinants, M, FM, and Fisher Rigidity. RT Chrom., one of these variables, differentiates between the two groups in a direction opposite to that predicted. There are three variables which do not meet the criterion of the 5% level for significance but fall between the 5% and 10% levels. These are: the reaction time, F%, and T/R. Reaction time differentiates the two groups in the direction opposite to that which was predicted while the other two are in the predicted direction. CF + C does not differentiate between the two groups of subjects used in this study.

Ambiguous Figure Findings. A response was scored as a "success" if the subject interpreted the figure as people in action—a swimmer and diver—and as a "failure" if such a response was not given. As described in the procedure section, if the subject did not interpret

TABLE 4a

Frequency Distribution of Rorschach Variables for the Kohnstamm-Positive Subjects

Subject	R	RT *	Total * Time	T/R	RT Chrom.	F%	CF/C	Sum C	M	FM	Fc/cF	Variety of Determinants	Fisher's Rigidity Score
1.	22	39.1	2456	111.6	47	18	2	3	6	3	2	9	7
2.	31	16.9	1066	34.4	20	48	1	3	2	8	1	9	6
3.	38	15.6	1545	40.7	19	39	0	3	5	9	2	7	0
4.	81	8.2	1372	16.9	12	30	5	6.5	14	18	2	9	9
5.	29	13.1	2110	72.8	19	14	1	4	9	5	2	8	6
6.	49	20.2	2922	48.7	24	20	12	18.5	5	6	2	8	18
7.	96	7.7	3057	31.8	10	68	3	5	10	6	11	10	10
8.	20	33.1	1328	66.4	23	55	0	5	4	4	1	4	36
9.	51	4.8	2045	40.1	5	27	4	6.5	12	10	7	7	9
10.	74	15.7	2744	36.3	10	61	2	4.5	4	7	5	7	10
11.	101	28.1	4536	44.9	20	61	3	5.5	3	10	10	11	12
12.	73	20.8	3802	52.1	26	30	1	4	17	13	6	11	11

* All time is reported in seconds.

Note: The same number refers to the same subject throughout the personality measures. The skewness of the distributions can readily be seen.

TABLE 4b

Frequency Distribution of Rorschach Variables for the Kohnstamm-Negative Subjects

Subject	R	RT	Total Time	T/R	RT Chrom.	F%	CF/C	Sum C	M	FM	Fc/cF	Variety of Determinants	Fisher's Rigidity Score
1.	26	17.2	1290	49.2	20	88	0	0.5	1	0	1	4	39
2.	30	15.0	1448	48.3	20	47	1	1.0	6	4	2	7	12
3.	21	7.5	707	33.7	8	43	2	2.5	1	2	2	7	43
4.	12	10.5	605	50.4	12	25	2	2	3	2	2	5	24
5.	13	42.6	1026	78.9	51	46	2	2	1	3	0	5	62
6.	13	9.7	281	21.6	18	62	0	0	1	2	2	4	51
7.	16	19.5	339	21.2	18	56	2	2	1	3	0	5	50
8.	48	13.6	2115	44.1	17	51	1	1	4	3	7	6	23
9.	17	19.6	859	50.5	22	53	2	2	1	2	0	5	38
10.	30	27.2	1960	65.3	20	48	2	3.5	2	2	3	10	12
11.	18	7.0	450	25.0	8	39	0	1	6	1	1	5	24
12.	65	6.4	1591	24.5	6	46	5	6.5	10	3	8	12	5
13.	41	7.5	767	18.7	8	64	3	4	2	4	2	7	22
14.	25	9.1	760	30.4	11	40	4	5.5	2	2	1	8	28
15.	37	15.6	1268	34.3	14	54	4	4	2	2	5	9	24
16.	74	8.3	3147	42.5	8	59	6	8	4	4	5	11	9
17.	30	10.5	708	23.6	13	53	4	6	2	1	3	6	27
18.	27	8.3	853	31.6	7	56	3	3	2	0	2	7	24
19.	35	4.8	1658	47.4	5	46	0	0.5	8	5	3	7	19

TABLE 5

The "z" Value and "P" Value Obtained by Applying the Mann-Whitney Test to the Rorschach Variables Concerning Which Predictions Were Made, and the Direction of the Differences between the Two Groups (Kohnstamm-Negative and Kohnstamm-Positive Subjects)

Rorschach Variable	z	P	Direction of Difference
Reaction Time	1.50	.0668	K Pos. greater
R	2.62	.0044 *	K Pos. greater
Total Time	3.285	.0005 *	K Pos. greater
T/R	1.298	.0968	K Pos. greater
RT Chrom.	1.602	.0548 *	K Pos. greater
Sum C	1.967	.0250 *	K Pos. greater
CF + C	0.040	.4840	
F%	1.541	.0618	K Pos. lower
Fc + cF	1.196	.1151	K Pos. greater
Variety of Deter- minants	1.967	.0244 *	K Pos. greater
M	3.042	.0012 *	K Pos. greater
FM	4.258	<.0001 *	K Pos. greater
Fisher Rigidity Score	3.366	.0004 *	K Pos. lower

* The results starred are those which meet the 5% level of significance.

the ambiguous figure "successfully" on its first presentation, he was presented with photographs of more clearly structured doodles easily perceived as people in action and then again presented with the ambiguous figure. Presentations of well-structured figures were interspersed with those of the ambiguous figure in a systematic fashion until either "success" was obtained or all of the well-structured figures had been presented without success on the critical figure.

It was predicted that Kohnstamm reactors would perceive the ambiguous figure more readily as people in action than would the nonreactors.

None of the Kohnstamm-positive subjects used in this study required more than one well-structured photograph after the Key Test Figure in order to achieve a "success" response, whereas nine Kohnstamm-negative subjects required more than one, and two Kohnstamm-negative subjects never did attain "success" under the conditions of this experiment.

A chi square test reveals that the differences are significant at the .04 level (P < .035). From this, we may infer that it is quite improbable that the differences obtained in the readiness of the Kohnstamm-positive and Kohnstamm-negative subjects to perceive people in action in the ambiguous figure would occur by chance more than four times in one hundred, and the greater readiness of the Kohnstamm-positive subjects to perceive the people in action would be expected to occur by chance less than two times in one hundred. Thus it is reasonable to believe that there is a significant difference between the two groups in their performance on this task after a brief "structuring" experience.

It was predicted that Kohnstamm-negative subjects would adhere to more liberal, concretistic reports of what the ambiguous figure "looked like" as reflecting their hesitancy about taking chances. This was true mostly of those Kohnstamm-negative subjects who did not perceive the ambiguous figure as people in action. Responses such as "rope with a loop in it," and "two pieces of rope," were quite characteristic.

Guilford-Martin Personality Inventories. The three personality inventories (Guilford STDCR; Guilford-Martin GAMIN; Guilford-Martin OAGCo), were filled out by 12 of the Kohnstamm-positive subjects and 19 of the Kohnstamm-negative subjects. These were the same subjects who were given the Rorschach test. Some predictions had been made concerning factors R, N, I and Co on these inventories which appeared to be directly related to control and security aspects of personality functioning which were hypothesized as being of importance in differential Kohnstamm reactivity.

Only Co differentiated between the two groups at less than the 5% level ($P = .045$).

One prediction had been made about the difference in security or self-confidence between those subjects who shifted their Kohnstamm reactivity when informed and those who did not. The nonreactors had been separated into two groups on this assumption with the presumably "secure" nonreactors and "secure" reactors being used as the groups for comparative personality studies. It was predicted that those who shifted in their Kohnstamm reactivity would differ significantly from those who did not on the factor I which the investigators refer to as the "Inferiority" factor. All of the subjects in the Kohnstamm-negative and Kohnstamm-positive groups (as defined for purposes of the personality studies) were compared with those subjects who shifted in Conditions III or IV. A t test on these two groups, shifters vs. nonshifters, gave a "t" value of 2.405 which is significant on the two-tail test at the .028 level.

DISCUSSION

Individual Differences

Individual differences in Kohnstamm reactivity to controlled Kohnstamm situations were found among the subjects used in the study. Only 27% (11 subjects) gave a positive Kohnstamm reaction when completely naïve concerning the phenomenon. There were 49% (20 subjects) who did not give a positive reaction even after they were informed of the normalcy of such a reaction and had been given a demonstration. There were 24% (10 subjects) who shifted from a negative to a positive reaction after they were reassured as to the normalcy of the Kohnstamm-positive reaction.

Among this latter group there were also differences in the amount and kind of information necessary before a shift in reaction occurred. One subject changed when given only the information that some people have something happen to their arm when they relax. Five subjects (12%) did not change until they had been told that some people have something happen to their arm, what that something was, and also were given a demonstration. Four subjects (10%) did not change even then but needed the additional information that an arm-elevation under these circumstances was a perfectly normal reflex reaction which some people showed while others did not. At no time was it implied by the experimenter that the subject's initial reaction was deviant. The subjects were only given information about *other possibilities of "normal" reaction.* Those who responded with an arm-elevation in the naïve state did not change their reaction when told that there were some normal people who did not react in this fashion. This information was accepted with the frequent interpretation that those persons who did not show arm-levitation must be preventing it. These subjects implied that they too could prevent their arms from rising if they tried.

The positive Kohnstamm reactivity in Condition I (the naïve state) is not adequately explained by such a concept as suggestibility (if suggestibility is defined as the influence on behavior by verbal cues). In no way, either verbally or behaviorally, did the experimenter indicate to the subjects any preferred mode of responding to the voluntary contraction. Moreover, when the experimenter did inform those subjects that there were some normal people who did not have their arm rise once they relaxed, the Kohnstamm-positive subjects were uninfluenced in their subsequent reactions to the

Kohnstamm situation. They continued to give an arm-elevation. A differential suggestibility would have to be invoked to explain the failure of this additional information to influence the Kohnstamm-positive reactors and yet attribute their naïve Kohnstamm reactivity to suggestion. Autosuggestibility, the reaction of the subject in such a way as to conform to his own expectations of the outcome (i.e., that the arm-rise is a reaction to the pressure exerted in the voluntary contraction, because of his knowledge that "to every reaction there is an equal and opposite reaction") also seems inadequate as an explanation for the following reasons: (1) the subjects' apparently genuine experience of surprise when their arms rose, and (2) manifestations of the phenomenon despite anticipations of something else happening (e.g., of becoming dizzy and maybe falling, an expectation spontaneously volunteered by one of the subjects).

A suggestion hypothesis also seems inadequate as an explanation for those who shifted their reactions after they were informed of the possibilities of "normal" reactions different from those which they gave. While they were told that there were some normal people who reacted differently than they had, they were also informed that there were other normals who reacted as they had. There was no implication made that their initial reaction (absence of an arm-elevation) was less preferred than the presence of levitation. A more tenable explanation for the change in reactions is that the added knowledge and increased familiarity with the total situation made it possible for these subjects to be less guarded and to relax, since any reaction seemed acceptable to the examiner as "normal."

The naïve state, Condition I, could therefore be viewed as an inhibiting one for 24% of the subjects in this study. They were not free to be themselves in this situation, an interpersonal one, where there was an observer of their reactions and they had no guide for acceptable behavior. Instructions to relax, i.e., to be "spontaneous," and react immediately to whatever impulse they might have, was not sufficiently reassuring until some idea of the possibilities of normal reactions had been given. While other conditions might be even more effective in bringing about a change from immobility to mobility in Kohnstamm reactivity, it is our hypothesis that all such conditions would have as a common factor the capacity to induce an attitude in the subject which enabled him to divorce himself temporarily from feelings of responsibility for his behavior.

Alcohol ingestion succeeded in changing immobility to mobility quite strikingly in one pilot subject (the only one with whom this technique was tried). This subject, who has been undergoing psychoanalytic psychotherapy for five years, did not give a positive Kohnstamm reaction under any of the four standardized conditions used in this experiment while sober. After two drinks containing alcohol, her arm flew upward very freely. There was evident delight on the part of the subject in response to her experience of the freedom of movement. She described herself as having the same kind of "irresponsible" feeling as she had once experienced under hypnosis. She ascribed her delight with both experiences to the effect they seemed to have of temporarily removing from her the controls which she felt so compulsively necessary to maintain even when it might seem appropriate to relax these controls.

Many subjects attributed differences in Kohnstamm reactivity to differences in degrees of subjective control—voluntary as the Kohnstamm-positive subjects perceived it and involuntary as the Kohnstamm-negative subjects perceived it. These suggested interpretations were given by the subjects spontaneously when they were told that there were people who reacted differently than they had. The Kohnstamm-positive subjects described the vivid experience of having their arms rise as one in which they exercised no control. They explained its absence in others on the basis of an intervention of control factors. They felt that they too could counteract the upward arm movement by a voluntary effort after they had once experienced the reaction. Some of those who did not initially react with an arm-elevation also associated their behavior in the situation with control factors—an inability to relinquish control voluntarily. One subject spontaneously asked (after her arm had finally risen), "Do you suppose I was unconsciously keeping it down before?" Another said that her arm did not go up at first "because I wouldn't let it; I thought it wasn't supposed to." This subject was one who gave an arm-elevation on the second trial in the naïve state but not in the first. She had felt that her arm wanted to go up in the first trial, but had consciously prevented it from so doing. She explained nonreactivity of others by saying that they were "not letting themselves relax." When informed that there were some persons who did not have their arm go up, she commented, "I don't see how they can prevent it." In contrast to this voluntary-control explanation for nonreactivity given by the Kohnstamm-positive subjects, the Kohnstamm-negative subjects offered an involuntary-control hypothesis to explain nonreactivity. They felt that they were relaxing as much as they could and that any control factors which might be present to prevent response must be on an unconscious level.

The above discussion does not mean to imply that control factors were completely in abeyance in the Kohnstamm-positive subjects; but rather that they could be diminished sufficiently not to interfere with arm-levitation. One Kohnstamm-positive subject who had both arms rise while being tested in the naïve condition described her subjective experience as follows: "You feel they're going up and you're on a stage and it's not right for them to do so and then you think maybe that's what's supposed to happen." She then described her experience as one in which she first had difficulty accepting for herself a state of being in which she relinquished control. However, she was able to relax and yield to the moment.

It is our hypothesis that Kohnstamm-positive subjects are less hesitant about relinquishing control than are Kohnstamm-negative subjects; that they can give up their control and allow themselves to be reactors rather than actors. It is our belief that this readiness to relinquish some control was evidenced by the Kohnstamm-positive subjects in some of the other experimental situations to be discussed below. Thus, this readiness to relax controls, evidenced in the Kohnstamm situation, appears to be a more general personality factor.

Aniseikonic Illusion

The Kohnstamm-positive subjects seemed to be freer to experience the unusual and seemingly impossible in the external world. There was a significantly greater number in this group who reported a desk as being in a tilted position while a tennis ball resting on it remained stationary on the incline. This occurred in spite of the rational awareness that the ball should be going downhill. They knew that their perceptual experience differed from objective reality since they had seen the desk and ball prior to putting on the aniseikonic lenses. Yet they were not so bound by past experience and constriction as to deny their immediate perceptions and to be dominated by their knowledge of what the experience should be. The change in perceptions by some of the Kohnstamm-negative subjects, after they had been informed of the possibilities of normal reactions, suggests that their constriction and guardedness is associated with their general mode of responding to strange or unknown situations. They were able to experience at first, in terms of past conventionality. When informed as to the various possibilities of normal reactions, they were then able to experience the uniqueness of the present. It might be postulated that these subjects are unduly afraid of being wrong; that they perceive new internal and environmental situations as "threatening" until they are tested and proved otherwise.

While the interpretations that have been given are inferences only, they gain support from such comments as the following, which was made by one of the Kohnstamm-negative subjects who did not, on the first trial, perceive the tilt illusion. After being informed that some normal persons perceive the desk as tilting when they view it through the glasses, he commented that he was sure he wouldn't see anything *because he knew what the table was like.* Interestingly enough, despite this conviction of his own logical reaction to situations, this subject did perceive the tilt after the information had been given him. He was quite surprised and pleased when he saw the illusion. His expressed resistance against giving up what he knew of objective reality seems quite evident.

The perception of a tilt by 10 of the 22 Kohnstamm-negative subjects and its absence in 2 of the 12 Kohnstamm-positive subjects suggests that the two situations tend to elicit different degrees of constriction from these subjects. These situations might have different meaning for the subjects involved. The two situations might reflect differences in the freedom with which people yield to changes within themselves as compared to those external to themselves. Both the desk and the self are objects of perception and one of the goals of perception is to maintain constancy of the objects which we perceive. While some individuals may experience themselves as still in a state of becomingness and yield to giving an arm-rise, they may attribute greater permanency and stability to objects outside themselves, more specifically to inanimate objects with which they have had prior experience. The reverse may be true of others. Those subjects not giving an arm-elevation but perceiving the aniseikonic illusion may feel more responsible for being in control of themselves than for controlling the environment.

The Kohnstamm-positive group is freer in their perception of the illusion than the Kohnstamm-negative group and the inference that they are able to be less controlled in situations where such behavior is appropriate seems tenable.

Rorschach Results

The differences in reactivity of the two groups of subjects to the Rorschach cards indicates a greater degree of freedom and spontaneity for the Kohnstamm-positive subjects. They react to more aspects of the situation and in a more differentiated fashion (greater number of determinants). They are, in general, more responsive (greater number of responses). The significantly greater amount of time which the Kohnstamm reactors spent with the cards suggests a greater ease in the situation with possibly less anxiety about the adequacy of their own performance. The Kohnstamm-negative subjects seemed uncomfortable in this situation and seven of them withdrew from one or more cards without giving a response (ten failures altogether). There were no failures for the Kohnstamm-positive subjects. The greater Sum C score of the Kohnstamm reactors also can be interpreted as reflecting a greater responsivity to stimuli originating from without (Klopfer and Kelley 1946; Klopfer et al., 1954). The relatively greater number of M responses among the Kohnstamm-positive subjects suggests that they are less bound by the concrete aspects of experience, that they are more imaginative and more apt to enrich their reactions with some personal touch, and that they can contribute to that which is given. The relatively greater number of FM responses for the Kohnstamm reactors is interpreted as a reflection of their awareness of impulses for immediate gratification (Klopfer et al., 1954), with the resultant implication that they might, therefore, react in a more "childlike" manner, and be more self-acceptant. Fisher's "personality rigidity score," a score which has received some experimental validation as an indicator of the constriction and guardedness which individuals used in coping with environmental demands, differentiates between the two groups significantly, with the Kohnstamm-positive subjects being the less "rigid." F% is one of the indices very widely used as a measurement of constriction. While there has not always been consistency in the findings appearing in the literature with respect to the correlation between high F% and constriction, there are studies which support this inference. Zelen (1954) found that when behavior criteria were correlated with Rorschach measures lack of spontaneity was related to a high F%, and concluded that "an excessively high F% indicates a narrow, constricted life, extreme intellectual control, and rigidity."

The finding that two of the indices concerning which predictions were made differentiated the two groups below the 10% level in the direction opposite to that which was predicted requires some explanation. These two indices are Reaction Time and Reaction Time to Chromatic Cards. One possible explanation is that the nonreactors in the Kohnstamm situation were so desirous of escaping this relatively unstructured situation that they responded quickly in order to be finished with it. The calculations, moreover, do not include the time spent with those cards which were "failures." This distorts the results in the direction obtained; however, since it is the method currently used of calculating reaction times, it was followed in this study. Since CF plus C is not significantly different between the two groups, it is inferred that the Kohnstamm-positive subjects used in this experiment are, in general, more reactive, but not more uncontrolled in their reaction, than are the Kohnstamm-negative group; the former can allow themselves to be uncontrolled when it appears to be appropriate. They fit the picture of the "spontaneous" reactors rather than that of the more immature, impulsive ones. In a less selected sample i.e., one including a random sampling of the population and not restricted to the college community, the prediction which was made might hold. There is, however, no support for it in this study.

The Rorschach results as interpreted thus differentiate the Kohnstamm-positive and Kohnstamm-negative groups with respect to their sensitivity and reactivity to the cards, and, it is assumed, to life situations. The Kohnstamm-positive subjects give indications of being more open to and responsive to their environment and more spontaneous and less guarded than the Kohnstamm-negative subjects.

Ambiguous Figure Situation

The performance of the two groups of subjects was found to vary significantly in their readiness to interpret as people in action a photograph of an ambiguous doodle made of thread and yarn after a single further exposure to a photograph of another more structured doodle. They again reacted in a manner consistent with the underlying hypothesis of "inner freedom." The Kohnstamm-positive group seem to have a greater readiness to perceive life and action in this ambiguous doodle and a lesser proclivity for responding with concrete descriptions of the photograph than do the Kohnstamm-negative subjects. It is suggested that this may reflect a greater freedom in taking chances for the former, one of the characteristics which was inititally hypothesized.

Guilford-Martin Inventories GAMIN, and OAgCo, and Guilford Inventory STDCR

Stagner (1948) points out that one's own account of his actions may be a valid indicator of the traits which he possesses. These inventories ask of an individual an account of certain thoughts, actions, and feelings presumed to be indicative of certain traits. To the extent that his answers give a valid picture of self-image, they may be said to measure personality differences.

There were a few factors which seemed directly pertinent to the control factor hypothesis being tested and predictions were made concerning these. Of four predictions made, only one was statistically significant. The Kohnstamm-positive group perceive themselves as being less critical of people and things than the Kohnstamm-negative group, more willing to accept people and things as they are. This could, in turn, lead to a state of lesser guardedness. The other three factors, R, I, and N, show differences between the two groups which could easily arise by chance. The restriction of the groups to college students contribute to this situation. Those subjects who would be expected to be highest in R are the "impulsive," immature subjects; those expected to be lowest in self-confidence or greatest in insecurity and those expected to be lowest in "relaxation" are the subjects who were excluded, those in the group which shifted their reactions. Between the groups tested, however, only Co differentiated at a level accepted as the criterion.

The group of subjects who shifted from immobility to mobility when they were informed of the normal reactions encountered in the Kohnstamm situation were differentiated from the others on the factor I, the only prediction made for them. This indicates that they perceive themselves as being more insecure than those who did not shift. The initial hypothesis thus seems tenable, i.e., that the non-reactors consist of two subgroups, (1) those insecure in the newness of the situation who would change when familiarized with the expectations of normal reactions, i.e., those striving to meet the demands of others, and (2) those who are meeting their own demands and are self-accepting but who characteristically are overcontrollers and cannot allow themselves to give up control even in the appropriate situations.

SUMMARY AND CONCLUSIONS

On the basis of the individual differences in Kohnstamm reactivity reported in the literature and the inability of physiologists thus far to explain these differences on a purely physiological level, the nature of some of the psychological factors which might be involved in the manifestation of the Kohnstamm phenomenon was investigated. It was postulated that "control operations" would be of importance in differential Kohnstamm reactivity on the basis of the following considerations: (a) the frequent references to the ease with which the Kohnstamm reaction could be blocked by voluntary control; (b) reports in the literature that there was facilitation of a positive Kohnstamm reaction when inhibitory controls were experimentally relaxed (e.g., by alcohol or hypnosis); (c) reported observation of a tendency toward decreasing reactivity as chronological age increased; (d) reports in the literature of exaggerated Kohnstamm reactivity in hysterical patients (i.e., in individuals in whom affectivity factors are presumably dominant over controlling intellectual factors). It was further postulated that such "control operations" were not idiosyncratic to the Kohnstamm situation but were more probably characteristic of an individual's broader mode of interacting with his environment, i.e., that Kohnstamm reactivity probably reflects a more general pattern of transactions with the world.

Individual differences in Kohnstamm reactivity were hypothesized to reflect differences in the degree to which individuals possess a psychological trait or attitude labeled "inner freedom." Behaviorally, this would be expressed in different measurable forms of "spontaneity." This spontaneity, in turn, was believed to be influenced by the degree of security or self-acceptance of the individual. A behavioral reflection and measure of this was to be found by (a) testing for the presence or absence of constriction in the readiness with which the subject responds to novel situations, and (b) the cognitive structure of the situations which elicit a Kohnstamm reaction from him. It was postulated that those persons manifesting a Kohnstamm reaction have a relatively greater degree of "inner freedom" than those not manifesting a Kohnstamm reaction; that persons who showed immobility in the Kohnstamm situation would show related perceptual rigidity and "personality rigidity," as defined by Cattell (1950), when confronted with situations in which such characteristics are said to be reflected. Insecurity was suggested as a possible inhibiting factor in the nonreactivity of some subjects.

Personality characteristics were thought to be significant psychological factors associated with the presence or absence of the Kohnstamm phenomenon. The investigation thus focused on some of the "control operations" manifested by the Kohnstamm reactors and nonreactors since such data here might permit inferences relevant to the hypotheses of "inner freedom" and "security."

The procedures included (1) a test of Kohnstamm reactivity for each of the subjects under several conditions so varied as to bring about progressively increasing degrees of relaxation of inhibitory controls; (2) an inquiry with those subjects who manifested a Kohnstamm reaction under any of the conditions to obtain their description of their experience; (3) a series of perceptual discrimination tasks—(a) looking at a desk through aniseikonic lenses, (b) interpreting an ambiguous figure, (c) responding to the ten Rorschach cards; and (4) the responses to the Guilford STDCR, Guilford-Martin GAMIN and OAgCo personality inventories.

Four standardized conditions were used for testing Kohnstamm reactivity. They were so designed as to give progressively increasing amounts and kinds of information about the phenomenon and the expectations of "normal" reactions. In this way, it was planned to reassure those subjects who tend to increase control when they become afraid of being considered different from others, and, if possible, induce sufficient psychological relaxation for them to react spontaneously. Changes in Kohnstamm reactivity under the more structured directions were considered a possible indication of an underlying insecurity factor and a means of differentiating between the secure and insecure subjects. For most comparative purposes only the results obtained with the secure subjects were to be used, i.e., those who did not change their Kohnstamm reactions under the varying conditions. Those who shifted their reactions were to be compared with the others only with respect to the I (Insecurity) factor on the Guilford-Martin GAMIN inventory. The Kohnstamm-positive group was to be composed of those individuals who, prior to any knowledge about the types of "normal" reactions, manifested an arm-elevation of at least 45 degrees and continued in the subsequent conditions to have an elevation at least that high. The Kohnstamm-negative group was to be composed of those individuals who gave no arm-elevation under any of the following four conditions:

Condition I—naïve state

Condition II—informed about the possibilty of something happening to the arm

Condition III—informed about the arm rise and given a demonstration

Condition IV—informed that the Kohnstamm phenomenon is a reflex reaction

The following order of experimentation was used.

First session—Condition I Kohnstamm, Aniseikonic Lenses, Condition I again.

Second session—Condition II Kohnstamm, Ambiguous Figure, Condition II Kohnstamm.

Third session—Condition III Kohnstamm.

Fourth session—Condition III repeated.

Fifth session—Condition IV.

Sixth session—Condition IV repeated.

The Rorschach was administered whenever a sufficiently long time interval was available, usually within the time period covering the other tests. On occasion it was delayed until everything else had been completed. The personality inventories were given the subjects to fill out at their leisure and then return.

The subjects were 50 University of Kansas students without previous knowledge about the Kohnstamm phenomenon. Both graduates and undergraduate students were represented. All except five were between 18 and 30 years of age. The five exceptions were between the ages of 35 and 55. There were 25 women and 25 men.

Twelve subjects fulfilled the criteria set up for membership in the "Kohnstamm-positive" group, i.e., they manifested an arm-elevation of 45 degrees or more prior to any knowledge about the types of "normal" reactions and continued to do so in subsequent conditions of Kohnstamm elicitation; 22 subjects fulfilled the criteria for membership in the "Kohnstamm-negative" group, i.e., they manifested no arm-elevation under any of the conditions. Rorschach tests and personality inventories were not obtained from three of the Kohnstamm-negative subjects.

EXPERIMENTAL RESULTS

Aniseikonic Lens Situation

1. The Kohnstamm-positive subjects more readily perceived the aniseikonic illusion than did the Kohnstamm-negative subjects when unaware of the possibilities of "normal" reactions. The difference was statistically significant at the .038 level.

2. Knowledge of the possibilities of "normal" reactions to the aniseikonic lens situation had no effect upon the resulting perception of the 2 Kohnstamm-positive subjects who had not initially perceived the illusion. Such information was associated with the experience of the illusion in 5 of the 12 Kohnstamm-negative subjects who had not initially perceived it. While the influence of information upon the Kohnstamm-negative subjects does not attain the 5% level of significance, it approaches this level ($P = .08$).

The Rorschach Psychodiagnostic Test

1. The Kohnstamm-positive subjects have a significantly lower Fisher "personality rigidity score" than have the Kohnstamm-negative subjects ($P = .0004$).
2. The Kohnstamm-positive subjects gave a significantly greater number of responses to the Rorschach cards than did the Kohnstamm-negative subjects ($P = .0044$).
3. The Kohnstamm-positive subjects spent a significantly greater amount of time with the Rorschach cards than did the Kohnstamm-negative subjects ($P = .0005$).
4. The Kohnstamm-positive subjects obtained a significantly higher Sum C score than did the Kohnstamm-negative group ($P = .0250$).
5. The Kohnstamm-positive subjects used a significantly greater variety of determinants than did the Kohnstamm-negative group ($P = .0244$).
6. The Kohnstamm-positive subjects gave significantly more M response than did the Kohnstamm-negative subjects ($P = .0012$).
7. The Kohnstamm-positive subjects gave significantly more FM responses than did the Kohnstamm-negative subjects ($P = .0001$).
8. The Kohnstamm-positive subjects had a tendency to study the cards for a longer period of time before responding ($P = .0668$).
9. The Kohnstamm-positive subjects tended to devote more time to each response than did the Kohnstamm-negative subjects ($P = .0968$).
10. The Kohnstamm-positive subjects had a longer reaction time to the chromatic cards than did the Kohnstamm-negative subjects ($P = .0548$).

11. The Kohnstamm-positive subjects tended toward having a lower F% than did the Kohnstamm-negative subjects (P = .0618).

12. There were 7 Kohnstamm-negative subjects failing to give a response to one or more of the Rorschach cards. There were no such failures among the Kohnstamm-positive subjects. This gives a chi square value of 3.768 which is significant at the .05 level.

Ambiguous Figure Test

1. Kohnstamm-positive subjects perceived the ambiguous figure as people in action more readily than did the Kohnstamm-negative subjects.

Guilford–Martin Inventories GAMIN, and OAgCo and Guilford Inventory STDCR

1. Co, Co-operativeness, was the only factor differentiating the Kohnstamm-positive and Kohnstamm-negative subjects at less than the 5% level of significance. The Kohnstamm-positive subjects described themselves as being less critical of people and things than did the Kohnstamm-negative subjects.

2. Those subjects who shifted their reaction from a Kohnstamm-negative to a Kohnstamm-positive one when given information about the expectations of "normal" reactions in the Kohnstamm situation perceive themselves as being less self-confident, and more insecure, than those who did not shift their reactions. A t test between the shifters and nonshifters for the factor I (Inferiority) gives a value of 2.045 which is significant at the .014 level for the direction predicted.

Subjective Experience of Those Subjects Manifesting a Kohnstamm Reaction

Both Kohnstamm-positive subjects and those who were initially negative but shifted when informed of the possibilities of "normal" reactions tended to implicate factors in their description of their subjective experience of the phenomenon.

(a) The Kohnstamm-positive subjects tended to attribute non-reactivity of others to the countereffect of voluntary control exercised by the nonreacting subject.

(b) Those subjects who shifted their reactions from a negative one in the naïve state to a positive one when informed of the types of reactions given by "normal" individuals tended to explain their initial immobility by involuntary control.

The results obtained in this study support the initial hypothesis relating to the greater freedom and spontaneity of the Kohnstamm-positive subjects and the inhibiting effect of insecurity. The Kohnstamm-positive subjects gave indications of being more open and responsive to their environment, more spontaneous, and less guarded than the Kohnstamm-negative subjects. The conclusions which follow seem justified by the results of this study.

CONCLUSIONS

1. Kohnstamm reactivity is not an isolated bit of behavior nor a neural process alone but is meaningfully related to currently used measures of perceptual rigidity and personality constriction. It may be considered a reflection of an individual's broader coping mechanisms which characterize his way of interacting with his environment.

2. "Control operations" are of importance in differential Kohnstamm reactivity. Kohnstamm-positive subjects are more open and responsive to novel inner experiences and to the environment than are Kohnstamm-negative subjects and may be considered as having a relatively greater degree of "inner freedom."

3. Feelings of insecurity appear to act as an inhibiting factor in the Kohnstamm situations.

4. A diminution of defensiveness and increased "inner freedom" may be induced in some individuals by removing the threat of their being deviant in behavior through acquainting them with the possibilities of "normal" reactions.

Correlates of Perceptual Change:
E. Self and Self-Products

· 12 ·

Modification of Manifest
and Implicit Perception of the Self *

The present study explores the relationship between the self-acceptance scale of the Bills Index of Adjustment and Values (Bills, Vance, and McLean, 1951) and measures obtained from the Thereness-Thatness Demonstration. The study also investigates modification of self-acceptance under a condition of praise of performance on an ego-involved task. A basic hypothesis is that praise increases acceptance of self.

METHOD

Subjects

The subjects were 18 female nurses employed by the East Orange Veterans Administration Hospital. All subjects were volunteers and possessed no knowledge of the purposes of the study. They were informed that they are to assist in the standardization of several tests for nurses.

Instruments

The self-acceptance scale of the Bills Index of Adjustment and Values was used as a measure of manifest self-acceptance. Settings on the Thereness-Thatness Demonstration were used as measures of latent perceptions of the self and of other objects.

The Aptitude Test for Nursing of the George Washington Uni-

* This chapter was prepared by Alfred L. Brophy and Eugene H. Walder.

versity Series was the ego-involved task for which the experimental subjects were praised. Areas assessed by this instrument are judgment in nursing situations, visual memory, memory for content, information, scientific vocabulary, and ability to understand directions.

Procedure

Each subject was administered the Bills Index of Adjustment and Values and exposed to the Thereness-Thatness Demonstration before and after the presentation of the ego-involved task. Immediately preceding the posttest session, subjects in the experimental group were praised for their performance on the ego-involved task. In order to eliminate influences arising from order of presentation of the instruments, half the subjects were administered the Bills Index followed by the Thereness-Thatness Demonstration, and the other half were administered the Bills Index and the instruments in reverse order. The subjects were randomly divided into these two groups. Code numbers were assigned to the subjects in order to stress the confidentiality of the results and to secure frank responses to the Bills Index.

The Bills Index was administered to the subjects in small groups, while the Thereness-Thatness Demonstration was administered individually to each subject. Before the administration of the Thereness-Thatness Demonstration, the subject was permitted to view the apparatus and its operation was explained to her. Trials with the Demonstration were run with the laboratory in darkness in order to minimize visual cues.

An undersized playing card was placed on the cart at a distance of 110 centimeters and the subject was asked if she recognized the object. She was then instructed to move the object so that it was at the same distance from her as the third illuminated post. This procedure was repeated at a setting of 320 centimeters. Settings from both positions were made again for a total of four trials. A photograph of a young woman, selected by the experimenters for its "average" tone and designated as the Neutral photograph, was introduced and the procedure employed for the playing card was repeated in detail. A self-photograph of the subject, obtained before the pretest session, was then mounted on the cart and the sequence of settings was repeated. Finally, a photograph of Adolf Hitler was introduced, recognition being requested, and the procedure again followed. The photograph of Adolf Hitler was reproduced from a full-faced portrait in order to correspond with the other photographs.

After the pretest was completed for all subjects, the subjects were divided into a control group and an experimental group. The division of subjects was made so that the mean self-acceptance score of the Bills Index was the same for the two groups and so that each group included four subjects who had received the Bills Index first followed by the Thereness-Thatness Demonstration and four who had been exposed to the reverse procedure. The next step involved the administration of the Aptitude Test for Nursing to all subjects. The Test was administered in small groups. Immediately preceding the posttest, each subject in the experimental group was praised by an experimenter for her performance on the Aptitude Test for Nursing. The experimenter said: "You remember the Aptitude Test for Nursing that you took last time? It was a test that measured judgment and skills in a variety of situations. Well, you did very well on it. As a matter of fact, your score was among the top fifteen scores of over one hundred nurses who have taken this test at this hospital and in other regions of the country. You did very well. It's something to be proud of."

Subjects in the experimental group were then administered the posttest in the same order as the pretest. Control group subjects were administered the posttest during the same time interval, but nothing was said regarding their performance on the Aptitude Test for Nursing.

RESULTS

The test-retest rank-order correlation for settings of the playing card on the Thereness-Thatness Demonstration was .71 for the 8 control subjects. The test-retest reliability of the self-acceptance scale of the Bills Index of Adjustment and Values was .76.

One measure obtained from the Thereness-Thatness Demonstration was the difference between each subject's mean setting of the self-photograph and her mean setting of the neutral photograph (N-S). The rank-order correlation between the N-S score and the self-acceptance score of the Bills Index was .29 for the 18 subjects on the pretest. The N-S measure, which was believed to be an index of the way the person perceived herself in relation to other, was, therefore, not significantly related to the phenomenological measure of self-acceptance.

The rank-order correlation between the Bills self-acceptance score and the settings of the playing card and of the three photographs were not significantly different from zero, but inspection of the data suggested that the regression was not linear. Therefore, the settings for each of the "thereness-thatness" objects were plotted against the Bills self-acceptance scores. The probability of the observed association of "thereness-thatness" settings above and below the median with the nine middle-range self-acceptance scores and the nine extreme self-acceptance scores was obtained by Fisher's exact method of computation.

The association between self-acceptance scores and settings of the playing card and of the neutral photograph was significant at the .006 level (two-tailed test); for the self-photograph, the significance level was .32 (two-tailed test). Subjects who rated themselves as being either very high or very low in self-acceptance tended to set the objects farther away on the Thereness-Thatness Demonstration than did subjects who rated their self-acceptance within the middle range. There was no evidence of a curvilinear relationship for the Hitler photograph or the N-S scores. The rank-order correlation of Hitler settings and self-acceptance scores was also not significant ($-.14$).

The mean pre- and posttest scores of the control and experimental groups on the Bills self-acceptance scale and for several objects on the Thereness-Thatness Demonstration are given in Table 1. (Because of the need to equate pretest means, the N's differ for some of the measures.) The experimental group evidenced a gain in the Bills self-acceptance score on the posttest significant at the .025 level, which, compared with the control group, is significant between the .05 and the .10 levels (one-tailed test). None of the Thereness-Thatness Demonstration measures was significantly different on the pretest and posttest.

DISCUSSION

The finding of a curvilinear relationship between the measure of a manifest self-acceptance and the measures of implicit perception of the self and the world is consistent with the studies dealing with the nature of phenomenological self-acceptance and with investigations of the relationship of adjustment to perceptual mode of response on the Thereness-Thatness Demonstration. Both high and low self-accepting subjects tended to perceive objects on the Thereness-Thatness Demonstration as larger (or closer) than did subjects who rated their self-acceptance on the middle range. Such perception has been found in previous studies to be characteristic of maladjustment. The low self-accepting subjects, in the light of their

TABLE 1

Pretest and Posttest Means, Standard Errors of the Differences between Means, and t's for the Experimental and Control Groups

Measure	Pretest	Posttest	s_d *	t
Bills Index				
Manifest Self-acceptance				
Control (N = 7)	168.3	171.9	4.1	
Experimental (N = 8)	172.9	185.5	4.2	
Between Groups			5.8	1.55 †
Thereness-Thatness Demonstration				
Neutral-Self-Photograph (N-S)				
Control (N = 7)	12.3	12.7	4.7	
Experimental (N = 5)	13.2	12.2	2.9	
Between Groups			5.5	.25
Self-Photograph				
Control (N = 6)	138.3	135.0	5.8	
Experimental (N = 7)	143.4	137.1	12.9	
Between Groups			14.2	.21
Mean of Three Photographs				
(Self, Neutral, Hitler)				
Control (N = 7)	135.7	134.3	4.5	
Experimental (N = 7)	136.8	135.7	8.5	
Between Groups			9.6	.03
Playing Card				
Control (N = 6)	118.5	110.8	10.6	
Experimental (N = 7)	114.4	112.3	3.9	
Between Groups			11.3	.50

* For the control and experimental groups the s_d's are those for correlated means; the between groups s_d's are for independent samples.

† Significant between the .05 and .10 levels (one-tailed).

self-acknowledged dissatisfaction, would be expected to perceive the world in such a fashion. For the high self-accepting subjects, it appears that defensive denial produced a distortion in responses to the Bills Index which may be seen as deriving from an inability to accept and integrate threatening self-perceptions. These subjects may have perceived objects as they did on the Thereness-Thatness Demonstration for a similar reason: they may have been threatened by the stimuli and may have attempted to reduce the threat by placing a distance between the objects and themselves.

The findings suggest that even a circumscribed praise experience produces an increase in manifest self-acceptance. The data afford no evidence, however, of change in implicit perception of the self and the world. These findings are similar to those reported by Diller (1954). Despite the fact that the more basic perceptual processes were unaffected, it should be expected that the observed modification in phenomenological self-acceptance would be accompanied by behavioral changes, though such behavioral concomitants would probably be transitory.

The occurrence of change in manifest self-acceptance in the absence of change in implicit self-perception supports the belief that the self operates so as to enhance the individual's self-picture. The observed change was evidenced in a perceptual situation that was within the individual's sphere of control and in which his need to enhance the self could be expressed more readily than in the less patent perceptual situations. Diller's finding that a *failure* experience results in change in unconscious self-evaluation and no change in manifest self-concept was probably based upon the fact that failure has a greater impact upon the individual than does an apparently similar praise experience. In the case of failure, too, manifest self-perception serves a defensive function, that of attempting to maintain, rather than to enhance, the self.

The anticipation that settings of the self-photograph on the Thereness-Thatness Demonstration would provide one of the most sensitive measures employed in the study was not fulfilled. This failure might have been due to partly uncontrolled differences in the brightness and size of the face in the self-photographs. The validity of settings of a self-photograph as a measure of implicit self-perception could be determined by relating settings of properly prepared photographs to ratings of latent self-acceptance based on protocols of projective techniques. For the present, however, the validity of these settings must remain in doubt.

Further research might equate the stimulus objects for the manifest and latent measures of self-perception by using ratings of the self-photograph as the phenomenological measure. Since the object of perception would be identical, the results would be more directly comparable for each of the measures. The number of subjects in the sample was small and no attempt was made to select subjects systematically on the basis of performance on the two instruments. The trends observed in the study require confirmation with larger samples. It might be fruitful to compare subjects with varying combinations of high and low standing on the manifest and latent measures of self-perception, both with respect to other personality variables and with respect to change in self-perception as a result of praise and failure experiences.

SUMMARY

The literature dealing with studies of modification of self-attitudes and the relationship of adjustment to perception of the self and of the world was reviewed. Previous research suggested that there is not always a direct relationship between manifest and latent self-reactions, and that high phenomenological self-acceptance may be associated with either good or poor adjustment and may serve a defensive function.

Self-acceptance was investigated experimentally within a perceptual framework by measures of manifest and latent self-perception. Eighteen subjects were administered the Bills Index of Adjustment and Values and the Thereness-Thatness Demonstration before and after the presentation of an ego-involved task. Preceding the posttest session, subjects in the experimental group were praised for their performance on the ego-involved task.

A curvilinear relationship was observed between manifest self-acceptance and several measures of implicit perception of the self and the environment. Both high and low self-accepting subjects implicitly perceived objects in a manner previously found to be characteristic of maladjustment. It appeared that defensive denial underlay the manifest self-reactions of the highly self-accepting subjects.

Praise of performances of an ego-involved task tended to effect an increase in manifest self-acceptance, but produced no measurable change in implicit perception of the self and the world. This finding appeared to support the belief that individuals seek to enhance the self concept.

· 13 ·

The Recognition and Evaluation of
Self-Products *

It is a common observation that people may not recognize some aspect of themselves, especially when their judgment of that aspect is unfavorable. Sometimes people may even fail to recognize their own faces. Clinical writings contain many descriptions of such phenomena. Franz (1933), for example, describes the following:

> Later, I led him into another room in which there was a mirror, and I suggested that he look into the glass. He appeared to be greatly upset . . . and after taking one look he said, "My God, is that me?"

It is less generally known, however, that the failure to recognize either one's self or one's own self-products is not necessarily a manifestation of pathology. Many normal people have had an experience similar to the one that Mach (1914) describes:

> Personally, people know themselves very poorly. Once, when I was a young man, I noticed in the street a profile of a face that was very displeasing and repulsive to me. I was not a little taken aback when a moment afterwards, I found that it was my face, which in passing a shop where mirrors were sold, I had perceived reflected from two mirrors which were inclined in the proper angle to each other.

It would seem strange that people, on occasion, do not recognize either themselves or their self-products. Such a lack of recognition, however, has been demonstrated in several studies.

---

* This chapter was prepared by Daniel Sugarman and represents a condensation of a doctoral dissertation entitled "The Relationship of Success and Failure to the Recognition and Evaluation of Self-Products by Normal and Schizophrenic Subjects."

If people are sometimes unable to recognize even physical aspects of themselves, it might be expected that they might likewise have difficulty in perceiving as their own something that they have produced. Studies of the recognition of self-products have ranged in scope from the mere reporting of the phenomenon to the exploring of possible connections between the recognition of self-products and other factors.

The earliest reported study concerned specifically with the problems of the recognition of one's own self-product is that of Eagleston (1937). Working with 60 college girls, he instructed them to pick out their own handwriting from among several samples. He found that only 50% of the girls could so so, and concluded:

> The data suggest that there may be many people who cannot recognize their handwriting. . . . There is also the suggestion that a larger number of pepole believe that they can recognize their handwriting than really can. (1937, p. 549.)

Perhaps the most extensive investigations concerning self-recognition, and the recognition of one's own products, have been carried out by Wolff and his associates (1943). He found that even though the judge failed in the majority of cases to recognize his own handwriting or other self-product, the subjective judgment of the product tended to be either extremely favorable or unfavorable. Wolff further noted that while some subjects could recognize their own product almost immediately, other subjects displayed great resistance to any type of self-recognition.

Although many of Wolff's experiments were merely exploratory, his work has suggested many possibilities for research. The technique of exploring a subject's attitudes towards himself by having him rate his own products in the absence of recognition stimulated several fruitful research studies.

Huntley (1938), in a prolonged and comprehensive study, confirmed Wolff's major findings. He demonstrated statistically that self-judgment of unrecognized self-products tended to be excessively favorable or unfavorable. He stated:

> Even when the judge, under conditions at the conclusion of the experiment, deliberately tried to choose his own samples, there were many instances in which he was not sure of his selection. There were also several cases of incorrect identification, and in some instances the judge was very sure that a mistaken sample was his own. (1938, p. 88.)

Epstein (1955), in a study designed to investigate the manner in which normal subjects evaluated their unrecognized self-products in comparison to schizophrenics, found that one's own judgments of unrecognized self-products were generally more favorable than judgments of the products made by others. His results were interpreted to mean that "unconscious over-evaluation of self is to a certain extent normal, but beyond that is associated with schizophrenia." (1955, p. 69.) His results differed from those of Wolff and Huntley in failing to indicate any tendency for self-judgments to be extreme in both directions.

In a study of the changes of self-attitude after success and failure experiences, Diller (1953) had subjects rate themselves and their friends before and after the experimental conditions. In an attempt to investigate more covert attitudes, he had the subjects rate their own unrecognized handwriting. He found success increased the amount of preference shown for the subject's own handwriting sample, but that failure produced no significant change in the subject's self-rating. In accounting for the phenomena of self-recognition and self-judgment, two major questions arise. One must explain the low incidence of self-recognition, and one must account for the strong affective nature of the self-judgments. Almost all psychologists who have conducted investigations in the area of recognition of self-products have stressed the difficulty that subjects seemed to have had in recognizing their own products. Wolff believed that:

> We may compare the lack of recognition or the retarded self-recognition with the suppression of associations or with the prolonged association time caused by "complex" words. (1943, p. 301.)

The Problem of the Present Study

The present study attempts to determine the effects of failure and success upon the subsequent rating of one's self-product, and the readiness to recognize it. In view of the evidence presented by studies of perceptual defense, Wolff's explanation of the marked lack of recognition of self-products as being related to the "suppression of association" (1943), seems to deserve empirical study. Much clinical and experimental evidence indicates that "we develop protective, defensive, nullifying techniques that help us retain approval and avoid self-castigation." (Cameron, 1947)

If Wolff's explanation for the striking lack of self-recognition of self-products is valid, then an individual who makes a self-product in an atmosphere that is unpleasant and charged with failure should subsequently experience difficulty in recognizing that self-product. Conversely, an individual who makes his self-product in an atmosphere of success should be able to recognize his product relatively rapidly.

The present study also attempts to investigate the self-evaluation of self-products after experimental failure and success have been induced. Previous studies in this area have all stressed the finding that the judgment of an unrecognized product was both quantitatively and qualitatively different from the judgment of a recognized product. The present study is designed to evaluate these findings and to ascertain if there are significant, observable differences in the self-ratings of unrecognized products by subjects who were exposed to different experimental conditions. Finally, the behavior of normal subjects is compared to the behavior of schizophrenics.

Hypotheses

The specific hypotheses of the empirical investigation are:

1. A negative relationship exists between antecedent failure experience and readiness to recognize self-products.

2. Conversely, a positive relationship exists between success experience and readiness to recognize self-products.

3. There is a negative relationship between antecedent failure experience and positive judgment of self-products.

4. Conversely, there is a positive relationship between antecedent success experience and positive judgment of self-products.

5. Under neutral conditions, schizophrenics recognize their self-products more readily than normals.

6. The major findings of Wolff (1943) and Huntley (1938) will be confirmed.

   (a) Judgment on one's own unrecognized product is more extreme than judgment of one's own recognized product.
   (b) Judgment of one's own product under neutral conditions is usually a positive one.

METHOD

Subjects

A total of 120 white, male, English-speaking hospitalized veterans were employed in this study. The 60 normal subjects were all hospitalized at the East Orange Veterans Administration Hospital for somatic, nonpsychiatric complaints. An attempt was made to eliminate as subjects any patients who had an illness which was considered to be psychosomatic in origin (i.e., colitis, ulcers, etc.). Almost all of the 60 normal subjects were postsurgical cases who had undergone surgery for conditions such as varicose veins, pilonidal cysts, or plastic repairs. No patient was tested during an acute phase of his illness and most were reasonably comfortable.

The 60 schizophrenic subjects were all hospitalized at the Veterans Administration Hospital at Montrose, N. Y. All of these subjects carried a staff diagnosis of schizophrenic reaction. Since schizophrenia describes an extremely heterogeneous group, only patients who met the following criteria were selected: (a) no known delusions or hallucinatory episodes; (b) no shock treatment for at least three months previous to the date of experimentation; (c) no known organic complications; (d) not receiving any medication with the exception of sedatives that were administered only in the evening.

All 120 subjects in the study, in addition, had to meet the following criteria. Each subject had to be between the ages of 19 and 50, smoke at least one package of cigarettes each day, and have adequate visual acuity without the use of glasses. The mean age of the normal subjects was 33.3 years and the mean age of the schizophrenic subjects was 33.6 years. In a short interview, the patient was told that the Psychology Department of the hospital was engaged in research with new tests and was asked if he would volunteer as a subject.

Design

The experimental design required each subject to be seen for two sessions. In the first session he made his self-products subject to the experimental conditions. During the second session, which was conducted exactly one week later, he was required to rate and to attempt to recognize the self-products which he had made the previous week.

Each subject was then placed, in a random fashion, into a success, failure, or control group within his appropriate population. Six groups were established:

1. Normal success group (NS)
2. Normal failure group (NF)
3. Normal control group (NC)
4. Schizophrenic success group (SS)
5. Schizophrenic failure group (SF)
6. Schizophrenic control group (SC)

Self-Products

In the previous investigations of self-rating and recognition of self-products, various forms of expressive movements and products have been employed. Epstein (1955), Huntley (1938), and Wolff (1943) used handwriting, drawings, a photograph of the subject's profile, and recordings of the subject's voice. In an attempt to find a series of tasks that would be satisfactory for the purposes of the present investigation, several pilot studies were conducted which tried many forms of expressive movements and products. It should be emphasized that a self-product, in this study, means merely a drawing, design, or other expressive object that is made by a subject himself.

Finally, the following six products were decided upon for inclusion in the present study:

1. figure drawing
2. reproduction of three Bender designs
3. handwriting
4. original design
5. coloring the mimeographed picture of a girl
6. clay man

These products were chosen for inclusion in the present study because they were simple and yet permitted individual differences to be manifested. In addition, all of the tasks seemed to have interest value and, in the pilot studies, engendered few refusals.

The instructions to the patient for the figure drawing were, "I'd like you to draw the picture of a man on this card. You may do it in any way you choose."

In a similar fashion, the patient was instructed to copy three Bender designs on another card, copy the phrase "New Jersey Chamber of Commerce" on a third, and draw an original design on a fourth. All of these were drawn with a number two black pencil on 3 by 5-inch white, unlined cards.

As a fifth self-product, the subject was presented with a mimeographed drawing of a girl holding an umbrella and 12 differently colored pencils. He was instructed, "Color this drawing in any way that you would like." For the sixth and last self-product, the subject was given one ounce of green artist's clay and instructed, "Make a man out of this clay in any way that you would like."

Procedure

First Session. In order to have a measure of each subject's initial tendency to rate his own self-products and to ascertain if the groups were initially equated in their tendency to rate their own self-products, a short questionnaire was constructed. This questionnaire consisted of six items which related to the six self-products that were to be made by the subject. The first item on the scale, for example, was,

> If you were asked to draw the picture of a man, and you were then to compare it to the drawings of other patients at this hospital, which of the above statements would you judge to be most correct? Place the number of that statement here.

The patient had the choice of rating himself at any point along a seven-point scale, ranging from "Mine would be the best (1)," to "Mine would be the worst (7)."

The initial questionnaire also served as a further screening device. Patients who seemed to have some visual difficulty when reading the questionnaire were eliminated from the study, as well as three schizophrenics who found it too complex to complete. The administration of the questionnaire to the patient was the first step in the experimental procedure and was the same for all six groups.

Control Groups

After the administration of the questionnaire, the subjects who had been placed in the control groups then made their six self-products without any interpolated experiences. When the subject finished the tasks, an appointment was made for the following week. The patient was told, "I'll see you again next week. We can finish then." Any questions were met with evasive answers.

Experimental Groups

In the pilot studies conducted prior to this investigation, several methods of inducing atmospheres of success and failure were used. Genuine stresses are not easy to induce ethically in an experimental setting. Therefore, a contrived, operationally defined, failure experience is frequently employed by investigators. For the purposes of the present investigation, it was found that giving or denying patients cigarettes for their performance on subtests of the Wechsler-Bellevue seemed to constitute a satisfactory experience of success or failure.

In order for a patient to make his self-product in an atmosphere of failure, without disparaging the product itself, the patients in the failure groups (NF, SF) made each of the six self-products interpolated between two failure experiences. In a like manner, the patients in the success groups (NS, SS) made each self-product between two success experiences. The basic procedure for the experimental groups, therefore, was the making of the self-products with interpolated success or failure experiences on the subtests of the Wechsler.

After the administration of the questionnaire, the subjects in the experimental groups (NS, SS, BF, SF) were given the following instructions:

> I have here some new tests that have been used with patients in other V.A. hospitals. Most of the patients who have taken these tests found that they could answer many of the questions. I have a table in this book here (examiner points to book) that tells me how many questions most people can answer. You will probably not be able to answer all of the questions, as many of them are quite difficult. The important thing is how you do in comparison with the others.

> Most patients find these tests pretty interesting, but just to add to the interest, you will be given some cigarettes each time that you do well— sort of as a sign to let you know how you are doing. One more thing, after each series of questions, and after I have told you how you have done on that series, I will ask you to do a little task for me. Most of the time this task will be a little drawing of some type. You cannot win any cigarettes for these tasks, only for the series of questions. Is it all clear now?

If the patient asked any questions, the instructions were repeated again. After it was clearly observed that the patient understood the instructions, the experimental procedure commenced.

Each patient was then given the Information and Comprehension subtests of the Wechsler-Bellevue (form II) in the standard fashion. He continued each subtest until he missed two successive answers. The examiner pretended to look into the book and gave each subject two cigarettes after each one of these two subtests. Each subject, therefore, regardless of whether he was in the failure (NF, SF) groups or the success groups (NS, SS) received two initial success experiences.

All of the subjects in the experimental groups were then administered a third subtest of the Wechsler. They were either given or denied cigarettes according to which experimental group they were in. The subjects in the failure groups (NF, SF) received no more cigarettes after the initial success experience. The subjects in the success groups (NS, SS) were given two cigarettes after their performance on each subtest. After the subjects either received or were denied cigarettes for their performance on the third subtest of the Wechsler, they made their first self-product.

This procedure of alternating the making of a self-product with a success or failure experience continued until all six self-products had been made. The subjects in the failure groups (NF, SF) received no more cigarettes after their initial success experience. The subjects in the success groups (NS, SS) received cigarettes for their performance on each subtest of the Wechsler.

The order of the administration of the subtest, as well as that of the making of the self-products, was rotated to control for any cumulative effect upon any single self-product. After a subject had completed this part of the procedure, an appointment was made for the following week.

The Second Session. The procedure employed for the second session, in which each subject was asked to rank and recognize the self-products that he had made the previous week, was the same for all groups (NS, NF, NC, SS, SF, SC). Each subject was seated comfortably in front of a perceptual apparatus that was constructed for the study.

The apparatus was a large, oblong, wooden box (36 by 24 by 12 inches). The top was glass so that the subject could see the interior. The two long sides of the box were cut away so that the subject could easily put his hands into the box and manipulate any material that was placed inside. The box was illuminated by seven low-wattage bulbs, so that constant illumination of one lumen was provided. As a result of a previous pilot study, the value of one lumen of illumination was decided upon as being most satisfactory for the purposes of the present study.

After allowing the subject two minutes for dark-adaptation, the experimenter placed seven samples of a product into the box in a rotated order. Six of these samples were standard ones and were used for all subjects. The seventh was the subject's own product that he had made the previous week. After the samples had been placed in the box, the experimenter slowly gave the following instructions to the subject:

I have placed in this box seven samples of handwriting that were made by patients at this hospital. I want you to rank them in the order that you like them, that you find most pleasing to you. I want you to put the one that you like best way over here on the right, the one that you like second best right next to it, and so on until you put the one that you like least way over here on the left. One of these samples of hand-writing may be yours. If you do find yours, let me know as soon as you see it.

The instructions were then repeated until it was clear that the subject understood the task. The illumination in the box was then turned on and the subject began to rate his products. If the subject did not pick out a product as belonging to him within 30 seconds, the experimenter said, "Pick out the one that looks most like yours." These instructions were repeated every 10 seconds until the subject made a choice. The instructions were repeated each time another one of the self-products was presented with six samples.

In a rotated order of presentation, the subject was asked to rank and to recognize each of the six self-products that he made in the previous week. Each of the subject's self-products was presented with the six standard samples of that product. The time required for the subject to make a choice as to which of the products was his own was recorded. Also recorded was the rank that the subject gave to his own product and the correctness of his choice.

After the conclusion of the experimental procedure, each subject was interviewed to ascertain his feelings about the experiment. The subjects who had been in the failure groups were told that the examiner had made a mistake the previous week and that actually they had done quite well. They were given the cigarettes that they did not win previously. Each subject was then taken back to his ward.

RESULTS

The present study raises four general questions. What are the effects of an atmosphere of success or failure upon the subsequent recognition of self-products? What are the effects of an atmosphere of success or failure upon the subsequent rating of self-products? How do schizophrenics differ from normals in recognizing and evaluating self-products? Finally, are Wolff's findings supported by the present data?

The experimental design employed in this study consisted of two different groups (normal and schizophrenics) and three different conditions (failure, success, and neutral, or control). The statistical technique of analysis of variance, which lends itself readily to this type of design, was, therefore, the primary technique employed in analyzing the data.

What are the Effects of Differing Atmospheres Upon Subsequent Recognition?

Failure. The first hypothesis states that subjects who make their self-products in an atmosphere of failure will experience difficulty when they subsequently attempt to recognize their products. Such difficulty should manifest itself in increased recognition times.

In order to evaluate this hypothesis, the average recognition time for each subject was calculated. This score was the average time that it took the subject to recognize all six of his self-products. In many instances, where the subject failed to recognize one or more of his self-products, the average recognition time was calculated only on the basis of those products that he did recognize. The average times required by subjects in each group to recognize their self-products are presented in Table 1.

TABLE 1

Average Times Required to Recognize Six Self-Products by All Groups

Group	Mean	S.D.
NS	16.2	4.5
NF	22.8	5.8
NC	18.4	4.2
SF	25.5	8.1
SC	16.8	6.4
SS	22.1	6.9

To test the hypothesis that subjects in the NF and SF groups took significantly longer to recognize their self-products, their recognition times were compared to those of the subjects in the NC and SC groups by means of analysis of variance.

A significant F was obtained (P .01) in the analysis of variance. It may be concluded, therefore, that subjects in the failure groups (NF, SF) took significantly longer to recognize their self-products than subjects in the control groups (NC, SC).

Success. The second major hypothesis states that subjects who made their self-products in an atmosphere of success should subsequently recognize their self-products more readily than subjects in either the control or failure groups. An analysis of variance which compares the success group (NS, SS) with the control group (NC, SC) in terms of average recognition times, reveals no significant F ratio for the experimental condition of success.

A significant F ratio for interaction, however, indicates a differential response to recognition by schizophrenic and normal subjects who made their self-products in an atmosphere of success.

The hypothesis that all subjects who make their self-products in an atmosphere of success will subsequently recognize them more readily than subjects in a neutral atmosphere is not, however, supported by the present data.

Success and Failure. The methods used for evaluating the first two hypotheses required the comparison of the experimental (success, failure) groups with the control groups. A comparison of the experimental groups was also made with significant difference between success and failure. A significant interaction was obtained.

In summary, the present results indicate that subjects who make a self-product in an atmosphere of failure will take longer to recognize that product than subjects who make their self-products either in an atmosphere of success, or in an atmosphere with no interpolated experience. The effects of an atmosphere of success are not the same for normal and schizophrenic subjects.

To determine whether there were any significant differences in the absolute number of products recognized by subjects in the different groups, a number of chi square tests were performed. None of these tests revealed any significant differences between the six groups.

What are the Effects of Differing Atmospheres upon Subsequent Rating?

In order to obtain an initial estimate of subjects' hypothetical ratings of their self-products, and to determine whether the groups were initially equated in their tendency to rate, a short questionnaire was used. The results support the necessary prerequisite assumption that the groups initially do not differ significantly from one another in their tendency to rate self-products.

In the actual ranking of self-products, each subject compared his own product to six samples. He, therefore, could give his own product a rank of from one to seven. A rank of one would indicate that the subject liked his product best. Conversely, a rank of seven would mean that the subject liked his product the least of the seven samples.

The average rank that was given to correctly recognized self-products was computed for each subject. The average ranks given by subjects in all groups to their self-products are listed in Table 2.

TABLE 2

Average Rank Given to the Self-Products by All Groups

	$\overline{X}$ rank	s rank
NS	3.2	.93
NF	4.2	.84
NC	3.5	.87
SF	4.3	1.4
SC	3.5	.79
SS	3.5	1.1

Failure. The third hypothesis states that self-products that are made in an atmosphere of failure will be ranked lower than self-products that are made in either a neutral atmosphere or in an atmosphere of success.

In order to evaluate this hypothesis, the average ranks of the subjects in the control groups (SC, NC) were compared to the average ranks of the subjects in the failure groups (SF, NF) by means of any analysis of variance which yielded a significant F value.

The hypothesis that subjects who make their products in an atmosphere of failure will subsequently rank them lower than subjects who make self-products in a neutral atmosphere was supported.

Success. The fourth hypothesis to be evaluated states that subjects who make their products in an atmosphere of success should subsequently assign a higher rank to their products than subjects who make their product in a neutral atmosphere. This hypothesis was evaluated by comparing the average ranks of the subjects in the success group (NS, SS) with the average ranks of subjects in the control groups (NC, SC) by means of an analysis of variance. The results of this analysis of variance indicate that there are no significant differences between the groups (NS, SS, NC, SC) as far as the ranks assigned to their products are concerned.

Unrecognized Products. Diller (1953), in his study of self-attitudes after success and failure, had subjects rate their unrecognized handwriting. He hoped to be able to delineate more valid attitudes towards the self in this fashion.

In order to determine if there was any differences between the groups in the ranking of products that a subject did not recognize, the following procedure was performed. The average rank given by each subject to the products that he failed to recognize was computed. A median test was then performed in order to determine if there were any differences between the groups in rating their unrecognized products. The first of these median tests was performed on the unrecognized ranks assigned by subjects in the failure group and control group. The second median test was performed on the unrecognized ranks assigned by subjects in the success group and control group. Chi square of .11 for the first test, and the chi square of .82 for the second, leads to the conclusion that making a product in either an atmosphere of success or failure had no demonstrable effect on subsequent rating of that product, when the product is not recognized by the subjects as being his own.

Do Schizophrenics Differ from Normals in Their Recognition and Evaluations?

Neutral Conditions. The fifth hypothesis predicts that under neutral conditions schizophrenics will recognize their self-products more readily than normals. In order to evaluate this hypothesis, a t test was performed on the difference between the means of the SC group and NC group. A t-ratio of .94 was obtained, hence the null hypothesis of no significant differences between the groups was not rejected. Apparently, therefore, under neutral conditions, schizophrenic subjects do not differ significantly from normal subjects in the time required to recognize their self-products.

Failure Conditions. The comparison of schizophrenics' and normals' average recognition time under failure conditions was made by means of an analysis of variance. The lack of a significant F ratio for diagnostic category would indicate that, while *both* normals and schizophrenics required more time for recognition of products when they were subjected to failure, they do not differ from each other.

In like fashion, a comparison of the average ranks assigned to the self-products of schizophrenics and normals, under conditions of failure, was made by means of an analysis of variance The lack of a significant F ratio for diagnostic category would indicate that under conditions of failure, normals and schizophrenics do not differ in the rating of their self-products.

Success. The significant F for interaction in an analysis of variance of the recognition times for subjects in the success (NS, SS) and control (NC, SC) groups suggests that schizophrenics and normals respond differently to the recognition of self-products under conditions of success.

A t test evaluating the significance of the difference between the mean recognition times of the normal success group (NS) and the normal control group (NC) was performed. The t ratio of 1.49 indicates that the null hypothesis of no difference between means of the schizophrenic success group (SS) and the schizophrenic control group (SC), reveals a t — ratio of 2.54, with P .01. This significant t value would indicate that schizophrenics in the success group, contrary to the proposed hypothesis, take significantly longer to recognize their products than schizophrenics in the control group.

A t test of the significance of the difference in means of the schizophrenic success (SS) group and the schizophrenic failure (SF) group ($t = .43$) reveals that there are no significant differences between these two groups.

In order to determine the relationship between "liking" or "disliking" one's own products and subsequent recognition of them, a product-moment correlation was computed between each subject's average recognition score and the average rank that he assigned to his products. For schizophrenics an r coefficient of .35, P .005 was obtained. The correlation coefficient for normals was $r = .25$, P < .025.

Are Wolff's Findings Supported?

Judgment of Unrecognized Products. In order to evaluate Wolff's findings (1943) that judgments of unrecognized products are more extreme than judgment of recognized products, the following procedure was employed.

The average extremity scores for each subject's recognized products and unrecognized products were computed. This extremity score was a measure of distance from the median rank, which was four. If, for example, a subject assigned a rank of one or seven to his product, this would give him an extremity score of three. A rank of two or six given to a product would be assigned an extremity score of two. A measure of each rank's distance from the median judgment was thus obtained.

A median test of extremity scores for recognized and unrecognized products in the normal groups was then performed. A significant chi square of 10.9 negates the null hypothesis of equal extremity of ranks assigned to recognized and unrecognized products. With normal subjects, therefore, Wolff's findings that judgment of un-recognized products is more extreme than judgment of recognized products is confirmed.

A median test of extremity scores of recognized and unrecog-nized products among schizophrenics does not reveal the same rela-tionship. The chi square of .202 does not permit rejection of the null hypothesis of equal extremity of judgment of recognized and un-recognized products.

Judgment of Recognized Products. In order to evaluate the hy-pothesis that under neutral conditions subjects tend to rate their products in a positive direction, the following procedure was em-ployed.

Each subject in the control groups (NC, SC) was considered to have given a positive judgment of his products if the average judg-ment of his products was between the range of 1 and 3.9. He was considered to have given a negative judgment of his products if the average judgment of his products was between the range of 4.1 and 7. A chi square test was then performed to evaluate the hypothesis that most of the judgments in the control groups were positive. The rejection of the null hypothesis of equal proportions of positive and negative judgments supports Wolff's findings.

SUMMARY

The present study attempted to determine the effects of atmos-phere of failure and success upon the subsequent rating of one's self-product and the readiness to recognize it. Six specific hypotheses were investigated:

1. A negative relationship exists between antecedent failure ex-perience and readiness to recognize self-products.

2. Conversely, a positive relationship exists between success ex-perience and readiness to recognize self-products.

3. There is a negative relationship between antecedent failure experience and positive judgment of self-products.

4. Conversely, there is a positive relationship between antecedent success experience and positive judgment of self-products.

5. Under neutral conditions, schizophrenics recognize their self-products more readily than normals.

6. The major findings of Wolff and Huntley will be confirmed.

   a) Judgment of one's own unrecognized product is more extreme than judgment of one's own recognized product.

b) Judgment of one's own product under neutral conditions is usually positive.

In order to test these hypotheses, 60 normal and 60 schizophrenic subjects were randomly placed into success, failure, and control groups. All of the subjects in the study were hospitalized veterans between the ages of 19 and 50 who smoked at least one package of cigarettes each day.

The experimental procedure required each subject to be seen for two sessions.

In the first session, he made his self-product (i.e., figure drawing, Bender designs, handwriting, original design and coloring) subject to the experimental conditions. Subjects in the failure groups made their products with interpolated failure experiences (i.e., withholding of cigarettes) on the subtests of the Wechsler-Bellevue Intelligence Scale. Subjects in the success groups made their products with interpolated success experiences (i.e., awarding of cigarettes) on the subjects of the Wechsler. The subjects in the control groups made their self-products without any interpolated experience.

During the second session, which was exactly one week later, the subject was asked to rank and to attempt to recognize the products that he had made the previous week. This second session was conducted under suboptimal illumination.

The following results were obtained:

1. Both normal and schizophrenic subjects who made their products in an atmosphere of failure took longer to recognize their products the following week than subjects in either the success or control groups. Subjects in the failure groups also rated their products more negatively than subjects in either the success or control groups.

2. Normal subjects in the success group did not significantly differ from subjects in the control groups in subsequent recognition or rating of self-products. Contrary to the prediction, schizophrenics in the success group took significantly longer to recognize their products than subjects in the control group.

3. Under neutral conditions, schizophrenics do not recognize or rate their products differently from normals.

4. Wolff's major hypotheses were supported in this study.

a) In a normal group, judgment of one's own unrecognized product is more extreme than judgment of one's own recognized product.

b) Judgment of one's own product under neutral conditions is usually positive.

These results were interpreted as supporting Wolff's hypothesis that people, on occasion, do not recognize either some aspect of themselves or something that they have made because that object or aspect has become associated with unpleasant experience.

Correlates of Perceptual Change:
F. Verbalization

· 14 ·

Changes in Perception
as a Result of Verbalization*

Verbalization is a salient feature of most forms of psychotherapy. Through this medium, the patient expresses to the therapist his thoughts, feelings, and perceptions. He thus releases these intrapsychic events from his private world, expresses them overtly, and shares them with the therapist. Partly as a result of such verbalization, and partly as a function of other aspects of the therapeutic relationship, he comes to "see" himself, others, and life itself in new ways. Verbalization is assumed, in other words, to be instrumental, under the special conditions of therapy, in altering perception.

The present research represents an attempt on a limited scale, and in a necessarily more artificial setting than in the actual psychotherapeutic situation, to study the effect of verbalization of perceptions under subsequent perceptions and ensuing behavior. A comparison of subjects' perceptions and handling of stimulus situations with and without having first verbalized their responses to them should thus afford a test of the assumption that verbalization, per se, has a differential effect. Since projective test materials are felt to tap areas of conscious and unconscious conflict, they provide convenient and meaningful stimulus material, the impact of which has been experimentally as well as clinically verified not only in psychodiagnostic testing but also in the modified use of these techniques in psychotherapy as well. With verbalization of responses to the projective test material (selected TAT cards) as the independent vari-

---

* The research was conducted by Leonard S. Abramson.

able, it is therefore possible to investigate its effects upon the subsequent perception and handling of these same materials in another context also evaluating perception. For the dependent variable, the "thereness-thatness" apparatus of the Ames demonstrations in perception affords a distance-setting measure of the subject's personal and idiosyncratic reactions to the stimulus materials when these materials are placed on the movable carriage and the subject asked to align them to a designated distance.

In Chapter IV, utilizing the "thereness-thatness" apparatus, no significant changes in perception were found between various experimental groups following verbalization. In this chapter it will be assumed that the effects of verbalization are to bring out and thereby heighten, in an idiosyncratic manner, already existing differences between persons, rather than to minimize differences. Greater communality between individuals can be expected initially. Increasing variability is expected to appear as deeper thoughts and feelings are brought out into the open and into a verbal communicative transaction with the experimenter. The direction of the change, further, cannot be predicted for the randomly selected individual subject and therefore for the subjects as a group, inasmuch as the direction of change is a function of many variables, for example, the varying personality orientation studied in Chapter IV.

The general hypothesis, then, is that verbalization of one's reactions to situations affects one's subsequent perception and ensuing behavior in the situations. More specifically, in our experimental settings subjects who do not verbalize their reactions will tend to respond similarly on test and retest. Subjects who do verbalize their reactions will change their perceptions as measured by their handling of the materials; this change will be idiosyncratic and therefore less highly correlated between test and retest.

The specific hypotheses are:

1. There is no significant difference in means between the pretest and posttest settings of the experimental TAT cards in the control group or the experimental group.

2. The experimental group is more variable in the posttest setting than is the control group.

3. The experimental group shows a greater variability in the posttest settings of emotionally valent stimuli as against the posttest settings of nonvalent stimuli than does the control group.

4. The individual effect of the experimental condition of verbalizing is idiosyncratic. It is therefore hypothesized that the experimen-

tal group shows signficantly lower correlations than the control group between the rank of the placement scores as to distance on the "thereness-thatness" apparatus and the rank of the magnitude of the change following verbalization, taking the direction of the change into account.

METHOD

Subjects

The population of the present study consisted of 40 nonneuropsychiatric veterans, ranging in age from 18 to 71, and in education from sixth grade to college graduate. Almost all of these patients (34 of the 40) were tuberculosis patients who had reached group V of the tuberculosis classification, i.e., they were negative on all tests of tuberculosis and at the most within a few months of discharge. They were therefore preparing to readjust themselves to living in the community and were facing their problems of readjustment without such a degree of adjustment difficulty as to constitute, and be evaluated as, psychopathology. In addition to these selection factors, since the experimental situation involved visual perception, patients with gross, uncorrected visual defects were excluded.

Procedure

The subjects were assigned alternately to a control group and an experimental group until 20 had been included in each. Each of the groups was put through three steps, a pretest on the "thereness-thatness" apparatus, an interstitial step during which the experimental group verbalized their responses while the control group did not, and a posttest to evaluate the effects of verbalizing and not verbalizing.

Specifically, the procedure and experimental materials were as follows:

With the Perception Laboratory room lights on, the experimenter introduced the individual subject to the "thereness-thatness" apparatus and explained briefly what he, the subject, would be expected to do. He was told that the experimenter would place certain objects on the movable carriage and the subject would be asked to place them at a certain distance along the table by turning a control wheel. The subject was then seated on a stool at one end of the table and asked to place his chin on the chin rest. The room lights were turned off. The time taken in the subsequent instructions and adjustment of the apparatus to the individual subject allowed for an adequate period of dark adaptation. The two switches on the apparatus illuminating the equally spaced posts on the subject's left and the movable carriage on the right were turned on. The subject was asked to keep both eyes open and to tell the experimenter when he just no longer saw the experimenter's hand as the experimenter lowered it behind the far end of the table. If the subject was able to see the experimenter's hand at the far edge of the table, the chin rest was lowered accordingly so that the subject could not quite see the far edge. The subject was then asked to close his right eye and to indicate if he could see with his left eye the five posts and the experimenter's hand, illuminated by flashlight, on the right side of the table-long partition. The same procedure was repeated for the left eye closed and right eye open. If necessary, the eye shield was shifted to adjust the apparatus so that the subjects were thus able to see both the posts and the experimenter's hand with the right eye but only the posts with the left eye. The subjects, then, could see the distance-standard posts with both eyes and the experimenter's hand (subsequently, the stimulus material to be manipulated) with only the right eye. This was checked periodically during the testing as a precaution against the subject having so moved his head in the chin rest as to change this alignment.

At this point, each of the subjects (both control and experimental) was asked to turn from the chin rest and the experimenter showed him, illuminating them by flashlight, each of the regular size Thematic Apperception Test cards in the following numerically ordered sequence: cards 1, 3BM, 4, 6BM, 7BM, 12BG, 13G, 13MF. These cards were selected to provide both meaningful, emotional valent stimuli and neutral stimuli. It was assumed that 1, 12BG and 13G would be relatively neutral. The subject was instructed to look at each card for about ten seconds, the experimenter indicating that he wanted the subject at this time only to become familiar with the cards. The subject was then requested again to place his chin on the chin rest and the larger screen in front of the subject was closed to shut off his view. The experimenter then brought out small-sized experimental TAT cards which had been mounted on stands for insertion onto the movable carriage. These were kept from the subject's view throughout the experiment, except under the specific experimental conditions. The screen was then opened for each trial. Each experimental card was placed on the movable carriage first at the near placement, a distance of 120 centimeters from the subject, and secondly at the far setting of 290 centimeters. The subject was

asked on each trial to line up the card with the third distance standard, the assumption being that the assumed size of the card and
therefore its placement to the fixed distance indicator would be
affected by the subject's reactions to the particular card.

Following these settings of the experimental TAT cards, the experimenter turned on the room lights and presented the regular-sized
TAT cards to the subject individually in the usual clinical testing
procedure. The subjects in the experimental group were given Mur-
ray's standard instructions: "This is a storytelling test . . . (etc.)."
The control group subjects were also given the cards, one at a time,
and in the same sequence. The instructions to the latter group were
altered as follows, to enlist involvement but preclude verbalization:
"This is a storytelling test. . . . Remember, just think up a story,
don't say it out loud. You have three minutes to think up a story.
See how well you can do." With both groups, the experimenter
started his stop watch as he handed the individual card to the subject and recorded the total time taken by the subject on the card
when the subject handed it back. Stories given by the experimental
group were recorded verbatim as given by the subject. Some of the
control group subjects asked whether they would be expected to
state later in the situation the stories which they had thought up;
all of them seemed to expect that they would be required to do so.
Judging from the concentration manifested by the control subjects
as they looked at the cards, they appeared on the whole to be as
much involved in developing stories to the cards as did the experimental group.

Following this intervening step of storytelling, verbalized vocally
or subvocally, the settings were repeated with the experimental
cards.

RESULTS

The two groups of subjects show no significant differences in their
mean placements of the experimental TAT cards on the pretest settings (see Table 1) and may therefore be assumed to have been
drawn from the same population.

There appears to have been a slight tendency for the experimental
group to be more variable initially than the control group. The comparable means accord with the hypothesis that in the random selection of subjects idiosyncratic performance would tend to cancel out
differences and comparable average placements of the experimental
cards would result. On the retest, the control groups' mean settings

TABLE 1

Means and Standard Deviations

Control Group

Card	Pre-Setting	S.D.	Post-Setting	S.D.	Mean Shift
1	109.3	24.9	109.6	30.0	−0.3
3BM	124.9	26.7	123.5	30.0	1.4
4	123.2	25.7	120.2	33.1	3.0
6BM	121.7	24.7	123.1	36.6	−1.4
7BM	131.9	26.6	133.5	35.1	−1.6
12BG	113.4	28.0	112.7	33.7	0.7
13G	127.0	25.5	127.8	29.5	−0.8
13MF	115.3	31.1	113.1	35.7	2.2
All Cards	966.5	601.8	963.5	804.9	3.0

Experimental Group

Card	Pre-Setting	S.D.	Post-Setting	S.D.	Mean Shift
1	111.1	39.6	108.5	32.5	2.6
3BM	118.6	32.3	123.3	33.3	−4.7
4	122.1	39.6	121.9	35.8	−.02
6BM	121.3	33.7	123.9	35.4	−2.6
7BM	130.5	29.4	138.3	37.3	−7.8
12BG	109.0	28.7	114.3	36.7	−5.3
13G	131.7	34.5	130.1	36.1	1.6
13MF	120.6	36.5	120.9	40.4	−.25
All Cards	965.5	784.22	981.0	881.1	15.5

were practically identical with those of the pretest. The experimental condition of verbalization also produced no significant shifts in the mean placement on the posttest settings, as may be seen upon inspection of Table 1. However, there was a tendency in the experimental group toward moving the cards further away from the subject. Six of the eight cards were placed further away on retest by the experimental group, four of the eight by the control group. The over-all difference for all of the cards combined appears particularly striking, suggestive of a systematic effect produced by the experimental condition in distancing the stimulus material which has by verbalization become increasingly ego-involved.

Inspection of the means placements shows consistent and apparently significant differences throughout the pre- and post-settings for both groups between the various TAT cards. The individual cards appear to vary in "pull," but not wholly in accord with the original expectation differentiating between those cards assumed to be emotionally valent and those assumed to be neutral. Card I, a relatively neutral card, first in the sequence of presentation and therefore without the cumulative effect of other card stimulation, was on the average placed closest by the subject. The most neutral card, 12BG which is a pastoral scene devoid of people, was also placed relatively closely. Card 7BM, the father-son stimulus card of the TAT series, was consistently placed the farthest away under all of the experimental conditions. In psychotherapy relationship terms, this latter finding might be interpreted as a transference effect. "Transference" produced a greater perceptual distortion than the condition of verbalization per se although the experimental condition produced the largest mean shift on this particular card. Conversely, however, card 13G which was assumed to be relatively neutral, was the second farthest card in mean placement. Card 13MF which was assumed to be emotionally valent was the third closest. The experimental cards were not equated in picture size and in clarity which differences were independent of the emotional valence dichotomization.

It was hypothesized that the experimental condition would enhance idiosyncratic differences in the placement of the experimental cards. If this is the case then the experimental group subjects should show greater variability on the retest. The *direction* and amount of the change has been shown above to be unpredictable but the variability of the shift may be greater in the experimental group.

Table 2 presents *F* tests of the significance of the differences

TABLE 2

Significance of Differences in Variabilities per Card between E and C Groups

	F	P
All Cards	2.07	.05-.06
1	3.31	<.01
3BM	1.44	—
4	3.16	<.01
6BM	1.21	(Reversed direction C > E)
7BM	1.61	—
12BG	2.97	.01
13G	1.03	—
13MF	1.02	—

All cards but 6BM E > C.

between the variabilities in the shift from pretest to posttest between the control and experimental groups. The subjects in the experimental group did prove to be more variable in their changes from the first to the second settings. Large shifts in both directions of card placement were made by this group as a whole. This was the finding in seven out of the eight cards, significantly so at the 1% level on three of the cards, and at the 5% level on all of the cards summed together. The probability of seven out of eight being in the postulated direction is in itself significant at beyond the 5 per cent level. In terms of the individual TAT cards, the three significant differences again do not appear to be a function of the distinction between assumed emotionally valent cards versus emotionally neutral cards (although one might question how neutral 12BG, a scene showing a stream in the woods, might be for recovering tuberculosis patients who had been hopsitalized continuously for many months).

Table 3 presents the total amount of change, regardless of sign, from test to retest for the 20 subjects in each group for each of and all the cards. The mean change on the eight cards is seen to be significantly greater in the experimental group at between the 1 and 5% levels of confidence.

Clearly, the experimental condition produced greater variability. There was more gross change in the experimental than in the control group. This was idiosyncratic and thereby cancelled mean dif-

TABLE 3

Magnitude of Change—per Card, Over-all

Cards	Experimental Group	Control Group
1	420	269
3BM	384	300
4	423	282
BM	297	353
7BM	302	262
12BG	405	214
13G	230	202
13MF	345	313
Total	2806	2195
Mean	350.8	274.4
	.05 > p > .01	

$F = 2.70.$

ferences between the two groups. This was true in spite of the finding that subjects in both groups who originally placed the experimental cards in near positions tended to place them near on retest
and those who placed them far did similarly on retest (Table 4).

TABLE 4

Rank-Order Correlations between Pre- and Post-Settings

Cards	Control Group	Experimental Group
1	.74	.79
3BM	.82	.72
4	.85	.77
6BM	.76	.83
7BM	.84	.85
12BG	.82	.77
13G	.91	.85
13MF	.73	.81
All Cards	.90	.86

The experimental condition did result in disruptive effects on the
retest in that predictability from the one setting to the other was
somewhat poorer for the experimental group. Inasmuch as the test-
retest reliabilities were high, the placement scores were summed for
each subject.

Table 5 presents rank-order correlations between the ranks of
these total placement scores and the ranks of the amount of shift
from the first to the second settings, taking the direction of the change

TABLE 5

Rank-Order Correlations between Total Placement Scores and the Direction and
Amount of Shift between Placements

Cards	Control Group	Experimental Group
1	.02	.04
3BM	.05	.08
4	.43	.08
6BM	.43	−.17
7BM	.60	.31
12BG	.43	.17
13G	.42	.16
13MF	.44	.33
All Cards	.55	.37

into account. The nearest total placement and the largest shift in the near direction were ranked at first rank. The disruptive effect of the experimental condition of verbalization of the stories is most patent here. Using a correlation of .44 (the 5% level of confidence) as a cutoff point, six of the eight individual card correlations and the correlation for the sums of all of the cards are significant in the control group. None of the correlations are significant in the experimental group.

DISCUSSION

The rather minimal difference in the intervening experimental conditions between the two series of card placements produced significant differences between the two groups. What factors might be adduced to account for the marked difference in the variability of the change from test to retest?

The major difference between the two conditions was in the fact of verbalization of the stories by the experimental group. The effect was relatively independent of what were assumed to be emotionally valent and nonvalent stimuli. The patients were selected from a nonpsychiatric population as a further means of precluding excessive and unpredictably varying degrees of emotional involvement, thus providing a more pure measure of the effects of verbalization *per se*. If there had been clear-cut differences between the emotionally valent and nonvalent cards, further analysis could have been undertaken between more and less affectively laden stories given by the experimental group.

It is recognized that the experimental condition did not provide a refined test of verbalization to the exclusion of other variables. The instructions to verbalize the stories also implied organization of the stories elicited by the stimuli into coherent, sequential, and presentable form, from the more rambling perceptions and thoughts which tend to develop first. This second-order response to the card stimuli is, in a sense, rather akin to the secondary elaboration in dreams—the thoughts are arrayed and fixed by this ordering and repetition, even though the original impact is thereby lost. It is possible, however, that the control group subjects also prepared their responses in sequential storytelling, as indeed they were requested to do. Although stories were not subsequently elicited from the control group, as they might have been following the second settings, the subjects of this group may have expected (and most of them indicated that they did expect) to tell the stories they thought of at some point in the proceedings. The experimental condition, further, required explicit speech and communicative expression directed to the experimenter, behavioral aspects which are subsumed in the fact of the verbalization of the stories. Coincident to the verbalizing, the time spent looking at the cards and relating the stories was generally, although far from consistently, longer in the experimental group. The experimenter wrote out the stories which were told to him, duplicating the conditions under which the Thematic Apperception Test is generally given as a projective diagnostic device, but also lengthening somewhat the time spent with the card by the subject. It seems unlikely that the brief difference in viewing time per card (generally less than one minute) would in itself account for the differences between the two groups. A more rigorous and exacting equation of the two groups in terms of time spent in viewing the card might have been preferable. Such equation, however, would have introduced extraneous and irrelevant ideation in the control group, once these subjects finished their thinking of the requested stories and viewing time remained.

Whether one or more of these factors were involved, over and above the fact of verbalization per se, it seems correct to conclude that a rather minor amount of added participation by the experimental group subjects resulted in significant alterations in perception and in the related handling of the stimulus material. To the limited extent of this experiment, participation in an interpersonal exchange, verbalizing sequentially ordered personal and idiosyncratic ideation, does seem to affect perception.

It might be argued that the experimental condition had a distracting and disruptive rather than a facilitating effect, and that the inherent perceptual tendency was enhanced by diverting the subject's attention, decreasing recall, and, in all, allowing for a more full emergence of the phenomenon. In such a case, however, the rank-order correlations between total placement scores and change from test to retest would be higher in the experimental group between test and retest, whereas in fact they were markedly lower. It may be assumed, therefore, that the results are idiosyncratically based, rather than based on the inhibitions of competing response tendencies.

SUMMARY

The essential hypotheses of the study are supported by the findings. Contrary to the stated hypotheses, there was a tendency in the experimental group, on the average, to place the experimental cards farther away, and a priori assumptions as to the emotional impact of the various cards were not confirmed. In essence, however, the experimental condition of adding verbalization to the subject's responding to the standard stimuli of the TAT cards produced greater idiosyncratically-determined perceptual change and related handling of the stimulus materials. In this sense, disruption of habitual modes of perception, in subjects who are the more amenable to perceptual flexibility and change, may be seen as the psychotherapeutic matrix in which personality development and change can occur.

References

Chapter 1

BENTLEY, ARTHUR F. "The Fiction of 'Retinal Image,'" in *Inquiry into Inquiries; Essays in Social Theory,* ed. Sidney Ratner (Boston: Beacon Press, 1954), Chapter 15.

BRIDGMAN, PERCY W. "Science and Common Sense," *Scientific Monthly,* July, 1954, pp. 32-39.

BRUNSWIK, EGON. *Perception and the Representative Design of Psychological Experiments* (Berkeley, Cal.: University of California Press, 1956).

DEWEY, JOHN, AND BENTLEY, ARTHUR F. *Knowing and the Known* (Boston: Beacon Press, 1949).

ITTELSON, WILLIAM H. *Visual Space Perception* (New York: Springer, 1960).

SCHILDER, PAUL. *Medical Psychology,* trans. David Rapaport (New York: International Universities Press, 1953).

WHITEHEAD, ALFRED NORTH. *The Aims of Education* (New York: Mentor Books, 1949).

Chapter 2

BLAKE, ROBERT R., AND RAMSEY, GLENN V. (eds.). *Perception: An Approach to Personality* (New York: Ronald Press, 1951).

MASLOW, ABRAHAM HAROLD, AND MITTELMANN, BELA. *Principles of Abnormal Psychology* (Rev. ed., New York: Harper Bros., 1951).

WITKIN, HERMAN A., LEWIS, H. B., HERTZMAN, M., MACHOVER, KAREN, MEISSNER, P. B., AND WAPNER, S. *Personality Through*

Perception: An Experimental and Clinical Study (New York: Harper Bros., 1954).

CHAPTER 3

BRUNER, JEROME S. "Personality Dynamics and the Process of Perceiving," in *Perception, an Approach to Personality*, ed. Robert R. Blake and Glenn V. Ramsey (New York: Ronald Press, 1951), pp. 121-47.

CAMERON, NORMAN A. *The Psychology of the Behavior Disorders* (Boston: Houghton Mifflin Co., 1947).

GOTTSCHALK, L. "Über den Einfluss der Erfahrung auf die Wahrnehmung von Figuren," *Psychol. Forsch.*, 1924, *8*, 261-317.

KLOPFER, BRUNO, AND KELLEY, DOUGLAS M. *The Rorschach Technique* (Yonkers, N. Y.: World Book Co., 1946).

RAPAPORT, DAVID. *Diagnostic Psychological Testing* (Chicago: Year Book Publishers, 1946), II.

RAUSCH, H. "Perceptual Constancy in Schizophrenia," *Journal of Personality*, 1952, *21*, 176-87.

SCHAFER, ROY. *The Clinical Application of Psychological Tests* (New York: International Universities Press, 1948).

SINGER, J. "Personal and Environmental Determinants of Perception in a Size Constancy Experiment," *Journal of Experimental Psychology*, 1952, *43*, 420-27.

WITKIN, H. "Individual Differences in Ease of Perception of Embedded Figures," *Journal of Personality*, 1950, *19*, 1-15.

CHAPTER 4

HORNEY, KAREN. *Our Inner Conflicts* (New York: Norton, 1945).

ITTELSON, WILLIAM H. *The Ames Demonstrations in Perception* (Princeton, N. J.: Princeton University Press, 1952).

KILPATRICK, FRANKLIN P. (ed.). *Human Behavior from the Transactional Point of View* (Hanover, N. H.: Institute for Associated Research, 1952).

TWITCHELL-ALLEN, DORIS. *Three-Dimensional Apperception Test* (New York: The Psychological Corp., 1948).

CHAPTER 6

ADORNO, THEODORE W., FRENKEL-BRUNSWIK, ELSE, LEVINSON, D., AND SANFORD, R. N. *The Authoritarian Personality* (New York: Harper Bros., 1950).

BALES, ROBERT F. *Interaction Process Analysis* (Cambridge: Addison-Wesley, 1950).

BECKER, W. C. "Perceptual Rigidity as Measured by Aniseikonic Lenses," *Journal of Abnormal and Social Psychology,* 1954, *49,* 419-22.

BOVARD, E. W. "Group Structure and Perception," *ibid.,* 1951, *46,* 398-405.

BROWN, R. W. "A Determinant of the Relationship between Rigidity and Authoritarianism," *ibid.,* 1953, *48,* 469-76.

ITTELSON, WILLIAM H. *The Ames Demonstrations in Perception: A Guide to Their Construction and Use* (Princeton, N. J.: Princeton University Press, 1952).

LIPPITT, R. "An Experimental Study of the Effects of Democratic and Authoritarian Group Atmospheres," *University of Iowa Studies in Child Welfare,* 1940, *16,* 45-194.

MARTIN, B. "Intolerance of Ambiguity in Interpersonal and Perceptual Behavior," *Journal of Personality,* 1954, *22,* 494-503.

McCARTY, GERALD J. *Small Group Interaction and Perceptual Changes* (Washington, D. C.: Catholic University of America Press, 1956).

O'CONNER, PATRICIA. "Ethnocentrism, 'Intolerance of Ambiguity,' and Abstract Reasoning Ability," *Journal of Abnormal and Social Psychology,* 1952, *47,* #2 (Supplement) 526-30.

PITCHER, B., AND STACEY, C. L. "Is Einstellung Rigidity a General Trait?" *ibid.,* 1954, *49,* 3-6.

ROKEACH, M. "Generalized Mental Rigidity as a Factor in Ethnocentrism," *ibid.,* 1948, *43,* 259-78.

CHAPTER 7

BERNSTEIN, L. "The Effect of Pre-Operative Stress on the Alleged Rorschach Signs of Anxiety," unpublished doctoral dissertation, Fordham University, 1951.

EYSENCK, HANS J. *The Scientific Study of Personality* (New York: Macmillan Co., 1952).

GOLDSTONE, S. "Flicker Fusion Measurements and Anxiety Level," unpublished doctoral dissertation, Duke University, 1953.

GRANGER, G. W. "Personality and Visual Perception: A Review," *Journal of Mental Science,* 1953, *99,* 8-43.

GRAVELY, A. M. "An Investigation of Perceptual Tests as Measures of Temperament," unpublished doctoral dissertation, University of London, 1950. Quoted in G. W. Granger, *loc. cit.*

KLEIN, GEORGE S. "The Personal World Through Perception," in *Perception, an Approach to Personality*, ed. Robert R. Blake and Glenn V. Ramsey (New York: Ronald Press, 1951), pp. 328-55.

KRUGMAN, H. E. "Flicker Fusion Frequency as a Function of Anxiety Reaction: An Exploratory Study," *Psychosomatic Medicine*, 1947, 9, 269-72.

LANDIS, CARNEY. "Something About Flicker-Fusion," *Scientific Monthly*, LXXIII (1951), 308-14.

MAY, ROLLO. *The Meaning of Anxiety* (New York: Ronald Press, 1950).

MISIAK, HENRYK. "The Decrease of Critical Flicker Frequency with Age," *Science*, 1951, *113*, 551-52.

PULLEN, M. S., AND STAGNER, R. "Rigidity and Shock Therapy of Psychotics: An Experimental Study," *Journal of Consulting Psychology*, 1953, *17*, 79-86.

RICCIUTI, H. N. "A Comparison of Critical Flicker Frequency in Psychotics, Psychoneurotics, and Normals," unpublished doctoral dissertation, Fordham University, 1949.

SIMONSON, E., AND BROZEK, J. "Flicker Fusion Frequency: Background and Applications," *Physiological Review*, 1952, *32*, 349-78.

CHAPTER 8

ALLPORT, FLOYD HENRY. *Theories of Perception and the Concept of Structure* (New York: Wiley Book Co., 1955).

AMES, ADELBERT, JR. "Aniseikonic Glasses," in *Human Behavior from the Transactional Point of View*, ed. Franklin P. Kilpatrick (Hanover, N. H.: Institute for Associated Research, 1952).

BECKER, W. C. "Perceptual Rigidity as Measured by Aniseikonic Lenses," *Journal of Abnormal and Social Psychology*, 1954, *49*, 419-22.

BUHLER, R. A. "Flicker Fusion Threshold and Anxiety Level," unpublished doctoral dissertation, Teachers College, Columbia University, 1954.

GOLDSTEIN, KURT. *The Organism: A Holistic Approach to Biology* (New York: American Book Co., 1939).

KILPATRICK, FRANKLIN P. (ed.). *Human Behavior from the Transactional Point of View* (Hanover, N. H.: Institute for Associated Research, 1952).

MARTIN, B. "Intolerance of Ambiguity in Interpersonal and Perceptual Behavior," *Journal of Personality*, 1954, *22*, 494-503.

MAY, ROLLO. *The Meaning of Anxiety* (New York: Ronald Press, 1950).

CHAPTER 9

HASTINGS, P. K. "An Investigation into the Relationship between Visual Perception and Level of Personal Security," in *Human Behavior from the Transactional Point of View*, ed. Franklin P. Kilpatrick (Hanover, N. H.: Institute for Associated Research, 1952).

WITTENBORN, J. R. "Factorial Equations for Tests of Attention," *Psychometrika*, 1943, 8, 19-35.

CHAPTER 11

ALLEN, F. "The Post-Contraction of the Muscles of the Arm," *Quarterly Journal of Experimental Physiology*, 1936-37, *26*, 305-17.

ALLEN, F., AND O'DONOGHUE, C. H. "The Post-Contraction Proprioceptive Reflex, its Augmentation and Inhibition," *ibid.*, 1927, *18*, 199-242.

AMES, A., JR. "Binocular Vision as Affected by Relations between Uniocular Stimulus-Patterns in Commonplace Environments," *American Journal of Psychology*, 1946, 59, 333-57.

ASCHER, E. "Motor Attitudes and Psychotherapy," *Psychosomatic Medicine*, 1949, *11*, 228-35.

BECK, S. J. "Personality Research and Theories of Personality Structure," *Journal of Projective Techniques*, 1955, *19*, 361-72.

BECKER, W. C. "Perceptual Rigidity as Measured by Aniseikonic Lenses," *Journal of Abnormal and Social Psychology*, 1954, *49*, 419-22.

CATTELL, R. B., AND TINER, L. G. "The Varieties of Structural Rigidity," *Journal of Personality*, 1947, *17*, 321-41.

COCHRAN, W. G. "The Comparison of Percentages in Matched Samples," *Biometrika*, 1950, *37*, 256-66.

FISHER, S. "Patterns of Personality Rigidity and Some of Their Determinants," *Psychological Monographs*, 1950, *64*, No. 1 (Whole No. 307).

FORBES, A., BAIRD, P. C., AND HOPKINS, A. McH. "The Involuntary Contraction Following Isometric Contraction of Skeletal Muscle in Man," *American Journal of Physiology*, 1926, *78*, 81-103.

GUILFORD, J. P. *An Inventory of Factors STDCR: Manual of Directions and Norms* (Rev. ed.; Beverly Hills, Cal.: Sheridan Supply Co., 1944).

GUILFORD, J. P., AND MARTIN, H. *The Guilford-Martin Inventory of Factors GAMIN: Manual of Directions and Norms* (Beverly Hills, Cal.: Sheridan Supply Co., 1943a).

GUILFORD, J. P., AND MARTIN, H. *The Guilford-Martin Personnel Inventory: Manual of Directions and Norms* (Beverly Hills, Cal.: Sheridan Supply Co., 1943b).

JOHNSON, L. C., AND STERN, J. A. "Rigidity in the Rorschach and Response to Intermittent Photic Stimulation," *Journal of Consulting Psychology*, 1955, *19*, 311-17.

KAPLAN, J. M. "Predicting Memory Behavior from Cognitive Attitudes toward Instability," *American Psychologist*, 1952, I, 322 (Abstract).

KLOPFER, BRUNO, AND KELLEY, DOUGLAS McG. *The Rorschach Technique* (Yonkers, N. Y.: World Book Co., 1946).

KLOPFER, B., AINSWORTH, M. D., KLOPFER, W. G., AND HOLT, R. *Developments in the Rorschach Technique* (Yonkers, N. Y.: World Book Co., 1954).

KOHNSTAMM, O. "Demonstration einer katatonieartigen Erscheinung beim Gesunden (Katatonusversuch)," *Neurol. Zentralbl.*, 1915, *34*, 290-91.

MARTIN, B. "Intolerance of Ambiguity in Interpersonal and Perceptual Behavior," *Journal of Personality*, 1954, *22*, 494-503.

MATTHAEI, R. "Nachbewegungen beim Menschen. (Untersuchungen über das sog. Kohnstammsche Phänomen), I. Vorkommen und Wesen der Erscheinung," *Pflügers Archiv für die Gesamte Physiologie*, 1924a, *202*, 88-111.

MATTHAEI, R. "Nachbewegungen beim Menschen. (Untersuchungen über das sog. Kohnstammsche Phänomen), II. Nachbewegungen und Kraftsinn," *ibid.*, 1924b, *204*, 587-600.

MORENO, JACOB L. *Who Shall Survive?* (New York: Beacon Press, 1953).

PEREIRA, J. R. "Les contractions automatiques des muscles striés chez l'homme," *Journal de Physiologie et de Pathologie Générale*, 1925a, *23*, 30.

PEREIRA, J. R. "Sur les Phénomènes d'automatisme," *ibid.*, 1925b, *23*, 795.

PINKHOF, J. "Contraction residuelle de muscles voluntaires après un raccourcissement tétanique energique," *Archive néerlandaise de physiologie*, 1922, *6*, 516-27.

REICH, WILHELM. *Character Analysis: Principles and Technique for Psychoanalysis in Practice and Training*, trans. T. P. Wolfe (New York: Orgone Press, 1945).

RORSCHACH, HERMANN. *Psychodiagnostics* (4th ed.; Berne, Switzerland: Verlag Hans Huber, 1949).

Salmon, A. "Nouve osservazione sui movimenti automatici che si compiono dope gli sforzi muscolari e del loro valore in neuropatelogia," *Atti della Accademia Medico-Fisica Fiorentina,* 1914.

Salmon, A. "Les mouvements automatiques qui suivent les efforts musculaires voluntaires chez les sujets sains," *J. Physiol. Path. gén.,* 1925, *23,* 790-94.

Schachtel, E. O. "On Color and Affect: Contributions to an Understanding of Rorschach's Test, II," *Psychiatry,* 1943, *6,* 393-409.

Scheerer, M., and Austrin, H. "A Study in the Post-Contraction of the Arm," unpublished honors paper, College of the City of New York, 1945.

Schwartz, A. "Le phénomène du 'Bras qui se lève tout seul,'" *Memoires de la Société de Biologie,* 1924, *91,* 1431-33.

Stagner, Ross. *Psychology of Personality* (New York: McGraw-Hill, 1948).

Strauss, E. W., and Griffith, R. M. "Pseudoreversability of Catatonic Stupor," *American Journal of Psychiatry,* 1955, *111,* 680-685.

Werner, R., and Wapner, S. "The Innsbruck Studies on Distorted Visual Fields in Relation to an Organismic Theory of Perception," *Psychological Review,* 1955, *62,* 130-38.

Whisler, R. G. "Modification of the Post-Contraction Reflex," *Abstracts of Doctors' Dissertations* (Ohio State University Press, 1931), #7, 295-300.

Zelen, S. "Behavioral Criteria and Rorschach Measures," *Journal of Personality,* 1954, *23,* 207-14.

CHAPTER 12

Bills, R. E., Vance, E. L., and McLean, O. S. "An Index of Adjustment and Values," *Journal of Consulting Psychology,* 1951, *15,* 257-61.

Diller, L. "Conscious and Unconsciousness Self-Attitudes," *Journal of Personality,* 1954, *23,* 1-12.

CHAPTER 13

Cameron, Norman A. *The Psychology of Behavior Disorders* (Boston: Houghton Mifflin, 1947).

Diller, L. "A Study of Self-Attitudes After Success and Failure," unpublished doctoral dissertation, New York University, 1953.

Eagleston, O. W. "The Success of Sixty Subjects in Attempting to

Recognize Their Handwriting," *Journal of Applied Psychology,*
1937, *21,* 546-49.

EPSTEIN, S. "Unconscious Self-Evaluation in a Normal and Schizophrenic Group," *Journal of Abnormal and Social Psychology,*
1955, *50,* 65-70.

FRANZ, SHEPHERD I. *Persons One and Three* (New York: McGraw-
Hill, 1933).

HUNTLEY, C. W. "Judgments of Self Based Upon Records of Expressive Behavior," unpublished doctoral dissertation, Harvard
University, 1938.

MACH, ERNST. *The Analysis of Sensations and the Relation of the
Physical to the Psychical* (Chicago: Open Court, 1914).

WOLFF, WERNER. *The Expression of Personality* (New York, Harper
Bros., 1943).

Index